KT-474-345

ABSOLUTELY EVERYTHING YOU NEED TO KNOW

Written by
LIZ MARSHAM
MELANIE SCOTT
LANDRY Q. WALKER
STEVEN WIACEK

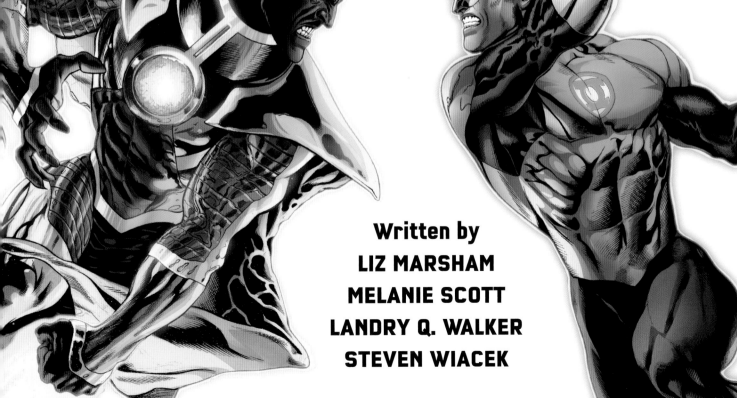

CONTENTS

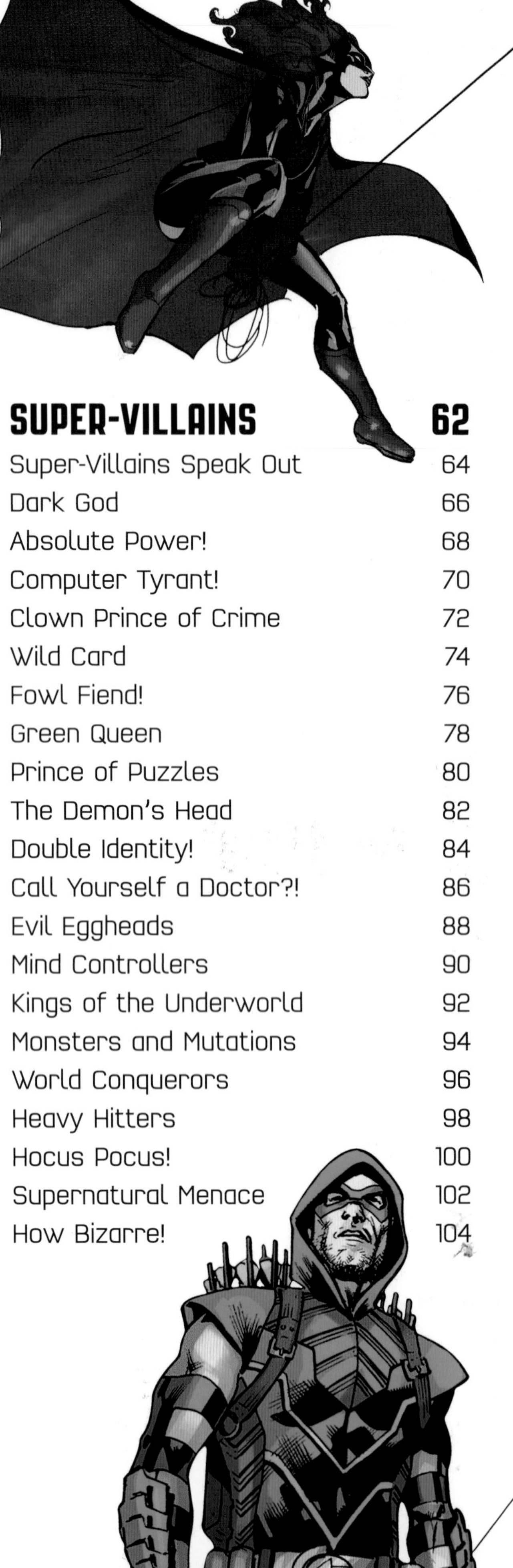

CHAPTER ONE CHARACTERS

CHAPTER TWO
TEAMS

CHAPTER THREE
SCIENCE AND MAGIC

CHAPTER FOUR
FROM HERE TO ETERNITY

CHAPTER FIVE
THE MULTIVERSE

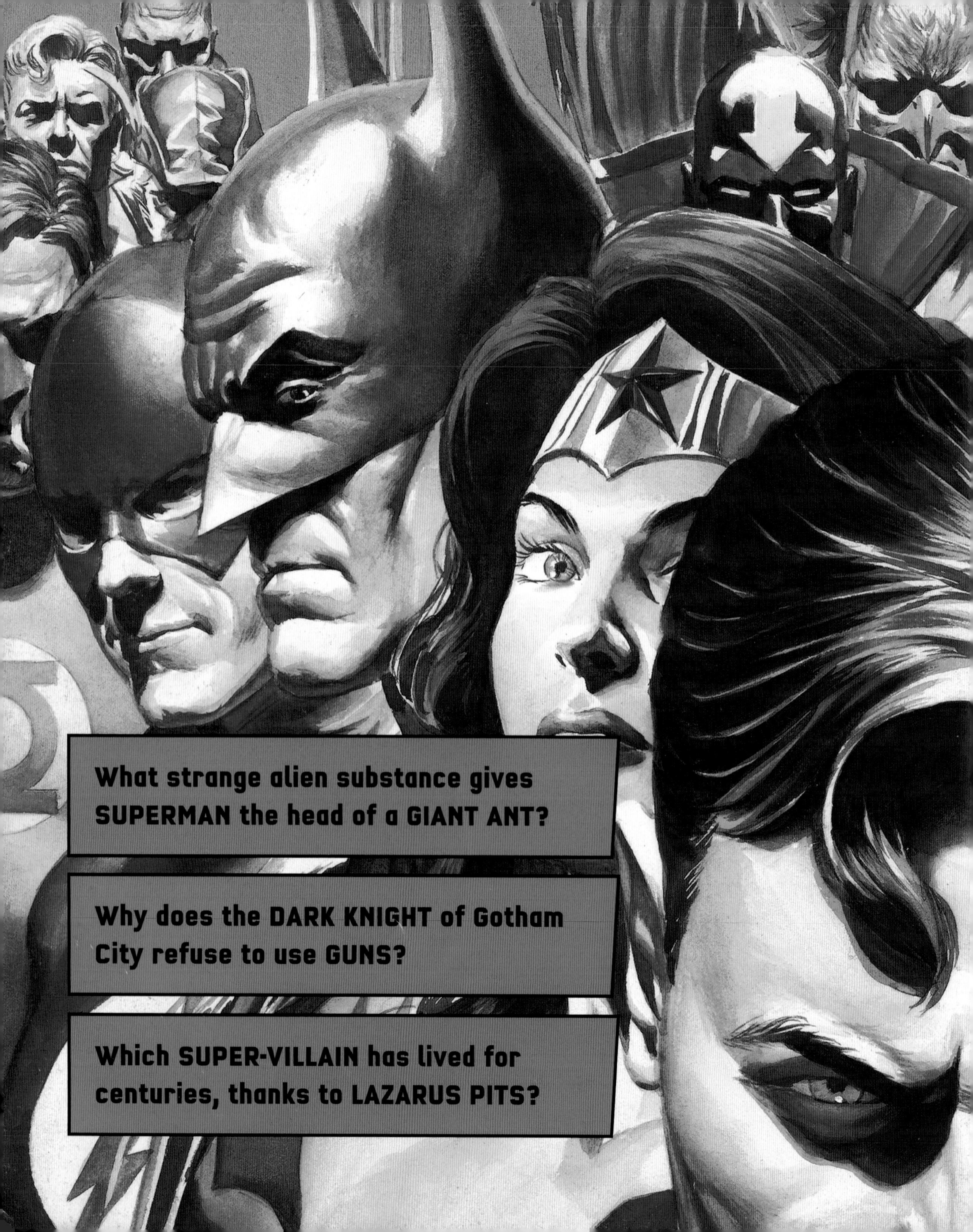
What strange alien substance gives SUPERMAN the head of a GIANT ANT?
Why does the DARK KNIGHT of Gotham City refuse to use GUNS?
Which SUPER-VILLAIN has lived for centuries, thanks to LAZARUS PITS?

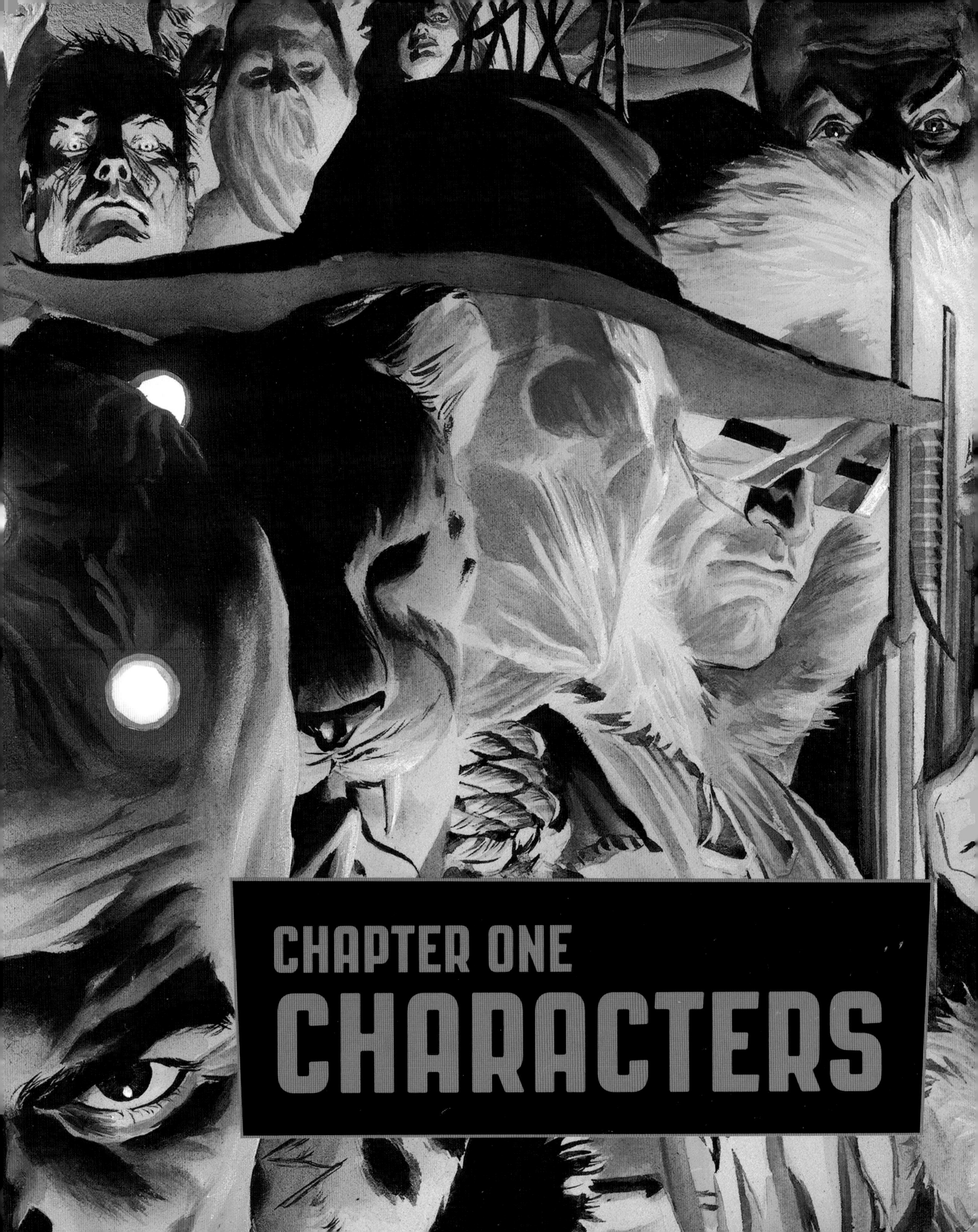

CHAPTER ONE
CHARACTERS

SUPER HEROES

SUPER HEROES SPEAK OUT!

They are defiant in their unending fight for justice. Their brave words are often as inspiring as their world-saving deeds!

THIS FIGHT CAN'T BE WON IF WE PULL OUR PUNCHES.
NIGHTWING

Life is locomotion. If you're not moving, you're not living.
THE FLASH

The medal can wait, sir! If the fightin's here—then here's where Easy's stayin'!
SGT ROCK

IS THERE SOMETHING WRONG WITH "GIRL" STUFF?
WONDER WOMAN

The country needs me and I need you. It is an urgent matter of national security.
UNCLE SAM

LIGHTNING STRIKES TWICE IN THIS TOWN— AND THE SECOND TIME I STRIKE— IT'S FOR KEEPS!
BLACK LIGHTNING

I'M GOING TO HIT HIM REALLY, REALLY HARD WITH A BIG GREEN BOXING GLOVE. I'M KIDDING.
GREEN LANTERN (HAL JORDAN)

Batman **NEVER** kills. Life is sacred to him.
ROBIN (TIM DRAKE)

I'M A CRIME-FIGHTER AND A DETECTIVE. I DON'T CALL MYSELF A HERO.
BATMAN

Consider this a practical demonstration of how judo really does work!
BLACK CANARY

TO ME, YOUR ANGRIEST BLOWS ARE NO MORE THAN THE WHISPER OF SNOWFLAKES.
SPECTRE

MY MEN BEAR ALLEGIANCE TO ONLY ONE RULER... JUSTICE!
BLACKHAWK

HEROES **ALWAYS** MAKE A DIFFERENCE.
HAWKMAN

THE SEAS WERE MY MOTHER AND FATHER. SO NO MATTER WHERE I GO IN THEM, I'M AT HOME.

AQUAMAN

No thug is going to kidnap me! I've worked out with the best!

LOIS LANE

THERE'S MORE TO LIFE THAN FIGHTING AND TRAINING AND—Y'KNOW—THE WHOLE BAT THING.

BATGIRL (CASSANDRA CAIN)

Just once I'd like to see something where cyborgs aren't the enemy.

CYBORG

I'm Kara Zor-El of Kandor. I'm a Super Hero. I don't scare easily.

SUPERGIRL

I'M WARNING YOU... DON'T BACK ME INTO A CORNER!

CATWOMAN

I don't think the human race understands just how PRECIOUS this planet is.

MARTIAN MANHUNTER

IT WAS KRYPTON THAT MADE ME SUPERMAN... BUT IT IS THE EARTH THAT MAKES ME HUMAN!

SUPERMAN

A Gotham City **without** Batman...will **always have** me!

ROBIN (TIM DRAKE)

Tell your friends there's a **HUNTER** on the streets. This is **MY** town now, and creeps like you are an **ENDANGERED SPECIES.**

GREEN ARROW

HE CAME FROM KRYPTON!

Before **Superman** bursts onto the world stage, **star-born orphan Kal-El** spends his early years in **a loving home.** As farmer's son **Clark Kent,** he learns about his **unique past** and how to **master his superpowers.**

DID YOU KNOW?

Kal-El comes from the planet **Krypton,** and he isn't the only one! His dog **Krypto** is in a test rocket that also lands on Earth. In addition, **Jor-El's** lab monkey **Beppo** actually stows away in **baby Kal's** escape ship!

FAST FACTS

REAL NAMES: Kal-El; Clark Kent

NICKNAMES: Superboy; The Man of Steel; The Man of Tomorrow; The Last Son of Krypton

PARENTS: Jor-El; Lara (Krypton); Jonathan and Martha Kent (Earth)

OCCUPATION: Super Hero

STRENGTHS: Powers growing under Earth's yellow sun

WEAKNESSES: Kryptonite; magic; unreliable superpowers

FOES: Lex Luthor; Kryptonite Kid; Dev-Em, the Knave from Krypton

NOTHING'S WRONG WITH YOU. YOU'RE SPECIAL. YOU'RE THE MOST SPECIAL BOY IN THE WHOLE WIDE WORLD.

A.I. EDUCATOR

Superboy is visited by a **robot teacher** built by **Jor-El.** The machine is built to ensure that the **Last Son of Krypton** will not misuse the powers granted by **Earth's yellow sun.**

POWER UP!

An alien teenaged criminal and his dog are irradiated by passing through a Green Kryptonite cloud. As Kryptonite Kid and Kryptonite Dog, they regularly make trouble for Superboy.

TOP 3

Clark's High School Goofs

1. Accidentally setting the school on fire with heat vision when Lana Lang kisses him.
2. Accidentally breaking his friend Pete Ross's arm while playing football.
3. Literally seeing through his classmates when his X-ray vision first kicks in!

WOW!

27.1

The number of light years Kal-El travels from Krypton to reach Earth!

MEGA MAKEOVER

Clark Kent's appearance has always been designed to help him blend in without being noticed, but that look has changed in the decades since Superman began!

1930s

1950s

1980s

2010s

BAD DAY

Superboy puts out **a fire** in young Lex Luthor's lab, but **spilled chemicals** make **Lex's hair** fall out. Lex blames Superboy and **hates him** from then on.

YESSS!

Lana Lang *is Clark's* ***first girlfriend*** *and knows all about his powers. She learns his secret after he saves her from being* ***chopped up*** *by* ***farm machinery!***

JLA FILES

Kal-El's ship crashes in rural Smallville, Kansas, and the baby is adopted by Jonathan and Martha Kent. They bury the rocket in their barn until little "Clark" is old enough to understand his uncanny origins. These are revealed years later when the vessel projects a holographic message from his Kryptonian parents, scientist Jor-El and his wife, Lara.

★ TEAM PLAYER ★

Clark doesn't realise that he's a member of the 31st-century **Legion of Super-Heroes.** After each adventure into the future, telepath **Saturn Girl** suppresses his **memories!**

DASTARDLY DEED

Kryptonian teenaged bully **Dev-Em** reaches Earth and frames **Superboy** for many cruel pranks before returning to space, forcing Superboy **to lie!** He claims that **Red Kryptonite** made him act **out of character.**

MAN OF STEEL

Clark Kent is **Superman**, the world's **greatest hero.** He rocketed to **Earth** as a baby from **planet Krypton**, minutes before it **exploded!**

SHOOTING FOR THE MOON
Superman once hit a baseball into space – at a target placed on the moon!

FAST FACTS

REAL NAME: Kal-El

ADOPTED NAME: Clark Kent

HEIGHT: 1.9 metres (6 ft 3 in)

WEIGHT: 106.6 kg (235 lb)

EYES: Blue

HAIR: Black

POWERS: Super-strength; super-speed; flight; invulnerability; heat vision; freezing breath; X-ray vision

ALLIES: Batman; Wonder Woman; Supergirl

ENEMIES: Lex Luthor; General Zod; Doomsday; Brainiac

HANDLE WITH CARE!

The **one substance** that can weaken, even **kill,** Superman, is **Green Kryptonite** from Krypton's **radioactive core.** Villains, such as **Metallo** use this to their **advantage.**

YESSS!

Superman can not only **hear** the heartbeat of **everyone in the world**, he can even **tell them apart**!

IN REAL LIFE

Superman creators Jerry Siegel and Joe Shuster first worked together in high school in Cleveland, Ohio. They created a story called "The Reign of the Superman" for a sci-fi magazine they self-published.

It's Only Love

Mermaid **Lori Lemaris** is one of Superman's **great loves.** He even considers **marrying her!**

WOW!

3

The number of eyes Superman has after Brainiac zaps him with Green and Red Kryptonite radiation!

TELL ME MORE

Under a yellow sun, Superman can function without food or sleep far longer than an ordinary human being.

WHENEVER THERE ARE PEOPLE WHO NEED MY VERY SPECIAL KIND OF HELP, IT WON'T BE A JOB FOR PLAIN, ORDINARY **CLARK KENT...** IT'LL BE A JOB FOR **SUPERMAN!**

Q&A

Q: Superman's dead?!?

A: Superman has died more than once. On one occasion he is killed by Kryptonian killing machine Doomsday. On another, he uses too much power and his body turns to dust!

TOP 5

Strange Stories

1. **MINI-SUPERMEN:** Superman gains the ability to fire mini-Supermen from his hands!
2. **SPLITSVILLE:** An accident turns Superman into two different versions of himself.
3. **LION MAN:** Superman is transformed into "Lion-Man", after refusing to marry a Greek goddess.
4. **ENERGY CRISIS:** Superman has to keep eating to maintain his powers.
5. **SUPER-ANT:** Exposure to Red Kryptonite gives Superman an ant's head!

DID YOU KNOW?

Superman wears his **indestructible uniform** beneath his ordinary **Clark Kent** clothes. He can activate it with a **single thought.** His **S-Shield** is the crest of the House of El, and is the Kryptonian symbol for **"hope"**.

ALTERNATE EARTHS

In another reality, **Superman** and **Lois Lane** marry and have a superpowered son, **Jonathan,** who has become the new **Superboy.**

SUPER SCOOPER!

Lois Lane is the finest **investigative reporter** in **Metropolis.** She's a determined **seeker of truth**—and Superman's **one true love!**

FAST FACTS

FULL NAME: Lois Joanne Lane

HOMETOWN: Pittsville

STRENGTHS: Pulitzer Prize-winning investigative journalist; trained in unarmed combat; courageous

WEAKNESSES: Superman

ALLIES: Jimmy Olsen; Perry White

FOES: Lex Luthor; Brainiac

It's Only Love!

Lois Lane's romance with **Superman,** and his alter ego **Clark Kent,** is one of **the great love stories.** There have been **major bumps** in the road, but they always **end up together!**

IN REAL LIFE

Lois Lane debuted along with Superman in *Action Comics* #1 (June 1938). She was based on Joanne Carter, a model who became co-creator Jerry Siegel's wife, and the crusading journalist Nelly Bly.

ALTERNATE EARTHS

On the **evil world** of **Earth-3,** Lois Lane is **Superwoman,** a manipulative, **amoral villain,** who comes to Earth-1 as part of **the Crime Syndicate.**

Q&A

Q: Who are Lois' family?

A: Lois is the daughter of Sam and Ella Lane. Army general Sam has a stormy relationship with Lois, whom he had wanted to be a boy! Lois' sister, Lucy, has dated Jimmy Olsen and taken on the mantle of Superwoman for a time.

DID YOU KNOW?

Science or magic often transforms **Lois** in **weird ways.** In one adventure, a magician turns her into a centaur – **half woman, half horse!**

YESSS!

Daily Planet editor ***Perry White*** tells ***Lois*** that he will only hire her if she brings him ***three great stories*** in ***three days*** – she does, of course, and ***the rest is history!***

SPECIAL *MOVES*

Lois doesn't (usually) have **superpowers,** but she can look after herself! While spending time in the bottled city of **Kandor,** Lois becomes **a master** of the Kryptonian martial art **Klurkor!**

IT'S NOT WRONG IF IT'S THE TRUTH!
AAARGH!

TOP 5

Lois' Super Hero Shots

1. **POWER GIRL:** Believing she's been given Superman's blood, Lois dreams that she has taken on his powers and is protecting Metropolis as Power Girl!
2. **LEOPARD LADY:** Hit with a ray that brings out her wicked side, Lois becomes a gang boss who marries Lex Luthor; in reality, "Leopard Lady" is a robot!
3. **KRYPTON GIRL:** On Earth-47, Lois Lane is the hero Krypton Girl, who struggles to keep her identity a secret from her *Daily Planet* colleague Clark Kent.
4. **ELASTIC LASS:** Borrowing Jimmy Olsen's elastic serum, Lois temporarily becomes Elastic Lass to track down the Wrecker.
5. **SUPERWOMAN:** Lois has been Superwoman many times, but only gets powers permanently when Superman seemingly dies.

NEWS

THE ONE THAT GOT AWAY

For years, the one big story that Lois is unable to crack – despite numerous close attempts – is the mystery of Superman's secret identity...

POWER UP!

When her son Jon is threatened by a Kryptonian Eradicator robot, Lois dons a hi-tech Hellbat suit to protect her boy, snarling: "Never mess with the baby bear when the mama bear's nearby!"

WHAT THE..?!

As a child, Lois goes exploring in the woods and comes across a **rattlesnake.** She manages to frighten the snake away using **a colourful toy,** which just happens to belong to a young **Kal-El!**

Lois is taken over by ***Brainiac,*** who uses her to turn the world ***against Superman.*** He has to battle her ***psionic powers*** to free her!

DID YOU KNOW?

The ***Daily Planet*** was originally named the ***Daily Star.*** The *Daily Star* later appeared as a rival newspaper.

ALTERNATE EARTHS

In an alternate reality, **Superman** takes his **friends** and **allies** to his **Fortress of Solitude**. It's the only way to save them from **an army** of his **greatest foes!**

MUTATION ALERT!

Jimmy Olson is Superman's best pal. That never changes, but a multitude of mutations means the boy photographer's body often does!

- A gorilla: When Jimmy's mind is switched with a gorilla's, his body follows suit!
- Elastic Lad: Jimmy drinks a special serum and gains fantastic stretching powers.
- Speed Demon: A potion gives Jimmy incredible – but hard to control – super-speed.
- A werewolf: Magic transforms Jimmy into a wild-eyed wolf man.
- Giant Turtle Man: Messing about with a growth ray makes Jimmy part man, part turtle – and all giant!

TOP 6

Daily Planet friends

1. **PERRY WHITE:** The paper's irascible, but good-hearted, Editor-in-Chief.
2. **LOIS LANE:** Top reporter; does everything she can to discover Superman's real identity.
3. **JIMMY OLSEN:** Excellent photographer and Clark's first friend in Metropolis.
4. **CAT GRANT:** Gossip columnist and good friend of Clark's.
5. **RON TROUPE:** Political columnist specialising in hard-hitting investigative pieces.
6. **LANA LANG:** Business editor; formerly Clark's Smallville girlfriend.

JLA FILES

JOHN & NATASHA IRONS

Engineer John Henry Irons quits his job designing weapons, dons an armoured suit, and helps his hero Superman defeat the cyborg Metallo. As Steel, he becomes a frequent crime-fighting partner of Superman. His niece Natasha assists at his Steelworks and has adventures in her own armoured suit as Steel, Starlight, Vaporlock, and under her own name.

Ron Troupe

Lana Lang

Perry White

Lois Lane

Jimmy Olsen

Cat Grant

SUPERMAN FAMILY

Superman is known as the **Last Son of Krypton,** but he's not the planet's **sole survivor.** Other Kryptonians reach Earth to become **heroes** alongside him. Superman also makes friends in **Metropolis** when, as **Clark Kent,** he joins the staff of the ***Daily Planet...***

I.D. CRISIS

When the Supergirl from the realm of Earth-2 arrives on Earth, she is surprised to discover another, younger, version of herself already battling evil there. Making the best of it, she drops her original moniker and adopts the name Power Girl. Then she starts doing what she does best – being a Super Hero!

WHAT THE..?!

Mon-El arrives on Earth with **amnesia.** His **superpowers** suggest he's from **Krypton,** but he's from **the planet Daxam. Lead** makes him very sick, so he has to stay in the **Phantom Zone** until **Brainiac 5** finds a cure – in the **30th century!**

SUPERGIRL

Supergirl is rocketed to Earth as a teenager to watch over her baby cousin Kal-El. Her rocket arrives late – Kal-El has already grown up to become Superman! Adopting a similar costume, Supergirl now fights for hope, humanity and compassion for all.

DID YOU KNOW?

SUPERGIRL is Superman's cousin from Krypton, and she may be **EVEN STRONGER** than he is!

SUPERBOY

Ten-year-old Jon Kent inherits Kryptonian powers from his father, Superman. His super-speed, strength and hearing are developing well, as is his heat and X-ray vision. His invulnerability is lagging behind a little, as he discovers when a fall from a tree knocks him unconscious!

YESSS!

To keep ***Superman*** safe, ***Supergirl*** dons a ***forcefield belt*** and flies a meteor of ***Green Kryptonite*** to a distant universe and ***buries it!***

BILLIONAIRE BY DAY...

Bruce Wayne, brilliant owner of **Wayne Enterprises,** is well known for being **a philanthropist** and **world traveller.** He's also the **Super Hero Batman** – but that's **a secret!**

IN REAL LIFE

In the comics, the Waynes are killed on their way home after seeing the movie *Zorro*. A masked, black-clad vigilante protecting the innocent, Zorro was created in 1919 by Johnston McCulley.

WOW!

$9.2 BILLION

Bruce Wayne's wealth—and Wayne Enterprises is worth $31.3 billion!

HOME SWEET HOME

Bruce lives in **WAYNE MANOR,** his family mansion just outside **GOTHAM CITY.** The mansion sits above a large **CAVE SYSTEM** that Bruce has converted into **THE BATCAVE!**

FAST FACTS

HEIGHT: 1.9 metres (6 ft 2 in)

WEIGHT: 95.3 kg (210 lb)

HAIR: Black

EYES: Blue

OCCUPATION: CEO, Wayne Enterprises

HELPING HAND

Bruce relies strongly on **Alfred Pennyworth,** the Wayne family's butler. Alfred looks after Bruce and all of his (and Batman's!) belongings, helps **Batman** on cases and even **cooks** for the **bats** in the **Batcave!**

NOOOO!

When Bruce Wayne's ***parents*** are killed by ***mugger Joe Chill, young Bruce*** vows that someday he will protect ***Gotham City*** from crime.

BACK FROM THE DEAD!

When Bruce **seemingly dies,** Robin tries to reanimate him using a **Lazarus Pit.** However this Bruce is an **insane clone,** created in **Darkseid's Evil Factory!**

A GENUINE GOOD GUY
Bruce doesn't just **save lives** as Batman. His **Wayne Foundation** funds **scientific breakthroughs** and **supports charities,** so he can do good **24 hours a day!**

POWER UP!

To prepare for life as Batman, Bruce studies chemistry, forensics, criminology and multiple martial arts in several countries. He also takes archery lessons from Green Arrow.

EVERYTHING'S IMPOSSIBLE UNTIL SOMEBODY DOES IT.

TOP 7

Bruce's girlfriends

Secret crime-fighting and romance don't really mix – but that doesn't stop Bruce from trying...

1. **JULIE MADISON:** Loses patience with Bruce when he keeps standing her up!
2. **VICKI VALE:** Ace photojournalist for the *Gotham Gazette*; figures out Bruce's secret ID and decides to pass!
3. **JEZEBEL JET:** A supermodel who turns out to be an agent of the evil Black Glove organisation.
4. **VESPER FAIRCHILD:** Bruce tries to protect her by ending their romance. She's murdered just the same, and Bruce is accused!
5. **SASHA BORDEAUX:** Bruce's bodyguard; romance dwindles when she's held as a suspect for Vesper's murder, along with Bruce.
6. **SHONDRA KINSOLVING:** A brilliant physiotherapist, she's turned evil by her brother and suffers a mental breakdown.
7. **SILVER ST CLOUD:** Put off when she learns that Bruce is Batman; when she reconsiders, she is tragically murdered!

ALTERNATE EARTHS

Elsewhere in the **Multiverse,** Bruce Wayne has some very **different destinies.** Instead of being Batman, he's a **magician** known as **Batmage,** one of **King Arthur's knights** and even **a vampire!**

DID YOU KNOW?

When **Bruce** first sets out to **fight crime,** he wears ordinary street clothes. But **a bat** crashing through a window at Wayne Manor gives him **a better idea...**

DARK KNIGHT

When the sun goes down and the **criminals** of **Gotham City** hit the streets, **Batman** is there to stop them with a combination of brilliant **detective work,** cutting-edge **technology** and relentless **fighting style!**

FAST FACTS

REAL NAME: Bruce Wayne

STRENGTHS: Martial arts; deduction; genius-level intelligence

WEAKNESSES: Slow to trust; no physical superpowers

KEY ALLIES: Robin; Nightwing; Alfred Pennyworth; Batwoman; Batgirl; Justice League; Commissioner James Gordon

KEY FOES: The Joker; Two-Face; The Penguin; Poison Ivy

★ TEAM PLAYER ★

Batman has inspired heroes around the world. Together they fight **global crime** as the **Batmen of All Nations!** Batman is also a major figure in the **Justice League**, along with **Superman, Wonder Woman, The Flash** and **Aquaman.**

TOP 3

Other Batmen

Bruce Wayne's Batman is a tough act to follow, but a few characters have tried...

1. **AZRAEL:** A badly injured Bruce Wayne gives this red-caped vigilante the role of Batman – but unruly Azrael is just too rough in his methods.
2. **JAMES GORDON:** In Batman's absence, James Gordon reluctantly dons an armoured Batsuit and does his best to fill Batman's boots.
3. **NIGHTWING:** Former Robin Dick Grayson grabs a Batsuit when Batman is believed dead – and does a decent job!

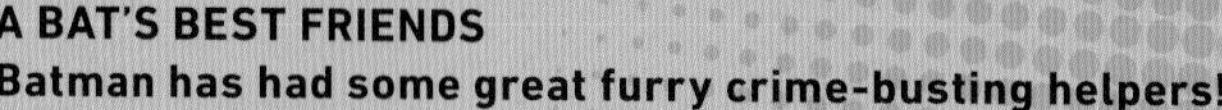

A BAT'S BEST FRIENDS
Batman has had some great furry crime-busting helpers!

ACE THE BAT-HOUND
One of Batman's several canine allies.

MOGO THE BAT-APE
A gorilla Batman rescues from a circus.

BAT-COW
A "Battlin' Bovine" saved from slaughter.

CRIMINALS ARE A SUPERSTITIOUS, COWARDLY LOT... I MUST BE A CREATURE OF THE NIGHT, BLACK, TERRIBLE...

It's Only Love

Batman and **Catwoman** are often on **different sides** of the law... but they're **irresistibly attracted** to each other!

MEGA MAKEOVER

Darkseid time-travels Batman back into the distant past, and the Dark Knight has to find his way back to the present! Along the way, Batman has to create new identities to fit the time period he's in, including a caveman, a witch-hunter, a pirate, and a gunfighter – who won't use guns!

NOOOO!

Brutal super-villain ***Bane*** breaks ***Batman's back!*** Batman can't move his legs – until his spine is healed by ***telekinesis!***

DID YOU KNOW?

Commissioner James Gordon is Batman's chief ally in the G.C.P.D. When he was a beat cop, Gordon discovered the bodies of Bruce Wayne's parents in Gotham City's Crime Alley.

KA-POW!

Backed by Bruce Wayne's billions, Batman can afford any weapon. But because his parents were killed with a gun, he refuses to use firearms.

UNLIKELY *ALLIANCE*

When they are both infected with a deadly virus, Batman has to team up with his archenemy the Joker to find a cure!

BACK FROM THE DEAD!

When the **Black Glove** organisation drugs **Bruce Wayne** to give him **amnesia,** Batman disappears and is believed to be **dead**... but Bruce recovers and Batman returns to **dispense justice** once again!

With Friends Like These...

Batman's **biggest fan** (or so he says!) is **Bat-Mite,** an imp from **the Fifth Dimension.** Bat-Mite likes to use his incredible **reality-altering powers** to cause **chaos,** so he can see his hero **spring into action!**

YESSS!

Batman can escape ***any trap*** – even from a chamber filled with ***water*** and rigged with ***machine guns.*** He traps air in his cape to ***breathe underwater!***

It's Only Love

Tim Drake has had **several girlfriends,** but the one who seems to have made the **biggest impression** is fellow crime-fighter **Spoiler (Stephanie Brown).**

KA-POW!

As well as Batarangs, Robin (Tim Drake) uses a battle staff. It was given to him by martial arts supremo Lady Shiva and he uses it as a weapon and a pole vault. It also makes a scary whistling sound when swung, intimidating foes.

FAST FACTS

REAL NAMES: Dick Grayson; Tim Drake; Jason Todd; Stephanie Brown; Damian Wayne; Carrie Kelley

NICKNAMES: The Boy Wonder; The Girl Wonder

STRENGTHS: Acrobatics; martial arts; detective skills

WEAPONS: Martial arts weaponry, such as bo staff, escrima sticks, and swords

WEAKNESS: Keeping identity secret from super-villains

FOES: The Joker; Two-Face; The Penguin; other Batman foes

WHEN GOOD GUYS GO BAD

His mind **poisoned** by being brought back to life in a **Lazarus Pit, Jason Todd** becomes the villainous **Red Hood,** seeking out **Batman** for not avenging his **death** at the hands of **the Joker!**

WHAT THE..?!

When **Batman** mysteriously vanishes from **Gotham City, Robin (Tim Drake)** takes over with his own **"R"** searchlight signal and red **"Robinmobile"!**

HOT WHEELS

When adventuring around Gotham City, Robin (Tim Drake) drives a red sports car called the Redbird. He also glides around the night sky, using a special hang-glider.

TITANIC TEEN WONDERS!

Every nightfall must be balanced with **the brightness of day.** No wonder the grim **Dark Knight** wants **a Robin** to fight alongside him! Many **teenage heroes** have donned the mantle, all of them **brave, bold** and **ready for battle!**

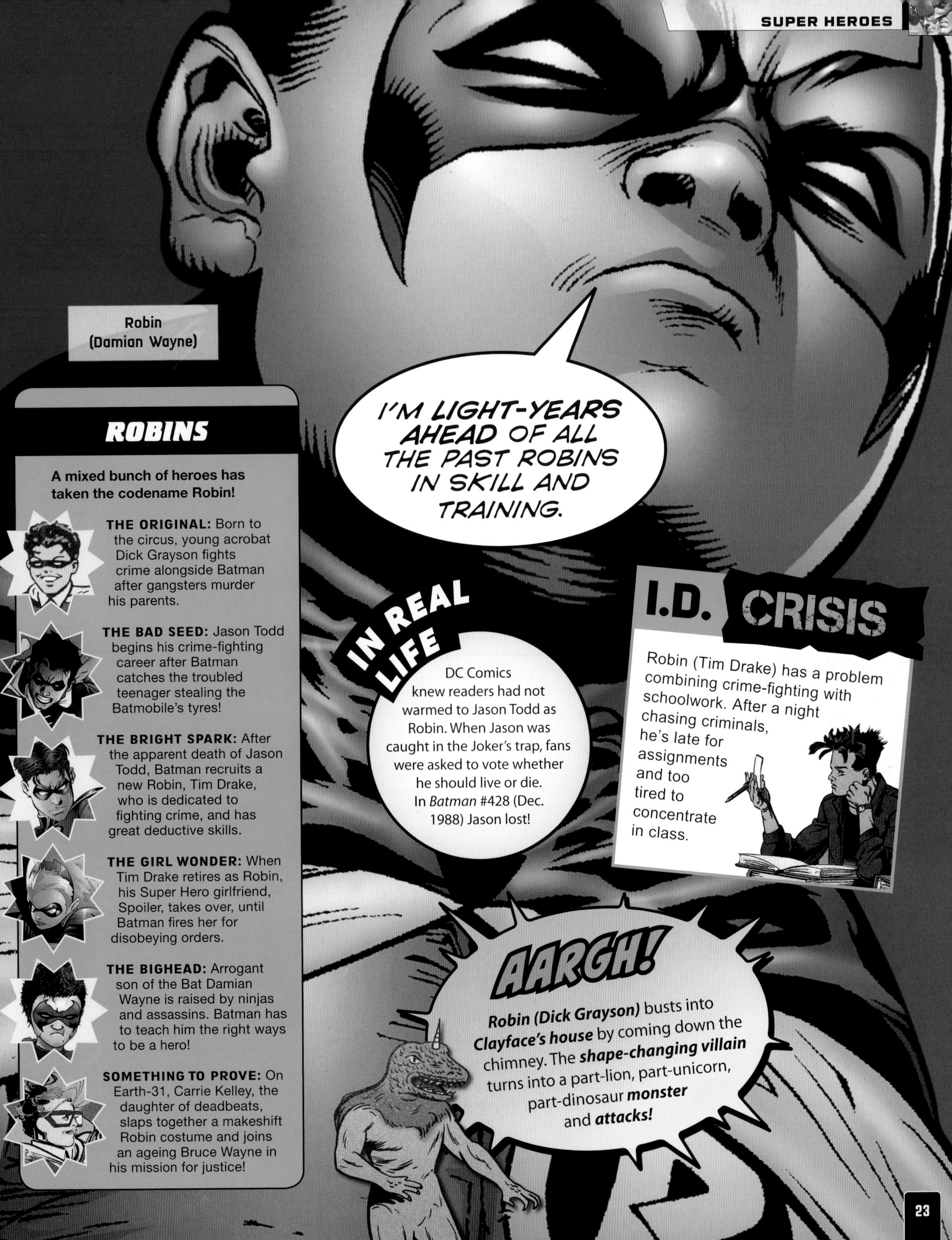

I'M LIGHT-YEARS AHEAD OF ALL THE PAST ROBINS IN SKILL AND TRAINING.

Robin (Damian Wayne)

ROBINS

A mixed bunch of heroes has taken the codename Robin!

THE ORIGINAL: Born to the circus, young acrobat Dick Grayson fights crime alongside Batman after gangsters murder his parents.

THE BAD SEED: Jason Todd begins his crime-fighting career after Batman catches the troubled teenager stealing the Batmobile's tyres!

THE BRIGHT SPARK: After the apparent death of Jason Todd, Batman recruits a new Robin, Tim Drake, who is dedicated to fighting crime, and has great deductive skills.

THE GIRL WONDER: When Tim Drake retires as Robin, his Super Hero girlfriend, Spoiler, takes over, until Batman fires her for disobeying orders.

THE BIGHEAD: Arrogant son of the Bat Damian Wayne is raised by ninjas and assassins. Batman has to teach him the right ways to be a hero!

SOMETHING TO PROVE: On Earth-31, Carrie Kelley, the daughter of deadbeats, slaps together a makeshift Robin costume and joins an ageing Bruce Wayne in his mission for justice!

IN REAL LIFE

DC Comics knew readers had not warmed to Jason Todd as Robin. When Jason was caught in the Joker's trap, fans were asked to vote whether he should live or die. In *Batman* #428 (Dec. 1988) Jason lost!

I.D. CRISIS

Robin (Tim Drake) has a problem combining crime-fighting with schoolwork. After a night chasing criminals, he's late for assignments and too tired to concentrate in class.

AARGH!

Robin (Dick Grayson) busts into ***Clayface's house*** by coming down the chimney. The ***shape-changing villain*** turns into a part-lion, part-unicorn, part-dinosaur ***monster*** and ***attacks!***

HERE COME THE BATWOMEN!

They may come from **wealth,** an order of **assassins** or from **police and military** families. But **whatever** their **backgrounds,** they're all called to join **the Bat-family** and become **crime-fighting Super Heroes!**

DID YOU KNOW?

When heiress Kathy Kane (Batwoman) and billionaire Bruce Wayne (Batman) first meet, they both rush off when the Bat-Signal appears in the sky. Neither knows the other's secret identity...

TELL ME MORE

Batman learns Kathy Kane's **secret ID** and pompously convinces her to **give up** crime-fighting for her **own good** – but **not for long...**

Batwoman (Kathy Kane)

HANDLE WITH CARE!

The contents of Kathy Kane's purse may look normal, but that **powder puff** is full of **sneezing powder,** that **perfume dispenser** contains **tear gas**, and her **hair nets** expand into **actual nets!**

YESSS!

Librarian ***Barbara Gordon*** becomes a ***Super Hero*** by accident when she dresses up as a ***female Batman*** at a fancy costume party and rescues ***Bruce Wayne*** from a ***kidnapper!***

FAST FACTS

REAL NAME: Kathy Kane

TRAINING: Trapeze; stunt cycling

ABILITIES: Acrobatics; martial arts

EQUIPMENT: Gadgets made to look like cosmetics or jewellery

POWER UP!

To keep criminal Elton Craig from swallowing his super-power capsule, Kathy Kane takes the pill herself... and gets the powers of Superman for 24 hours!

JLA FILES

CASSANDRA CAIN

A future Batgirl, Cassandra is raised by her assassin parents, David Cain and Lady Shiva, who never teach her to speak or read. Instead, they enhance her fighting ability by teaching her to predict opponents' moves from their body language. When Cassandra later learns to read, she is extremely dyslexic.

A BAT IS BORN

Kate Kane is inspired to become a Super Hero when she is mugged one night and saved by Batman!

FAST FACTS

REAL NAME: Kate Kane

TRAINING: Military school; gymnastics

ABILITIES: Acrobatics; criminology; hand-to-hand combat; stealth techniques

EQUIPMENT: Modified military tech

WHEN GOOD GUYS GO BAD

The Teen Titans discover that **Cassandra Cain** is working with the villain **Deathstroke! Robin** soon realises that Deathstroke is **drugging her** in order to **control her.** He injects her with an **antidote.** When she comes to, she **seeks revenge!**

NEW AGE OF CRIME... MEET NEW AGE OF CRIMEFIGHTER.

Batwoman (Kate Kane)

I.D. CRISIS

Cassandra Cain seems to lose hope when Bruce Wayne is thought to be **dead**, and she gives **Stephanie Brown** her **Batgirl** costume. After fighting crime as **Spoiler** and then **Robin**, Stephanie becomes **Batgirl!**

It's Only Love

After her romance with **G.C.P.D. cop Maggie Sawyer** is complicated by her secret life as **Batwoman, Kate Kane** solves the problem by revealing her **double life** and proposing **costume!**

BATGIRL FAST FACTS

BARBARA

REAL NAME: Barbara Gordon

ABILITIES: Martial arts; photographic memory; computer hacking

CASSANDRA

REAL NAME: Cassandra Cain

ABILITIES: Martial arts; body language reading; stealth techniques

STEPHANIE

REAL NAME: Stephanie Brown

ABILITIES: Martial arts; acrobatics; escapology

WHAT THE..?

Batgirl (Barbara Gordon) tracks down her first super-villain, **Killer Moth,** with her sense of **smell!** Some of her **perfume** has **rubbed off** onto the criminal!

DID YOU KNOW?

Catwoman knows **Batman's true identity,** but her lips are sealed. **Talia al Ghūl** teaches her a **meditation technique** to prevent her revealing it, even when under the influence of **mind control** or **truth serums.**

SPECIAL *MOVES*

Catwoman is such an **incredible acrobat** and **so fast** on her feet she can **dodge a hail of bullets!**

WOW!

3.7

The length in metres of Catwoman's whip (12 ft)!

AARGH!

While trying to purloin an ***ancient Egyptian relic,*** Catwoman accidentally revives a mummy who's been dead for ***4,796 years.*** The mummy thinks Selina is a reincarnation of his ***long-dead love!***

Q&A

Q: Is Catwoman a hero or a villain

A: Both – and neither! Slinking through Gotham City by night, Selina Kyle loves the thrill of stealing from the rich. Howev she also has a strong, if unpredictable, moral code of her own.

Cat and Bat

When **Batman** meets **Catwoman,** he stops her stealing a diamond. To **Robin's disgust,** he then lets her **escape.** He eventually **proposes** with a ring displaying the **very same diamond** she once **tried to steal!**

BEST KNOWN F

Being Gotham City's premier ca burglar—and always landing on her feet!

NO ONE WOULD EVER MISTAKE ME FOR A **HERO**, BUT I DO HAVE **SOME** STANDARDS.

CATWOMAN'S PETS

Not surprisingly, Catwoman has shared her home with many cats, including **Hecate,** who she has trained to **steal** for her. She has also been accompanied by larger, more savage felines, including **a tiger called Rajah!**

Cracking the whip

Catwoman is a superb acrobat and martial arts fighter. She also employs some tricksy gadgets and weapons...

A LEATHER BULLWHIP: her signature weapon; carried in her boot or in a backpack.

KNOCKOUT POWDER: in her compact; puts foes to sleep in seconds.

CLAWS: forged from titanium; retractable; for climbing, or scratching!

CAT-GRAPNEL: fired from a wrist device; for climbing or descending tall buildings.

BOOT PITONS: spring loaded; for extra grip when climbing.

STUN GUN: concealed in boot; delivers 75,000 volt shock.

FAST FACTS

REAL NAME: Selina Kyle

NICKNAMES: Princess of Plunder; the Cat; Plundering Kitten

STRENGTHS: Superb gymnast and martial artist

FOES: Joker's Daughter; Black Mask; Dollhouse; Bone; Scarecrow

★ TEAM PLAYER ★

Seeing the good in **Poison Ivy** and **Harley Quinn,** Catwoman suggests that they team up to form the **Gotham City Sirens.** The trio fights for justice, but their **methods** are sometimes **extreme!**

TOP 5

Feline Fashions

Catwoman is best known for her black catsuit, but she has worn a variety of outfits over the years.

1. **MASKED MOGGY** One of Catwoman's first costumes consists of an evening dress and a very realistic cat's head mask.

2. **CAPED CAT** Catwoman later adopts a whole costume for her persona, including a flowing purple dress, green cape, boots and a cat-eared mask.

3. **GOING GREEN** For a short time Catwoman wears a green, scaly-looking catsuit. It also has an eye mask, complete with cat ears.

4. **PURPLE REIGN** Still in a catsuit, but back in purple, Catwoman now has long sharp claws on her gloved fingers.

5. **LEATHER LOOK** Catwoman rocks a "biker chic" look, in black leather with added cat-ear mask and signature goggles.

PRINCESS OF PLUNDER

Catwoman Selina Kyle has been one of Batman's most **tricky foes,** but she is also one of the people he **trusts most.** An **expert thief** who loves **diamonds,** Catwoman is also a **fierce protector** of Gotham City's **most vulnerable citizens.**

BACK FROM THE DEAD!

Cats are supposed to have **nine lives,** and Catwoman uses up one when the villain **Hush** cuts her heart out! Thankfully, Selina and her heart are **kept alive** by machines. Batman defeats Hush and Selina **gets her heart back!**

SCARLET SPEEDSTER

Barry Allen, alias **The Flash,** has **saved the universe** many times. However, he's not the only **Scarlet Speedster,** he's just the **frontrunner** in a dynasty of **super-fast heroes!**

I HAVE TO RUN TOWARD DANGER... NO MATTER WHAT PRICE I HAVE TO PAY!

FAST FACTS

REAL NAME: Bartholomew "Barry" Allen

OCCUPATION: Police scientist; Super Hero

STRENGTHS: Extreme super-speed; super-fast healing

WEAKNESSES: Human biology

FOES: The Rogues; Gorilla Grodd; Reverse-Flash

ALLIES: Justice League; Green Lantern; Kid Flash

BEST KNOWN FOR

Being the Fastest Man Alive!

Q&A

Q: How does The Flash pass through solid objects?

A: By controlling the speed of his body's atoms, The Flash can phase them around the atoms of any obstacle in his path!

IN REAL LIFE

Jay Garrick was the original Flash, created by Gardner Fox and Harry Lampert, and debuting in *Flash Comics* #1 (Jan. 1940). The first hero with just a single superpower, Garrick was quickly followed by a wave of mega-fast mystery men from other comics publishers.

DID YOU KNOW?

The Speed Force is an extradimensional energy that propels all motion in the Multiverse. Through it, time itself moves forwards or backwards. The Flash, and all speedsters, access this energy when they run.

JLA FILES

Police scientist Barry Allen is struck by lightning and drenched in chemicals. Empowered by the cosmic Speed Force, he gains super-speed. He becomes Super Hero The Flash, after his favourite childhood comic book hero! His speed powers give him great endurance, but he still gets hungry, and must eat vast amounts to keep energised.

WOW!

200

The number of times The Flash races around foreign spy Dr Lu's island, making her missiles go haywire and blow the island up!

EWWW!

Gorilla Grodd is one of The Flash's ***scariest*** foes. This super-smart, evil ape wants to ***eat The Flash's brains!***

DASTARDLY DEED

On Barry Allen's **wedding day, Reverse-Flash** Professor Zoom tries to replace him. The villain plans to marry **Iris West** and **steal** The Flash's **life!**

SPECIAL *MOVES*

The Flash's brain and senses work at super-speed. If he's shot, he reacts faster than thought, vibrating the bullet through his body before he even realises he's been hit!

MUTATION ALERT!

Enemies delight in mutating The Flash. He's been...

- Afflicted with a giant head and crippling headaches by the Trickster
- Transformed into a wooden puppet by Abra Kadabra
- Turned into an old man by The Top
- Transformed into glass by Mirror Master
- Merged with Kid Flash into one body by The Turtle
- Shrunk to the size of a mouse by Mirror Master
- Evolved into a human lightning bolt by his own speed
- Reduced to a cringing coward by a telepathic alien
- Expanded to weigh 454 kg (1,000 lbs) by Gorilla Grodd

When ***Darkseid*** dies, the ***Justice League*** becomes the New Gods of Apokolips and ***The Flash*** becomes the inescapable ***God of Death!***

TOP 5

Ways to become The Flash

1. **FALL ASLEEP IN A LAB** and inhale radioactive fumes (Jay Garrick).
2. **STAND NEAR SOME CHEMICALS** and hope for a lightning strike (Barry Allen).
3. **STAND NEAR SOME CHEMICALS** in the same place and hope lightning strikes twice (Wally West).
4. **INHERIT SUPER-SPEED** from your grandfather (Bart Allen).
5. **GO BACK IN TIME**, getting charged up by speed-inducing Tachyon Particles (John Fox).

TELL ME MORE

When super-speed isn't enough, The Flash uses a special running machine to go even faster! The Cosmic Treadmill enables him to traverse time and space – and even to reach alternate dimensions.

DID YOU KNOW?

The Flash's wife, **Iris West,** comes from **1,000 years** in the **future.** When Barry and Iris retire there, they have speedster children **Don** and **Dawn Allen** – the **Tornado Twins.**

KING OF THE SEAS

Aquaman is like the waters he dwells in: **deep, mysterious,** sometimes **turbulent.** This Super Hero of the seas is the **King of Atlantis,** a protector of the world's oceans, and a founding member of the **Justice League.**

FAST FACTS

REAL NAME: Arthur Curry

HOMES: Amnesty Bay, Maine; Atlantis

STRENGTHS: Super-speed in water; bulletproof skin; control over marine life

KEY WEAKNESS: Powers diminish if out of water too long

ALLIES: Mera; Vulko; Garth (a.k.a. Aqualad); Justice League; Tula (a.k.a. Aquagirl)

It's Only Love

Powerful metahuman **Mera** is Aquaman's **true love.** Unfortunately, Atlantean laws prevent Aquaman **marrying** a **non-Atlantean,** such as Mera, so Aquaman makes her an **honorary Atlantean** – and **Queen of Atlantis.**

UPGRADE!

After **one** of **Aquaman's hands** is eaten by **piranhas,** the **Lady of the Lake** helps him by gifting him a magical **water hand.** This enables Aquaman to **control water** and **heal wounds,** among other powers.

AARGH!

Aquaman loses one of his ***hands*** when evil villain ***Charybdis*** forces it into a river teeming with vicious ***piranhas!***

MUTATION ALERT!

Shrunk to a tiny size by the water sprite Qwsp, Aquaman and his sidekick Aqualad are far from the ocean and in danger of drying out! They trick a pelican into dropping water on them to save themselves. Luckily, they are soon back to normal.

BACK FROM THE DEAD!

Aquaman is **resurrected** after the **Blackest Night event**. He has two normal hands again, until **Black Manta** slices one off!

TOP 5

Aquaman Foes

1. **BLACK MANTA:** Aquaman and Black Manta are locked in a cycle of revenge after the tragic deaths of their fathers.
2. **OCEAN MASTER:** Aquaman's half-brother, Orm, takes sibling rivalry to extremes.
3. **SIREN:** Mera's twisted twin sister's mystical powers enable her to create hard-water weapons. She hopes to seize the throne of Atlantis!
4. **CHARYBDIS:** A terrorist, driven insane with grief by the death of his wife, Scylla.
5. **THE DEAD KING:** Formerly Atlan, King of Atlantis who was usurped by his brother Orin. Centuries later, the Dead King returns to revenge himself on Orin's descendant, Aquaman.

I KNOW THE OCEANS BETTER THAN **ANYONE**, BUT THEY'RE **STILL** FULL OF SECRETS, EVEN TO ME.

IN REAL LIFE

Aquaman made a big splash when he debuted in *More Fun Comics* #73 in November 1941. The Super Hero swam solo for nearly two decades before helping to found the Justice League, in March 1960.

WOW!

3,048

The speed in metres per second that Aquaman ca[n] move through the water (10,000 ft per second)!

KA-POW!

In combat, Aquaman wields the Trident of Neptune. It's not just an iconic symbol of Atlantean power, it's also a potent and magical weapon.

SPECIAL *MOVES*

Aquaman can **communicate** with almost any **aquatic creature**. He can travel anywhere in the sea – even to its **deepest, darkest,** and **coldest** depths.

Q&A

Q: Who are Aquaman's parent

A: Arthur Curry is the son of Thomas Curry, a lighthouse keeper, and the amphibious Queen Atlanna of Atla Afraid her origins will put Arthur at risk, Atlanna flees back to Atlantis There, she marries and has anoth son, named Orm.

BAD DA

Aquaman accid kills **Black Ma** **father** while s revenge for h **father's death** start of a **lifelo** between t

NOOOO!

Ruthless, arms-dealer ***Scavenger*** orders a fleet of submarines to ***invade Atlantis. Aquaman*** summons ***Topo,*** a giant, tentacled sea monster, to fight them off, but the effort of controlling the beast sends him into ***a six-month coma!***

HANDLE WITH CARE!

Evil mastermind **Oran Dargg** teleports Earth onto **a collision course** with the planet **Rann. Hawkman** and **Hawkgirl** team up with **Adam Strange** to defeat the super-villain and return the planets to their natural orbits.

DID YOU KNOW?

Hawkman has mastered **every handheld weapon** ever created, but his **favourite method** of putting villains in their place is **whacking** them with his **battle mace.**

JLA FILES

Nth METAL
A mineral found exclusively on the planet Thanagar, Nth Metal negates gravity and enhances strength and healing ability. It also fortifies the wearer, enabling him or her to fly without feeling the effects of cold, friction, or lack of oxygen.

TELL ME MORE

Hawkgirl is a ferocious warrior and brilliant detective, every inch the equal of her partner Hawkman.

TOP 5

Hawkman foes

1. **HATH-SET:** An evil, reincarnating wizard who perpetually tries to murder Hawkman and Hawkgirl/ Hawkwoman throughout history!
2. **MANHAWKS:** Space-pirates with bird bodies and ray-blasting, humanoid face-masks.
3. **MATTER MASTER:** Elemental shaper who creates a duplicate Hawkman, Golden Eagle.
4. **BYTH ROK:** Shape-shifting Thanagarian warrior who becomes a crime boss in Chicago; works with another Hawkman foe, Shadow Thief.
5. **GENTLEMAN GHOST:** Phantom highwayman Jim Craddock seeks thrills and a way to become a living man again!

WOW!

362

Speed in km/h (225 mph) that Hawkman flies; however it's possible he can go faster...

HAWKS ARE NOT HUNTED. THEY'RE THE HUNTERS!

WHAT THE..?!

Katar Hol assimilates **all human knowledge** by scanning planet Earth with a Thanagarian **Absorbascon.** This device also enables Hawkman to **communicate with** and **control birds.**

WHEN GOOD GUYS GO BAD

Thanagar becomes a **military dictatorship** and its leaders try to covertly conquer **Earth,** forcing **Hawkman** and **Hawkwoman** to wage a secret **"Shadow War"** against their **own people** to save humanity from **alien domination!**

Q&A

Q: Who exactly is Hawkman?

A: It's hard to say. He could be...

- **Archaeologist Carter Hall:** A reincarnated Egyptian prince.
- **Katar Hol:** An intrepid Thanagarian police officer.
- **Katar Hol:** A disgraced Thanagarian soldier and political rebel.
- **Fel Andar:** A Thanagarian spy laying plans for an invasion by infiltrating the Justice League.
- **Katar Hol:** An amnesiac fugitive and Thanagarian royal consort.

IN REAL LIFE

The character of Hawkman took to the skies in *Flash Comics* #1 (Jan. 1940). The hero was later reinvented many times. All the different versions were merged (by the Thanagarian Hawk god) during DC Comics' Zero Hour event.

WINGED WONDER

With **wings** and **equipment** laced with a mysterious, gravity-defying metal, **Hawkman** delivers justice and vengeance with **ancient weapons** and **timeless fury!**

POWER UP!

Nth Metal eventually invades Hawkman's body. This grants Hawkman the ability to instantly sprout wings and generate Nth Metal weapons and armour.

FAST FACTS

REAL NAME:
Katar Hol

OCCUPATION:
Law officer on planet Thanagar

STRENGTHS: Superpowered physique; super-fast healing; combat training; communicates with birds

WEAKNESSES: Dangerously short-tempered

FOES: Hath-Set; Manhawks; Matter Master; Byth Rok; Shadow Thief; Gentleman Ghost

ALLIES: Justice League

It's Only Love

Time and again, Egyptian prince ***Khufu*** has been reborn and reunited with his love, ***Chay-Ara.*** As ***Carter Hall,*** he meets ***Shiera Sanders*** and they become ***Hawkman and Hawkgirl,*** a.k.a. ***Hawkwoman.***

FAMOUS LAST WORDS

"A Thanagarian does not shy away from a fight. A Thanagarian... savours it!"

Hawkman

AMAZING AMAZON

Diana of Themyscira is born on an island of **immortal women,** and sent out into the world on **a mission of peace.** She uses **gifts** from the **Greek gods** to fight **evil** as **Wonder Woman!**

MAKEOVER
Wonder Woman loses her superpowers when she opts to stay on "Man's World", instead of following the Amazons to another dimension. She updates her look and opens a boutique, but continues to fight crime using her superb martial arts skills.

JLA FILES

DIANA'S BIRTH
Wonder Woman's mother, Hippolyta, Queen of the Amazons, prays to Zeus, ruler of the Greek gods, to give her a child. He tells her to make a baby from clay, and breathes life into it. Little Diana grows up to be Wonder Woman.

TELL ME MORE

Wonder Woman's Lasso of Truth is forged by Hephaestus, the Olympian god of blacksmiths. Her Magical Gauntlets are made from the shield of Athena, goddess of wisdom.

IN REAL LIFE

Wonder Woman was created in 1941 by psychologist William Moulton Marston and artist Harry G. Peter to "save the world from the hatreds and wars of men in a man-made world!"

FACE OFF

WONDER WOMAN
Great knowledge of fighting techniques given to her by the goddess Athena and trained into her by the Amazons.

THE CHEETAH
Channelling the spirit of The Cheetah gives her super-speed, strength as well as razor-sharp claws.

WINNER: Wonder Woman – divine empowerment beats catlike reflexes.

UNLIKELY ALLIANCES

When **Harley Quinn** uncovers a plan to kill **Wonder Woman,** they **swap costumes** and shut the villains down. Then Harley steals "Wondy's" lasso to play **Truth or Dare**!

GOOD DAY

Wonder Woman defeats alien **fairy-tale-obsessed** sorceress **Queen of Fables** by imprisoning her in the **dullest book** she can find: the **U.S. Tax Code**!

WHAT THE..?!

In alternate histories, when **Diana** is growing up on the island of Themyscira, she builds a **plane** that is **completely invisible!** She uses it to travel long distances.

★ TEAM PLAYER ★

One of Wonder Woman's **best friends** is feisty student **Etta Candy**. In one adventure, Etta helps Wonder Woman **capture** a Nazi base and **rescue** Steve Trevor from evil **Doctor Poison**!

It's Only Love

Steve Trevor has **carried a torch** for **Wonder Woman** for years. She won't **marry** him until her job **fighting evil** is done!

WE WILL SHOW THOSE EVIL MEN THAT WOMEN FIGHT FOR PEACE HARDER THAN MEN CAN FIGHT TO SATISFY THEIR GREED!

TOP 4

Wonder Weapons

1. **LASSO OF TRUTH:** This cannot be broken and forces people to tell the truth.
2. **MAGICAL GAUNTLETS:** These deflect bullets, lasers and energy blasts.
3. **SWORD:** Wonder Woman prefers traditional Amazonian weapons to modern ones.
4. **SHIELD:** For deflecting objects in battle.

FAST FACTS

REAL NAME: Diana

POWERS: Super-strength and durability; super-speed; enhanced senses; flight, expert at unarmed combat

FOES: Ares, god of war; The Cheetah; Circe

ALLIES: Justice League; Etta Candy; Steve Trevor

HANDLE WITH CARE!

Wonder Woman's tiara is also a **weapon.** It has **razor-sharp edges** and can be thrown like a **boomerang.** She once even pierced **Superman's skin** with it!

WONDER WOMEN

Wonder Woman's stand for **peace, freedom** and **justice** has inspired **a host of heroes** to take on her **mantle,** either in **tribute,** in **challenge** – or in **another world!**

In an alternate timeline, ***Wonder Woman*** has a twin sister named ***Nubia.*** Baby Nubia is stolen by the ***god of war*** and raised to ***destroy the Amazons.*** Nubia later ***challenges*** Diana for the right to call herself ***"Wonder Woman"!***

GOOD DAY

After becoming **friends** with Wonder Woman, teenager **Cassie Sandsmark** discovers the **Sandals of Hermes** and the **Gauntlet of Atlas,** which give powers of **flight, super-speed and super-strength.** She decides to fight evil with her friend as **the second Wonder Girl!**

Cassie Sandsmark

MEGA MAKEOVER

When Diana briefly becomes a god of Olympus, her mother, Hippolyta, becomes Wonder Woman, joining both the JLA and JSA. Instead of a lasso, Hippolyta battles foes with a broadsword!

TOP 5

Alternate Earth Wonder Women

Wonder Woman appears in many forms throughout the Multiverse...

1. On Earth-3, Lois Lane is the villainous Superwoman of the Crime Syndicate of America.
2. On Earth-9, she's a super-strong psychic alien from Planet Gotham.
3. On Earth-18, she's a Wild West sheriff fighting mechanical gunslingers.
4. On Earth-19, Diana is an actor in a 19th-century U.K. ruled by Jack the Ripper.
5. On Earth-C-Minus, she's Wonder Wabbit, a member of the heroic team Just'a Lotta Animals.

POWER UP!

King of the Greek gods Zeus grants Cassie's fondest wish and makes her superpowers a permanent part of her. He then confesses that he's her father!

WE DIDN'T CHOOSE TO BE WHAT WE ARE... THIS LIFE CHOSE US. WE LIVE IT. WITH ALL ITS CHANGES AND CHALLENGES. OBSTACLES. DISAPPOINTMENTS. FAILURES. ITS SUCCESSES. ITS JOYS.
Donna Troy
Wonder Woman

I.D. CRISIS

Donna Troy can't remember her own childhood, and has confused memories of living in another universe. "I don't know where I'm from. I was adopted age seven. I have no memories prior to that. I don't even know where my powers come from."

TELL ME MORE

When Amazon Queen Hippolyta has a vision of her daughter Wonder Woman dying, she tries to save Diana by replacing her. A warrior named Artemis from the Bana-Mighdall Amazon tribe steps up and becomes the new Wonder Woman!

BACK IN TIME

As Wonder Woman, **Hippolyta** travels back in time to the 1940s and joins the **Justice Society.** She stays for eight years before coming back to the present!

DID YOU KNOW?

An Amazon sorceress creates a magical duplicate of Diana, so young Wonder Woman will have a playmate. This twin grows up to be a hero in her own right, super-powered Donna Troy!

BACK FROM THE DEAD!

Artemis dies battling the demonic **White Magician** and finds herself in the **Underworld.** She defeats one of the **Princes of Hell,** finds her way back to the **land of the living** and becomes **a demon hunter!**

WHEN BAD GUYS GO GOOD

After **Wonder Woman** frees **Nubia** from the war god's mind control, Nubia breaks off the fight with her twin. She and her band of warriors devote themselves **to peace!**

FAST FACTS

REAL NAME: Hal Jordan

OCCUPATION: Fighter pilot

KEY STRENGTH: Great willpower enables power ring to form objects from hard light, translate languages= and create a force field that allows intergalactic travel and protects against hostile environments

ALLIES: Green Lantern Corps; Justice League

FOES: Sinestro; Black Hand; Hector Hammond; Star Sapphire

WOW!

3,600

The number of space sectors across the universe protected by the Green Lantern Corps.

JLA FILES

INBUILT WEAKNESS
The Guardians of the Universe capture the yellow fear entity, Parallax, and imprison it inside the Central Power Battery. Because of this, the Green Lanterns' rings suffer from an "impurity". The rings are far weaker if the ringbearer is afraid, and they can be useless against the colour yellow.

WATCH THE CHARGE!

Green Lantern's power ring is charged up from a **lantern-shaped battery.** The more he uses the ring, the faster it **runs out of juice!**

WHEN GOOD GUYS GO BAD

Hal Jordan loses control and becomes **a villain!** it turns out that **Parallax** has escaped from the **Central Power Battery** on Oa, infected Hal and **taken over his body!**

It's Only Love

When Green Lantern **Hal Jordan** battles the villain **Star Sapphire,** he's unaware he's fighting his boss and on-off girlfriend, **Carol Ferris.** She's been powered up by **alien warrior women!**

TOP 4

Green Lantern members

The Corps includes some unusual-looking characters...

1. **SALAAK:** A brainy hero from planet Slyggia; four arms make him a great multi-tasker!
2. **MOGO:** A sentient planet, he can change his climate, gravity and surface; if a Green Lantern dies, he finds a replacement.
3. **KILOWOG:** A brilliant scientist from Bolovax Vik; 2.5 metres (8 ft 3 in) and hugely strong, he recruits and trains Corps members.
4. **LEEZLE PON:** This intelligent smallpox virus fights bravely for justice!

DID YOU KNOW?

The Guardians, leaders of the **Green Lantern Corps,** are the **oldest** living beings in the **universe!**

TOUGH BREAK

Green Lantern foe **Major Disaster** is well named. He hires scientists to invent a device that creates **natural disasters,** but **electrocutes himself** when **turning it on!**

GOOD DAY

Green Lantern **Abin Sur** crashes on Earth and is **mortally wounded.** His power ring seeks out **Hal Jordan,** who becomes **the first human Green Lantern!**

WHEN GOOD GUYS GO BAD

Hal Jordan's first teacher in the Corps is the headstrong **Sinestro**. However, Sinestro is **kicked out** of the Corps and banished to the **antimatter universe** – where he finds a **yellow power ring** and returns as one of Hal's most **dangerous foes!**

★TEAM PLAYERS★

As well as Hal Jordan, other strong-willed humans have been chosen to join the Green Lantern Corps…

Guy Gardner: A former police officer always ready for a battle.
Kyle Rayner: A former graphic designer and artist, sensitive and creative.
John Stewart: A former U.S. Marine and architect with a rebellious streak.

SPECIAL *MOVES*

Green Lantern can will his power ring to **take any shape.** When going undercover while investigating a group of **human-abducting aliens,** he transforms his ring into **a pair of sunglasses!**

A GREEN LANTERN ISN'T WITHOUT FEAR. A GREEN LANTERN OVERCOMES FEAR.

AARGH!

The Black Hand has a novel way of attacking ***Green Lantern.*** The villain possesses a device that ***divides the hero in two*** and sends one half to ***another dimension!***

GREEN POWER!

Fighter pilot Hal Jordan's extraordinary **willpower** enables him to wield a **Green Lantern ring.** He polices **the universe** as a member of the **Green Lantern Corps!**

FAST FACTS

REAL NAME: Oliver Queen

OCCUPATION: Industrialist; Super Hero

ABILITIES: Archery; martial arts; hunting skills

ARCHENEMIES: Merlyn; Count Vertigo; Killer Moth; Cupid

ALLIES: Green Lantern; Justice League; Speedy; Green Arrow II; Speedy II; Arrowette; Black Canary; Red Arrow; Batman

FILES

Wealthy playboy and heir to Queen Industries Oliver Queen is partying on an oil rig when terrorists attack and the rig explodes. Ollie is believed to be dead, but ends up on a desert island. To survive, he becomes an expert archer. He eventually returns to civilisation a changed man, and becomes crime-fighting Super Hero Green Arrow.

BEST KNOWN FOR

His incredible chili recipe—unequalled in the known universe!

ALTERNATE EARTHS

In an **alternate future,** an ageing **Green Arrow** helps **Batman** battle **Superman.** His reason? **Revenge!**

IN REAL LIFE

Created by Mortimer Weisinger and George Papp, Green Arrow was one of the few Super Heroes to be published throughout the 1950s. The hero first appeared in *More Fun Comics* #73 (Nov. 1941).

If things get ***really desperate,*** the Emerald Archer can blow the opposition to ***kingdom come*** with his ***Atomic Warhead Arrow!***

EMERALD ARCHER

Green Arrow was **born** the day that multi-millionaire **Oliver Queen** officially **"died".** With a **new purpose,** Queen honed his **archery skills** and then set out to **change the world!**

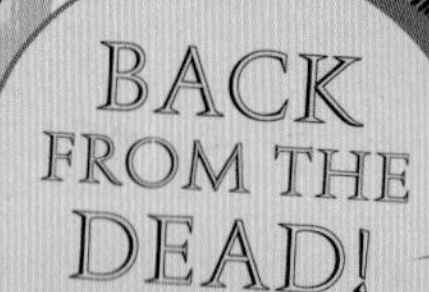

After being **blown up** by a bomb, **Oliver Queen** is revived by former Green Lantern **Hal Jordan** while Hal is imbued with **godlike powers** as the evil **Parallax!**

ANYONE DOESN'T WANNA BE A HUMAN PIN-CUSHION BETTER MAKE LIKE A STATUE!

AARGH!

Caught in ***a death trap***, Green Arrow must either ***lose his arm*** or cause ***Metropolis*** to be ***destroyed.*** Instead, he blows ***himself*** up!

KA-POW!

The Emerald Archer is such a good shot, he can even target a single drop of falling water!

DID YOU KNOW?

Oliver Queen loses **billions of dollars** after becoming a **hero**, and eventually chooses to **reveal his identity** to the public!

★ TEAM PLAYER ★

Green Arrow makes history and **saves galaxies** when he becomes a founding member of the **Seven Soldiers of Victory!**

TOP 10

Trickiest Trick Arrows

1. **BOXING GLOVE ARROW:** Knocks out bad guys with one punch!
2. **UMBRELLA ARROW:** Makes a handy parachute!
3. **JELLYFISH ARROW:** Fires a sticky jelly-like substance.
4. **JACK-IN-THE-BOX ARROW:** Packs a surprise punch.
5. **DRY ICE ARROW:** Creates an atmospheric cloud.
6. **FOUNTAIN PEN ARROW:** Shoots out ink for tracking down crooks.
7. **TUMBLEWEED ARROW:** Stirs up a dusty, concealing smokescreen.
8. **HANDCUFF ARROW:** Captures villains.
9. **BOLA ARROW:** Entangles fleeing bad guys.
10. **PAINTBRUSH ARROW:** Coats a getaway car's windshield with paint.

STRAIGHT ARROWS

Green Arrow has had several partners, all ready to launch themselves into danger!

SPEEDY: Roy Harper joins Green Arrow in his earliest crime-fighting days.

GREEN ARROW II: Son of Oliver Queen Connor Hawke follows in his father's footsteps.

SPEEDY II: Mia Dearden teams up with Oliver Queen after he is brought back to life.

ARROWETTE: Bonnie King is an Olympic-level archer, but a failure at fighting crime.

RED ARROW: Oliver Queen's half-sister Emiko may be an even better archer than he is.

BLACK CANARY: A powerful crime-fighting partner in every sense of the word!

THE MAN FROM MARS

J'onn J'onzz, the Martian Manhunter, stands up for **peace, love, honor, and justice**—no matter what the **cost!**

TOUGH BREAK

Accidentally **teleported to Earth** by scientist Saul Erdel, J'onn J'onzz's appearance provokes **a heart attack,** and Erdel dies before he can return the Manhunter to his place of origin: Ma'aleca'andra, or as we know it, **Mars!**

FAST FACTS

REAL NAME: J'onn J'onzz

OCCUPATION:
Martian peace officer; Earth police officer; Super Hero

STRENGTHS: Super-strength; speed; vision powers; durability; shape-shifting; density control; flight; regeneration; telepathy; telekinesis

WEAKNESSES: Fear of fire

FOES: Ma'alefa'ak (Malefic); White Martians; Despero

ALLIES: Justice League; Justice League of America; Stormwatch; Justice Experience

BAD BLOOD

On Mars, J'onn is a **truth-seeker** and **Manhunter.** However he has an **evil twin** named Ma'alefa'ak (Malefic), whom he arrests for **horrific crimes.** In retaliation, Ma'alefa'ak creates the **H'ronmeer's Curse plague** to wipe out all Green Martians!

IN REAL LIFE

The idea for J'onn J'onzz came from *Batman* #78 (Aug./Sept. 1953), when the Caped Crusader tracked down "The Manhunter From Mars"! The character was reimagined, debuting in *Detective Comics* #225 (Nov. 1955).

TELL ME MORE

Martians keep one shape just for family and friends. On Mars, J'onn only shares this secret form with his wife M'yri'ah and daughter K'hym, but on Earth, a few Justice League comrades know it, too.

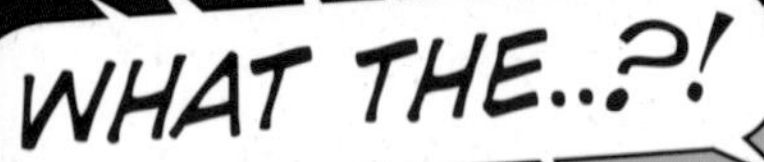

WHAT THE..?!

In Japan, J'onn is an **adored hero** with his own manga and anime franchises. Millions of fans keenly follow **street urchin "Jomo Atomo"** who melds with an alien parasite to become **Bio Armor Jade Warrior!**

JLA FILES

FEAR OF FIRE

Thousands of years ago, the Guardians of the Universe evolved the peaceful Green and the warlike White Martians from the Burning, a barbaric conquering race that needed fire to reproduce. All Martians now have a fear of fire. This phobia was instilled into all Green and White Martians by the Guardians to hamper them from using their powers to conquer other worlds.

EASY MONEY

The Martian Manhunter never needs to go short of cash. He can extract gold from seawater!

★ TEAM PLAYER ★

The **Martian Manhunter** has joined most **Justice League** lineups, leading **Justice League Detroit** and **Justice League International.** The **JLA founder** has also joined extraterrestrial defence force **Stormwatch,** federal agency **A.R.G.U.S.,** and 1960s super-team the **Justice Experience.**

I WILL PROTECT THE INNOCENTS OF THIS PLANET FROM MONSTERS. AND I SHALL WATCH AND LEARN.

SWEET TOOTH

J'onn loves Earth confectionary, especially **chocolate cookies!** Luckily he can reshape his **teeth** and **waistline** at will!

NOOOO!

When ***J'onn J'onzz*** attempts to cure his ***fire weakness,*** he accidentally devolves into an alien creature named ***Fernus.*** It takes the ***entire Justice League*** to defeat Fernus and restore J'onn to normal.

POWER UP!

While battling to stop time-shifted ancient Mars overwhelming Earth, J'onn integrates with the mechanical brain of a Martian City Mech to become a colossal war robot!

BACK FROM THE DEAD!

J'onn is **vaporised** while fighting **Ma'alefa'ak,** but **regenerates** when his own **severed arm** grows back into a **new body!**

TOP 10

Alter Egos

Shape-shifting J'onn J'onzz maintains many different identities to help him understand life on Earth. Some are heroes; some are not even people!

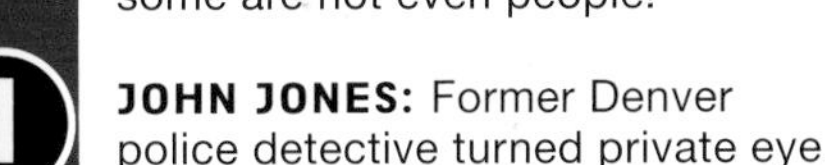

1. **JOHN JONES:** Former Denver police detective turned private eye.
2. **MARCO XAVIER:** International playboy and agent of crime syndicate Vulture.
3. **BRONZE WRAITH:** Super Hero in 1960s team the Justice Experience.
4. **TOMASO:** J'onn tests human kindliness as a Venetian street cat.
5. **BLOODWYND:** Sorcerer and occasional Justice League member.
6. **BIG DOOF:** Clumsy, super-strong minor villain who somehow never gets caught!
7. **ISOBEL DE LA ROSA:** Author and activist from Montevideo, Uruguay.
8. **MRS KLINGMAN:** Clark Kent's high school civics teacher.
9. **YUCHIRO TAKATA:** An elderly Japanese inventor.
10. **GOLDIE JOHNSON:** Star reporter for Chicago tabloid *The World Register.*

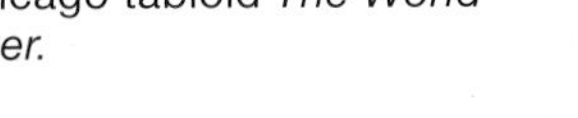
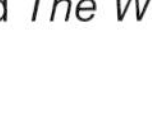

OUT OF THE SWAMP!

Evergreen warrior **Swamp Thing** is Earth's **elemental guardian.** He wages war against **devils, aliens, monsters** and, most of all, **greedy, polluting humans!**

IN REAL LIFE

Swamp Thing first appeared as a mucky man-monster in *House of Secrets* #92 (July 1971) in a story of thwarted love and revenge from the grave. A massive hit, a year later Swamp Thing returned in his own award-winning series by Len Wein and Bernie Wrightson.

POWER UP!

After passing trials set by the Parliaments of Stones, Waves, Air and Flames, Alec becomes an elemental god, not only controlling all terrestrial life, but also the primal forces that created Earth!

FAST FACTS

REAL NAME: Alec Holland

OCCUPATION: Botanist; biochemist

STRENGTHS: Human personality able to build bodies out of vegetable matter; control of plant life

WEAKNESSES: Vulnerable to pollution; magic; loneliness

FOES: Anton Arcane; Nergal; Sunderland Corporation; Floronic Man; Hunters Three

ALLIES: Justice League Dark; John Constantine; Phantom Stranger

SPECIAL *MOVES*

One of Swamp Thing's **greatest feats** is growing into a huge spider and carrying fabled **castle Camelot** away from a **besieging army!**

AAARGH!

Swamp Thing's arm** is **cut off,** but it soon **grows back.** However, the **lost limb** also **keeps growing** – becoming a near-mindless **duplicate** who **attacks the original Swampy!

WHAT THE..?!

Swamp Thing is one of a long line of protectors safeguarding **the Green** for the **Parliament of Trees.** His predecessors include **Lady Jane, Tree of Life Yggdrasil, Tree of Knowledge Tuuru,** and an ancient, weird-looking lifeform called **Eyam.**

GROWTH SPURT!

When searching for his lost love Abigail in Gotham City, Swamp Thing grows to the size of a skyscraper!

TELL ME MORE

The Green is a true force of nature, an ethereal network linking all plant life in a single, vast global community. It allows plant-consciousnesses to travel anywhere vegetation grows. It also enables the Parliament of Trees to contact and monitor their agents, such as Swamp Thing.

ALEC HOLLAND IS DEAD... AND IN HIS PLACE STANDS ONLY A... SWAMP THING!

OTHER PRIMAL FORCES:

THE RED
Connects all of Earths animal life

THE GREY
Connects funghi and lichens

THE BLUE
Or "Clear" protects the oceans and all life in them (supervised by a Parliament of Waves)

THE BLACK
Or "Rot" thrives on the death of all things (govern by a Parliament of Decay)

Q&A

Q: How does scientist Alec Holland become Swamp Thing?

A: Holland's lab is blown up by villains, his clothes catch fire and he throws himself into a Louisiana swamp. An experimental serum he has swallowed reacts with the swamp and out comes – Swamp Thing!

Swamp Thing loves **Abigail Arcane.** Unfortunately she's the daughter of his **great enemy, Anton Arcane.** Anton is the **Avatar of the Black**, the force of **death** and **decay**, and Abby eventually **takes his place!**

YESSS!

When **Superman** is infected with deadly **Kryptonian scarlet fungus,** Swamp Thing manages to bring the dying hero into Earth's **Green** to cure him.

HEAVY METAL KID

His body **shattered,** young **Victor Stone** is **cybernetically augmented** with **extraterrestrial technology** to save his **life.** Now he's **Cyborg** – half-man, half machine, **all hero!**

BEST KNOWN FOR

Upgrading himself to better defend Earth and humanity

IN REAL LIFE

When Cyborg debuted in 1980, he was a reluctant young hero who joined the New Teen Titans and the Justice League of America. In 2011's New 52 reboot, he was created just after Darkseid attacked Earth.

FAST FACTS

REAL NAME: Victor Stone

OCCUPATION: Super Hero; former student and athlete

STRENGTHS: Can interface with all electronic technology; augmented strength; enhanced reflexes and speed.

WEAKNESSES: Traumatised by the damage to his human body; vulnerable to hacking and malware attacks

FOES: Anomaly; Technosapiens

ALLIES: Justice League; Teen Titans; S.T.A.R. Labs

BACK FROM THE DEAD!

Technosapiens are cyborgs from another universe infested with a **cyber-parasite.** Drawn to Earth by modifications Silas Stone made to Victor they **kill Cyborg,** but a hidden program **regenerates** and **reboots** him. He gains the power to **change shape** and **mimic human form!**

WHAT THE..?!

Since his **near-death** and forced bonding with **extraterrestrial gadgets** Victor can't get **dizzy** any more!

AARGH!

Cyborg and Batman set up **the Grid** – software to alert Cyborg to crises. The Grid **rebels,** expels Cyborg's organic parts and uses his **metal and plastic** ones to build itself **a body!**

HUMAN. TECH.
I DON'T CHOOSE SIDES. I'M THE BRIDGE BETWEEN THEM.
I'M A CYBORG.

WOW!

1000

The number of teleports Cyborg's Boom Tubes can make before his systems reset and he and any passengers end up on the hellworld of Apokolips!

TOP 5

Cyborg's Enhancements

1. Infrared, microscopic, X-ray, and night vision.
2. Jump jets, to enable mile-long leaps.
3. Mechanised motors, providing super-strength.
4. Super-hearing and sense of smell.
5. No need to eat – but if he wants to his taste-sensors are hyper-keen!

JLA FILES

CYBORG
Teenager Victor Stone almost dies when Darkseid attacks Earth. His S.T.A.R. Labs scientist father Silas saves him by merging the remains of his body with alien applied science. As Cyborg, Vic is able to communicate with almost all technology. He soon joins with other Super Heroes to drive Darkseid from Earth.

MUTATION ALERT!

Silas Stone creates copies of himself to use as guinea pigs in his search for a cancer cure. One of these androids, craving revenge, eventually becomes the monster Anomaly and attacks Victor.

YESSS!

Originally upset that he's **a half-human monster,** Vic changes his attitude after meeting youngsters with missing limbs who think his prosthetics are **really cool!**

BACK FROM THE DEAD!

Cyborg worries that he's **really dead** and only exists as a **computer program,** until he joins **the Justice League** in the Valley of Souls. Fighting the ghostly **Pretas,** Victor learns that he has **a soul:** one that walks the line between the **living** and the **dead!**

DASTARDLY DEED

Impersonating Cyborg's father, **Anomaly** secretly installs a **cut-off switch** in Cyborg's operating system and **shuts Cyborg down!**

THIS IS OUR WAR. THE ONE WE'RE STUCK WITH. THE ONE WE'VE GOTTA FIGHT TO A FINISH.

YESSS!

During World War II, ***Sgt Rock and Easy Company*** team up with ***Batman*** in France to defeat a ***Nazi mastermind***. Years later, at Gotham Museum, Sgt Rock saves Batman from ***the same Nazi mastermind!***

TOP 5

Wartime Heroes

1. **SGT ROCK:** Leader of Easy Company, a crew of soldiers who overcome impossible odds so many times they make it look "easy"!
2. **THE BLACKHAWKS:** Ace pilots who fly top-secret missions in World War II.
3. **LIBERTY BELLE:** Super-strength and sonic powers help her protect leading figures, such as U.S. President Roosevelt and British Prime Minister Winston Churchill.
4. **UNCLE SAM:** "The spirit of the U.S.A." brought to life!
5. **MISS AMERICA:** Given powers to transmute matter by a secret experiment she can no longer recall.

IN REAL LIFE

Sgt Rock, who debuted in *Our Army at War* #81 (Apr. 1959), is one of DC Comics' most popular war heroes. Writer Robert Kanigher allegedly gave Sgt Rock his own dog tag number: 409966.

WHAT THE..?!

Sgt Rock and **Easy Company** dress as **clowns** in an effort to entertain some children. The costumes amuse **the Nazis,** too, allowing Easy Company to catch the enemy **off guard.**

DID YOU KNOW?

Heroes **Gunner and Sarge** have a German shepherd dog named **Pooch.** He later wins a **Purple Heart** for **bravery** with elite combat unit the **Losers.** He's also super-intelligent **Rex the Wonder Dog's brother.**

THIS MEANS WAR!

When **the world** is plunged into **war,** heroes of all kinds and from **all walks of life** willingly lay down their lives to end **suffering and oppression!**

TELL ME MORE

In World War II, most of America's Super Heroes are forbidden from serving on the front lines. This is to prevent them falling under the influence of Adolf Hitler's magic staff, the Spear of Destiny, which can control minds.

★ TEAM PLAYER ★

Rejected at first, **Zinda Blake** is finally admitted to the all-male **Blackhawk Squadron** when she rescues them from evil pirate **the Scavenger.** As **Lady Blackhawk,** she later joins the **Birds of Prey** Super Hero team.

DID YOU KNOW?

The Unknown Soldier is the "mystery G.I. of World War II". His face is destroyed in an explosion, but he's a master of disguise and carries on fighting as an undercover agent.

JLA FILES

ALL-STAR SQUADRON
After the attack on Pearl Harbor on December 7, 1941, which sparks the U.S.'s entry into World War II, President Franklin Roosevelt appeals to the Super Heroes of America to form a team to battle sabotage and defend the country. The team is named the All-Star Squadron!

YESSS!

The Losers are an elite unit of World War II soldiers famous for their ***bad luck.*** Yet, despite their name, they somehow manage to end up ***winners!***

WHAT THE..?!

The U.S. Army's **Prof. Mazursky** forms the **Creature Commandos** – super-soldiers transformed to look like **Frankenstein's monster,** a **werewolf** and a **vampire.** The aim: to frighten enemies **out of their wits!**

WILD IN THE WEST

These heroes stood up for **justice** in the **Old West,** using their **wits,** their **six-shooters** – and even the occasional **superhuman ability!**

IN REAL LIFE

Cowboy heroes were a DC Comics staple right from the start. The company's first publication, *New Fun* #1 (Feb. 1935), featured several, as well as a strip starring the movie cowboy Tom Mix.

YESSS!

Minstrel Maverick would rather sing than fight badmen, but, if trouble comes, he's ready with ***roaring guns*** and his ***steel-reinforced guitar,*** which he can swing like ***a baseball bat!***

WHAT THE..?!

Timid schoolteacher John Tane conceals his **crime-busting activities** by dying his blond hair black and calling himself **Johnny Thunder.** Nobody recognizes him, not even his father, **the local sheriff!**

FAITHFUL TO THE END

Iron Jaws the wolf is bounty hunter Jonah Hex's loyal companion. He saves Hex from death even while dying from a rattlesnake bite!

ALTERNATE EARTHS

On Earth-18, **the Justice League** are reborn as **western heroes,** protecting **life** and **liberty** as the **Justice Riders**. Their first leader is Wonder Woman **Diana Prince,** a sheriff leading the team against criminal **Maxwell Lord** and his gun-toting **clockwork men.**

THUNDERING HOOVES

A cowboy's greatest ally is often his horse...

- **THE GENERAL:** When Jonah Hex's magnificent stallion dies in a gunfight, Hex never again allows himself to get attached to another mount.
- **BLACK LIGHTNING:** Fiercely defends his rider, Johnny Thunder, from all manner of human and animal enemies.
- **LUCIFER:** El Diablo's night-black stallion's flashing hooves and blazing eyes proclaim that the vengeance of hell is coming!

MASKED AVENGER

Following a brutal bank robbery, clerk Lazarus Lane is stuck by lightning and in a coma. Native American Wise Owl uses magic to transform his spirit into righter of wrongs El Diablo!

IT AIN'T THE *SPEED* OF A MAN'S HAND WHAT KILLS YA... IT'S THA *BULLETS!*

Good or Bad

Tough hero Jonah Hex's visage is scarred. He has a good side and a bad side. You don't want to get on his bad side!

It's Only Love!

Jeanne Walker masquerades as an outlaw to track down her father's killers. Once **Madame .44** gets justice, she becomes **Johnny Thunder's crime-fighting partner**, and also **his wife!**

DID YOU KNOW?

Nurse **Bess Lynn** becomes America's **first costumed hero** when she dons a **star-spangled outfit.** As **Miss Liberty,** she fights alongside frontiersman **Tomahawk** during the **War of Independence.**

FREAKY FRONTIER FOES

Frontiersman Thomas Haukins, alias Tomahawk, has to deal with some unusual adversaries, such as a tribe of tiny warriors, dinosaurs, a sea monster, giant ape "King Colosso", the "Terrible Tree-Man", and a massive alien from outer space!

TOP 4

Crime-busting Cowboy Detectives

Many of the era's greatest heroes carry a badge as well as six-guns.

1. **POW-WOW SMITH:** The Sioux sheriff of Elkhorn City uses the wisdom of two races to solve crimes.
2. **ROVING RANGER:** Former confederate officer Jeffrey Graham is a wandering Texas Ranger.
3. **WYOMING KID:** Sheriff and army scout William Polk rides the range hunting bad men.
4. **COWBOY MARSHAL:** James Sawyer crosses state and territorial borders to stop greedy criminals and killers.

Seeing Double

THE TRIGGER TWINS

Rocky City Sheriff Walt Trigger is frequently outmatched by bandits. Luckily his twin brother Wayne is a much better fighter and secretly substitutes for him, when he's not running the family's general store!

Jonah Hex

Slam Bradley

★ TEAM PLAYER ★

Jason Bard, self-proclaimed **"best young detective in Gotham City",** doesn't think he needs to take on a partner – until he sees **Man-Bat** in action and realizes they'd make a **great team!**

It's Only Love

Old-school private eye **Slam Bradley** discovers **Catwoman's identity,** but keeps her secret as he develops a **soft spot** for Selina!

PRIVATE EYES HAVE A ***BAD RAP*** AS ***CREEPS*** WHO'LL DIG UP ***ANY KIND OF DIRT*** FOR A PAYCHECK.

POWER UP!

Gotham Academy student Olive Silverlock is not only a member of an unofficial Detective Club with her fellow students, she also starts to develop fiery superpowers, like her mother, former villain and Arkham Asylum inmate Calamity.

CRAZY GANG!

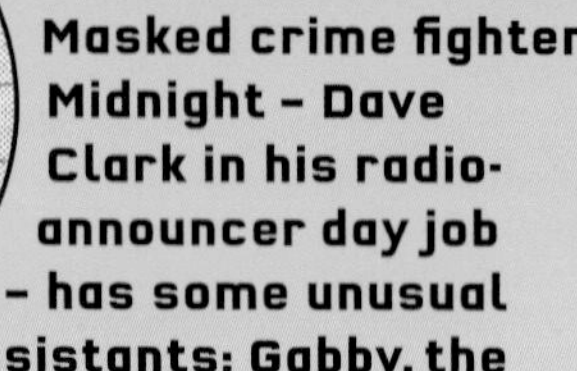

Masked crime fighter Midnight – Dave Clark in his radio-announcer day job – has some unusual assistants: Gabby, the talking monkey; nutty scientist Doc Wackey; hopeless private investigator Sniffer Snoop; and Sniffer's pet polar bear, Hot-Foot!

WHAT THE..?!

Originally part of a **sideshow act,** simian sleuth **Detective Chimp** gains eternal youth, genius-level intelligence and the ability to **talk to humans** and animals after a visit to **the Fountain of Youth** with **Rex the Wonder Dog!**

JLA FILES

TV DETECTIVES

Roy Raymond is known as the "TV Detective". To ensure that all the weird and wonderful stories that appear on his show are true, he roots out all the hoaxes. Many years later, Roy's grandson, Roy Raymond Jr., is also a TV presenter before taking to costumed heroics as Owlman of the Outsiders team.

BACK FROM THE DEAD!

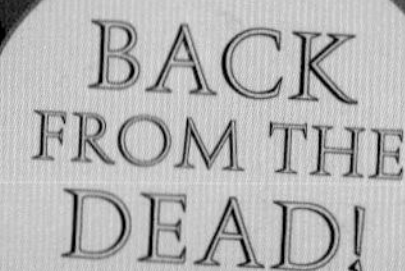

Crime reporter **Iris West Allen,** wife of **The Flash,** is killed by madly jealous **Professor Zoom.** She lives again when **her soul escapes** to her time of origin – **the 30th century** – and is implanted in a host body.

ON THE CASE

In a **world** full of **criminals,** there are always **crimes to solve.** What's more, to be **a detective hero,** you don't even have to be **human!**

SPECIAL *MOVES*

Captain Mark Compass is the man for all **nautical mysteries.** As well as being an **ace sleuth** and **bare-knuckle fighter,** Compass is also qualified to **command ships.**

EWWW!

The new **Crimson Avenger,** Jill Carlyle, has a permanent, bleeding **bullet wound** through her torso, like a **painful homage** to the symbol on the original's costume.

NOOOO!

Star Hawkins is a detective in the late 21st century, with a ***robot assistant*** called ***Ilda.*** Transported back to the 20th century, Hawkins is ***killed*** by a telepathic assassin as part of a plot to target his friend ***Captain Comet.***

IN REAL LIFE

Lee Travis, the Crimson Avenger, was the first ever masked Super Hero, debuting in *Detective Comics* #20 (Oct. 1938), written and drawn by Jim Chambers.

BAD DAY

Private eye Nathaniel Dusk finds happiness with a woman called Joyce Gulino. However, Joyce's ex is an underworld boss, who takes brutal revenge!

WHAT THE..?!
PREEEEEEESENTING... THE REAL ME, THE CHANGELING! IN THE VERDANT FLESH!
Beast Boy

SPECIAL *MOVES*

The hero **Metamorpho** can **reshape** and **transmute** different parts of his body into any **elemental substance!**

WHAT THE..?!

To cure his **son** of a **rare illness, Garfield Logan's father** gives him an untested **serum.** It cures Gar, but also turns him **green** and gives him the ability to **transform** into **any animal.** He becomes the hero **Beast Boy!**

TOP 6

Transformations

1 **FIRESTORM:** Ronnie Raymond and high school classmate Jason Rusch unleash the "God Particle" and fuse together into one entity with nuclear powers!

2 **CONGORILLA:** Explorer Congo Bill's magic ring enables him to switch minds with the fabled Golden Gorilla. He uses his new body to fight jungle crime!

3 **ELASTI-GIRL:** Exposed to volcanic gases, movie star and Olympic swimmer Rita Farr discovers that she can change size and starts a new life!

4 **BLACK ORCHID:** Experiments give Alba Garcia plant-based powers. She can change shape and even regrow limbs!

5 **ANIMAL MAN:** Buddy Baker sees a space ship crash in woods and passes out. He awakes to discover he can use the abilities of any animal!

6 **PLASTIC MAN:** Petty thief Eel O'Brian is doused with chemicals during a robbery. His body can now stretch any which way, and he becomes a crime-fighting hero!

★ TEAM PLAYER ★

Plastic Man sometimes fights evil with the **Justice League.** He even impersonates the **Joker** to sneak into the **Injustice League** and help thwart **Lex Luthor's** latest **dastardly scheme!**

DID YOU KNOW?

Ralph Dibny is one of the first heroes to publicly reveal his **secret identity** as the stretchy **Elongated Man**. Later, both he and his wife **Sue** use their real names to join the **Justice League!**

TOUGH BREAK

When Animal Man is stranded in space, he's only able to get home by using his special power, which enables him to "borrow" abilities from any nearby animals. The only creatures in range, however, are living space clouds, called Sun-Eaters!

SPECIAL *MOVES*

Element Woman (Emily Sung) can metamorphose all or parts of her form into **any element** found in the human body. Her **incredible powers** enable her to remove a deadly piece of **Green Kryptonite** from **Superman's brain!**

WHAT THE..?!

Danny the Street is a living, sentient stretch of neighbourhood who **communicates** via window displays and graffiti and can teleport **anywhere in the world!**

SHAPE CHANGERS

These heroes fight crime in incredibly **creative ways** – by altering their **bodies** in ways that their enemies **least expect!**

HANDLE WITH CARE!

Beatriz da Costa, a.k.a. **Fire,** can turn into a being of **dangerous green plasma** at will... and sometimes does it accidentally when she's **upset!**

IN REAL LIFE

Black Lightning was the the first African-American Super Hero to be given his own title by DC Comics, debuting in April 1977.

MY NAME IS CAPTAIN ATOM. AS IN A-BOMB... AS IN NUCLEAR FISSION... AS IN... THE END OF THE WORLD.

KA-POW!

Black Lightning's electricity manipulation powers are genetic and have been passed down to his two daughters, Super Heroes Thunder and Lightning.

Black Lightning

Captain Atom

SPECIAL *MOVES*

Teen Titan **Bunker** can construct **psionic energy bricks** with the power of his mind, and form them into **walls, giant fists,** or **shields.**

Bunker

DID YOU KNOW?

Black Lightning's alter ego, Olympic decathlete **Jefferson Pierce,** is a high school principal, and becomes Secretary for Education under **U.S. President Luthor.** Both men hail from Suicide Slum, one of Metropolis' **toughest districts.**

BACK FROM THE DEAD!

Legion of Super-Heroes member **Lightning Lad** sacrifices himself to save teammate **Saturn Girl,** but the Legion revives him with lightning. Sadly, **Chameleon Boy's** shape-shifting pet, **Proty,** dies in the process.

POWER-PACKED!

The ability to harness **pure energy** gives any hero a **serious advantage** in battle! The trick is to control the power so as not to become **highly dangerous...**

JLA FILES

CAPTAIN ATOM
U.S. Air Force pilot Captain Nathaniel Adam is the pilot of an experimental rocket designed by quantum physicist Dr Megala to explore parallel realities. The ship explodes and Adam's body is destroyed. However, his consciousness survives, and he later returns with a new, glowing, humanoid form as a living nuclear reactor.

POWER UP!

Left for dead by an alien parasite, Andrew van Horn finds he can convert matter to energy. He becomes the hero Gunfire, firing molecular projectiles like bullets from any object he picks up!

HANDLE WITH CARE!

The **Miraclo** pill, invented by **Hourman** (Rex Tyler), bestows superhuman strength, speed, and durability, night vision and the ability to survive underwater, but only for **one hour!** The drug also turns out to be **dangerously addictive.**

YESSS!

The ***military*** want to turn ***Captain Atom*** into a living ***weapon of mass destruction,*** but he is determined to use his ***nuclear powers*** for the ***good of humanity!***

★ TEAM PLAYER ★

Halo is a **dead woman** named Violet Harper who is inhabited by a light being known as an **Aurakle.** She joins the **Dead Heroes Club,** assembled by Batman to perform **ultra-secret missions.**

LOOK SHARP!

Bank clerk Emily Briggs is transformed by Halley's Comet into a metahuman with psionic powers. Calling herself Looker, Emily undergoes another dramatic metamorphosis when she becomes a vampire!

BEFORE

AFTER

Halo

WHEN GOOD GUYS GO BAD

Halo's aura gives her different powers depending on what **colour** it shows. If it is **violet,** it is a sign that the **sociopathic personality** of **Violet Harper** is in control!

FIGHTING MAD!

These Super Heroes spend years mastering ancient **martial arts.** They **battle evil and injustice** with nothing more to rely on than their **strength, speed, skills** and **sheer guts!**

Batgirl

KA-POW!

When Wonder Woman loses her mighty powers, she continues her crusade against evil thanks to Buddhist mentor I-Ching, whose martial arts crash-course turns Diana Prince into a high-kicking karate-fighter!

Wonder Woman

SPECIAL MOVES

TRAINED IN ISOLATION by her assassin father, **BATGIRL** Cassandra Cain never learns to speak, yet can **INFALLIBLY PREDICT** how opponents will act in combat by reading their **BODY LANGUAGE.**

IN REAL LIFE

Black Canary was the first DC Super Hero to exclusively use Eastern fighting techniques such as judo and ju-jitsu. She actually debuted as a villain, battling hero Johnny Thunder in *Flash Comics* #86 (Aug. 1947).

TOP 3

FACE TO FACE

1. **BATMAN VS BRONZE TIGER:** Winner: Bronze Tiger
2. **TIM DRAKE VS LYNX:** Winner: Tim Drake

3. **RICHARD DRAGON VS ARMY OF ASSASSINS:** Winner: Dragon

NOOOO!

After Green Arrow (Connor Hawke) battles Paper Monkey (secretly Lady Shiva) to a draw, Batman warns him that his martial arts skills have made him a target for every kung fu warrior on Earth!

Lady Shiva

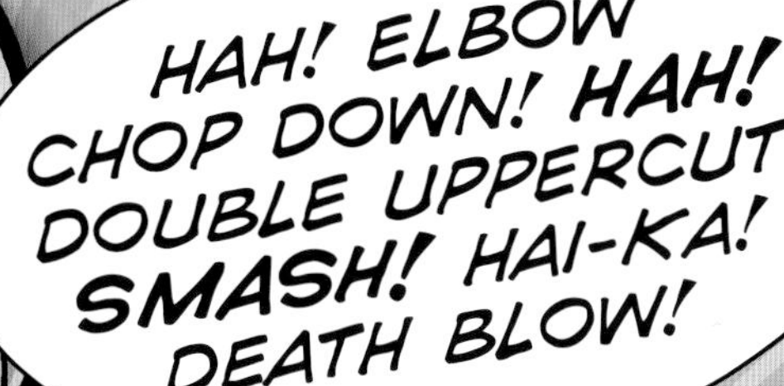

HAH! ELBOW CHOP DOWN! HAH! DOUBLE UPPERCUT SMASH! HAI-KA! DEATH BLOW!

Karate Kid

Black Canary

DID YOU KNOW?

Val Amorr is trained from infancy in every **earthly and alien** martial art known in the 30th century. As **Karate Kid,** he joins the **Legion of Super Heroes,** where he becomes their **greatest** combat specialist.

NOOOO!

Future Super Hero ***Karate Kid*** is expert in every martial art. However, his unmatched ***self-discipline*** almost ***kills*** him when he screens out the pain of a ***stab wound*** and nearly ***dies*** from his injuries!

TOP 3

Top fight

Lady Shiva is renowned as the world's deadliest assassin. But who has beaten her in a fair fight?

1. **ASSASSIN DAVID CAIN:** They later have a daughter, named Cassandra.
2. **CASSANDRA CAIN:** Both as Batgirl and as leader of the League of Assassins, but only after Shiva trains her.
3. **BATMAN**: Because he's Batman!

KA-POW!

Damian Wayne is the son of Bruce Wayne and the grandson of Rā's al Ghūl. His fighting style combines Batman's unique mixed martial arts training with disciplines taught by Rā's' ruthless League of Assassins.

Damian Wayne

SPECIAL *MOVES*

JUDOMASTER Sonia Sato is blessed with an **"AVERSION FIELD",** making it impossible for any blow to **TOUCH HER!**

DID YOU KNOW?

When not crushing crime, **Dinah (Black Canary) Drake** sings in punk rock band **Black Canary,** "The Most Dangerous Band in America!" She still ends up **fighting,** though, with **bandmates, rival acts, angry fans** – even **invading monsters.** And if fights get out of hand, she can use her metal-shredding **sonic cry!**

A KIND OF MAGIC

Tapping into **mystical powers** way beyond the **limits** of **scientific knowledge,** these **magical heroes** guard the realm of Earth from **supernatural threats**. Most are **kindhearted,** but some are **spooky** and **scary**!

STARE DEEP INTO MY EYES, EVIL ONE—AND WE WILL WALK INTO THE VALLEY OF DEATH TOGETHER!

The Spectre

DID YOU KNOW?

Paranormal detective **John Constantine** comes from **Liverpool** and used to play in a **punk rock band** called **Mucous Membrane.**

ALTERNATE EARTHS

Hoppy the Marvel Bunny is a **cartoon rabbit** from another dimension who gains the power of **Shazam.** In one adventure, he fights **Captain Carrot** over the right to date **Wonder Wabbit!**

★ TEAM PLAYER ★

Raven is the daughter of the **demon Trigon** and desperate to **shake off** his influence. She finds a new **"family"** when she joins the **Teen Titans.**

BAD DAY

Mystical energy fuses stuntman **Dan Cassidy** to his mechanical suit. He becomes the Super Hero **Blue Devil** – whether he **wants to or not!**

DASTARDLY DEED

The demon Eclipso makes **the Spectre** believe that **magic** is the root of all **evil.** The Spectre goes on a **vengeful rampage,** destroying **magic realms** and **magicians!**

YESSS!

Princess Amethyst is one of the many magical beings who help restore mystical realm ***the Rock of Eternity,*** shattered when ***the Spectre*** decides to destroy ***all magic!***

THE SHAZAM FAMILY

Teenager Billy Batson's journey to power begins when he meets the being known as the Wizard. After judging Billy worthy, the Wizard instructs him in the Power of Shazam, imbuing Billy with living lightning—the energy of the gods!

BILLY BATSON: When Billy yells "Shazam!" he becomes the superpowered adult Shazam.

FREDDY FREEMAN: After accidentally injuring Freddy, Billy saves his life by transferring some of his own power to him, turning him into Shazam, Jr.

MARY BATSON: Billy's younger sister begs the Wizard to grant her powers so she can help her family.

TAWKY TAWNY: Mary's plush tiger doll is turned into a living humanoid tiger by Ibis the Invincible!

TOUGH BREAK

Zatanna's father, **Zatara,** sacrifices himself to **save his daughter's life**. He draws the fire of **all-consuming celestial evil** away from **her** – and onto **himself!**

WHEN BAD GUYS GO GOOD

The demon Etrigan is one of **Hell's Rhymers,** cursed to forever speak in **verse**. Bonded with the mortal **Jason Blood,** Etrigan is often compelled by his **human half** to perform heroic deeds against his **evil wishes**.

Etrigan

AARGH!

Criminals drown cop ***Jim Corrigan*** in a barrel filled with ***liquid cement.*** They think they've seen the ***last*** of him, but he returns to take revenge as ***the Spectre!***

JLA FILES

NIGHTSHADE

Eve Eden, alias Nightshade, is a U.S. government agent, an early Suicide Squad recruit and a member of mystic superteam Shadowpact. Eve draws her shadow magic from the Land of the Nightshades, of which she is the lost princess.

IN REAL LIFE

Mary Batson is one of the first-ever female comic book Super Heroes. She made her debut as Mary Marvel in *Captain Marvel Adventures* #18 (Dec. 1942).

Mary Marvel

WHEN GOOD GUYS GO BAD

During the event known as **Final Crisis,** Mary Batson becomes possessed by the evil mind of the sinister **Desaad,** the cruel torturer from Apokolips!

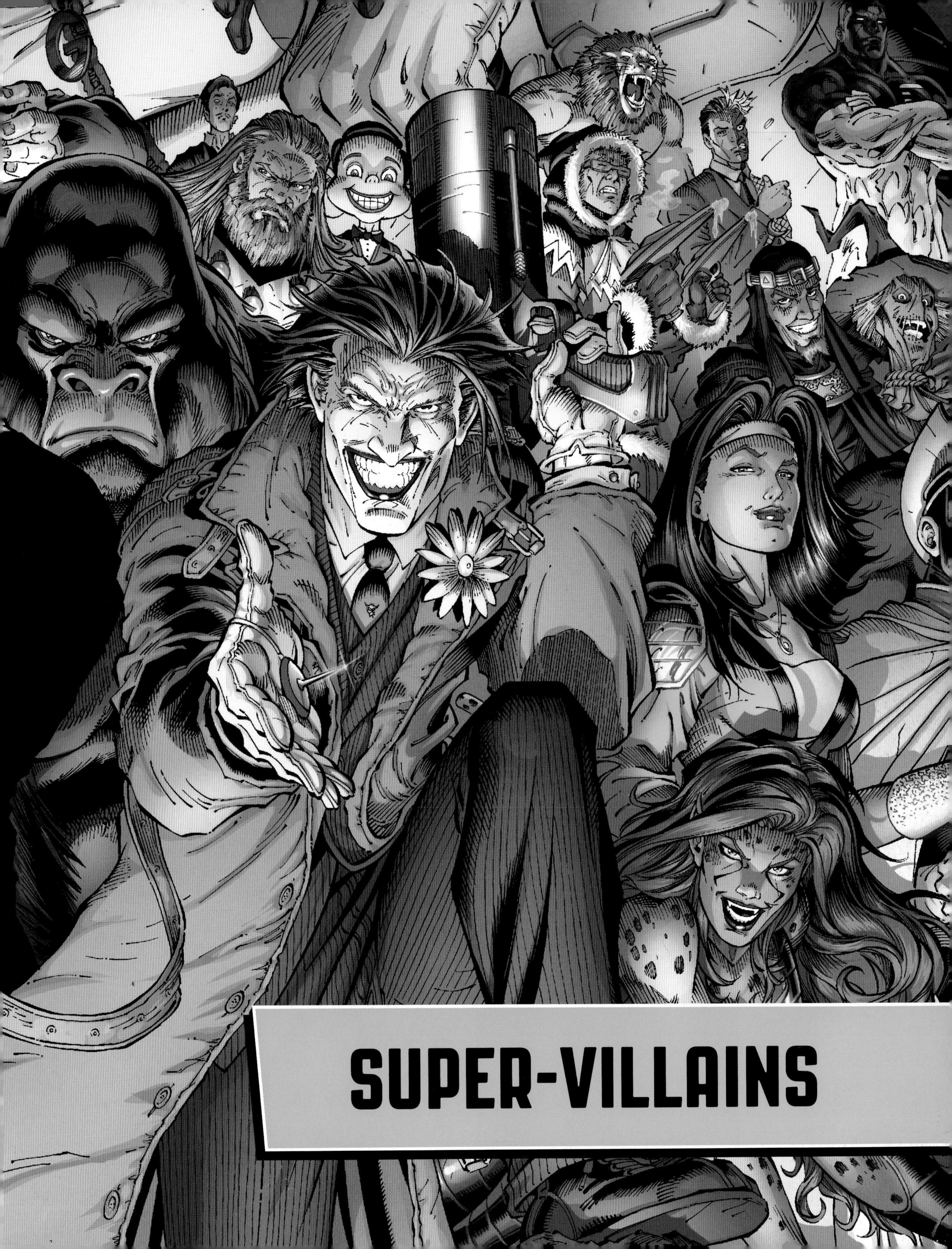

SUPER-VILLAINS

SUPER-VILLAINS SPEAK OUT!

They boast. They bully. They snarl. They hope to rule by fear. Yet their threats are usually empty, and only reveal their weakness!

I killed every living thing on Czarnia fer fun.
LOBO

WELCOME TO THE FUTURE OF VILLAINY!
CLOCK KING

WHEN I CAN'T BE THE TOUGHEST WITCH IN TOWN, I SETTLE FOR BEING THE SNEAKIEST.
ENCHANTRESS

THE JOKER beats any card in the deck!
THE JOKER

*I HAVE BEEN CALLED **CRIMINAL** AND **GENIUS**... AND I AM **NEITHER!** I AM AN **ARTIST!***
RĀ'S AL GHŪL

The future is a riddle only time can solve!
THE RIDDLER

Batman! Fah! An overrated athlete in fancy dress!
THE PENGUIN

ONCE YOU'VE BEEN TOUCHED BY POISON IVY, YOU CAN NEVER GET RID OF HER. NEVER, NEVER, NEVER!
POISON IVY

TO ATTAIN MY GOALS, I WOULD CRUSH THE VERY UNIVERSE, TO SEE IT REMADE IN MY IMAGE!
DARKSEID

SOON ALL HUMANS WILL JOIN OUR SPECIES—AND OUR CAUSE—OR DIE! GRODD HAS SPOKEN!
GORILLA GRODD

Me **Solomon Grundy!** Me mightier than **Superman!** Me mightier than **all** Super Heroes!
SOLOMON GRUNDY

I am everything this city deserves—and more. I am the darkness that fills the heart of every living soul in this sordid little town.
BLACK MASK

WHO... WHAT AM I? I'M NOT A MAN! I'M HALF A MAN... BEAUTY AND THE BEAST... GOOD AND EVIL! I'M A LIVING JEKYLL AND HYDE!
TWO-FACE

I DARE you to capture me, SUPERMAN! The moment you touch my ULTRA-FORCE SHIELD, even your invulnerable body will be DESTROYED!

BRAINIAC

The sinister Scarecrow is free once more—a living ***heart attack*** *loose in the dark!*

SCARECROW

DON'T STOP HITTING BIZARRO!! ME LOVE YOU!!

BIZARRO

Come on, SUPERMAN... fight back! The MORE energy you use, the FASTER I can drain YOUR strength into MY body!

PARASITE

Batman is no more. I have destroyed him. I rule these streets! I rule GOTHAM!

BANE

METROPOLIS AND HER PEOPLE ARE MINE—AND THEY'LL LIVE OR DIE AS I SEE FIT!

LEX LUTHOR

Why can't a girl be NICE to a guy without the mook trying to MOIDER her?

HARLEY QUINN

You have stopped me once, but you cannot stop me ***now!*** *I have slept in the* ***depths*** *with the* ***dazzling death,*** *and it has given me* ***more life!***

DR PHOSPHORUS

My name is Dr Psycho. And you're going to help me with a little experiment.

DR PSYCHO

FOOLS! SUPERMAN'S HEAT VISION DESTROYED MY SECRET WEAPONS—AND ACTIVATED AN EVEN MORE TERRIBLE DEVICE! HA! HA! HA!!

DOCTOR DESTINY

THERE IS NOWHERE TO RUN, JUSTICE LEAGUE. THE HATE OF DESPERO MOVES SLOWLY, BUT IT MOVES UNSTOPPABLY.

DESPERO

DARK GOD

He exists beyond the **boundaries** of the **Multiverse**. **Darkseid** is the **Lord of Apokolips,** the **blight** of the **Old Gods** and the **destroyer of all things!**

I AM FEAR ITSELF—THE TERROR HIDDEN IN YOUR DARKEST DREAMS.

Darkseid creates his **Evil Factory** to design powerful bioweapons, such as a **giant aquatic monster.** Shrunk to **microscopic size,** it is hidden in a lake in **Scotland!**

FAST FACTS

REAL NAME: Uxas

SPECIES: New God

OCCUPATION: Ruler

GOAL: The conquest of everything

ARCH-ENEMIES: Justice League; Highfather; New Genesis

KEY SUBORDINATES: Granny Goodness; Desaad; Virman Vundarbar; Glorious Godfrey

POWERS: Teleporting; fires disintegration beams from eyes; grows at will; regenerates from any wound

BEST KNOWN FOR

Wanting to boss everything in existence!

WHEN GOOD GUYS GO BAD

As a young man, **Darkseid** falls in love with beautiful, **peace-loving Suli.** Her **death** at the hands of **Desaad traumatises** him, turning him into the **super-villain** we know today!

SPECIAL MOVES

Darkseid's most powerful weapon are his **Omega Beams,** force blasts that he fires from his **eyes.** He can also generate **shock waves** from his **hands.**

WOW!

823

New God Darkseid is a real heavyweight champ—that's his weight in kg (1,815 lb). He's also 2.7 metres (8 ft 9 in) tall!

HANDLE WITH CARE!

Darkseid seeks one thing above all others – **the Anti-Life Equation.** With this, he hopes to conquer **all reality!**

DID YOU KNOW?

Darkseid commands an army of **Parademons.** These brainwashed warriors **live or die** only for their master.

AARGH!

In a ***future reality,*** where Darkseid rules everything, the godlike being is ***struck down*** by ***the Atom,*** the ***smallest*** of the ***JLA,*** who rides through Darkseid's forcefield on a ***photon*** and ***zaps him in the brain!***

BACK FROM THE DEAD!

One thing Super Heroes learn the hard way... Darkseid is virtually impossible to kill!

- **Darkseid** is killed by the **Black Racer,** an incarnation of **Death.** However, he is **reborn** as his **own son,** and raised by his own daughter, **Grail!**
- **Orion** hates his father so much he **tears out** his **heart!** Darkseid finds a human host for his consciousness and becomes crime lord **Boss Dark Side!**

WHAT A FAMILY!

The children of Darkseid are a very mixed bunch!

KALIBAK: Darkseid's brutish firstborn son is a ruthless commander of his father's armies.

ORION: Raised by the kindly Highfather of new Genesis, Orion is a heroic warrior. But, being Darkseid's son, he constantly wrestles with anger issues!

GRAYVEN: Darkseid's neglected third son hates his father and longs to conquer Apokolips for himself.

GRAIL: The daughter of an Amazon, Grail utterly despises her father, and wishes to destroy him.

CLOSE CALL

Apokolips and New Genesis seal a peace treaty by allowing each ruler to bring up the other's son. Darkseid enslaves Highfather's son, Scott, and tries to break him. He fails, and Scott becomes the hero Mister Miracle.

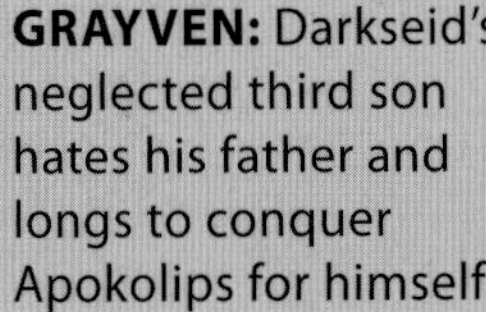

YESSS!

Wonder Woman stops Darkseid conquering her Themyscira homeland by using ***a mental link*** to make Darkseid more merciful, thus ***sapping his power!***

ABSOLUTE POWER!

Lex Luthor is **proud, smart** and **arrogant.** He's either the **planet's greatest genius** or the **greatest threat** to universal safety **ever born!**

IF IT WASN'T FOR **SUPERMAN,** I'D BE IN CHARGE OF THIS PLANET!

FAST FACTS

REAL NAME: Alexander Joseph Luthor

OCCUPATION: Scientist; former President; engineer; CEO

STRENGTHS: Extreme intelligence; ruthlessness; charisma; strategic planning

WEAKNESSES: Obsessed with proving he's the smartest man alive; overconfidence; blaming Superman for all his problems

FOES: Superman; Batman; Justice League; Crime Syndicate

ALLIES: Injustice League; Justice League; Secret Society

BIG BULLY

Unable to defeat an adult Man of Steel, Lex Luthor regresses Superman to a child. He still fails to kill his hated enemy!

BACK FROM THE DEAD!

Dying from **Kryptonite exposure,** Lex transplants his **brain** into a **clone body** and returns to Metropolis as his own son, **Alexander Luthor!**

WHAT THE..?!

Lex builds a **deadly robot bodyguard** and advisor. He makes it look like **Lois Lane** because he can't stand losing the real Lois to **Clark Kent!**

BEST KNOWN FOR

Trying to do almost anything to destroy Superman

Tough Break

Lex leaves Earth and becomes **a hero** on planet Lexor. He even has a wife, called **Ardora.** When the whole world is **accidentally obliterated** in a battle with his archenemy, Lex blames Superman, **of course!**

POWER UP!

The magic Powerstone enables Lex Luthor to survive anything and even steal Superman's powers. However, Lex's overconfidence allows the Man of Steel to trick him into missing out on the mystic mineral!

TOP 5

Lex Luthor inventions

1. **ATOMIC GRENADE:** Gives Lex a much bigger bang for his buck!
2. **4TH-DIMENSIONAL RAY PROJECTOR:** Just the thing to make the Man of Steel finally vanish.
3. **EVERYMAN PROJECT:** Gives anyone superpowers (which Luthor can then steal for himself).
4. **KRYPTONITE MAN:** Emits green Kryptonite radiation to threaten Superman.
5. **WARSUIT:** For taking on Superman in hand-to-hand combat, and winning!

IN REAL LIFE

lIn a 1944 story, Luthor used an atom bomb against Superman. Because of similarities to real nuclear weapons, the U.S. War Department asked for the tale to be suppressed until World War II was over.

Luthor for President!

Lex cheats his way to becoming U.S. President, but is thrown out and branded a criminal by Superman and Batman after conspiring with Darkseid.

AAARGH!

Learning that ***Kryptonite*** harms Superman, Luthor wears ***a Green-K ring*** to keep his enemy at bay. The radiation ***slowly poisons*** Lex, destroying his hand, and eventually his ***entire body!***

WHEN BAD GUYS GO GOOD

After the Man of Steel **seemingly dies,** Lex decides that the public deserves a truly human hero – **himself!** Using an alien reality-altering device, he becomes the new **Superman of Metropolis!**

UPGRADE!

When the **Justice League** battles the New Gods, Darkseid is killed. Luthor absorbs his **Omega Force energies** and briefly becomes the supremely evil **overlord of Apokolips!**

DASTARDLY DEED

Lex craves public praise. After saving Earth from the **Crime Syndicate,** he blackmails the **Justice League** into letting him join by threatening to expose **Batman's secret identity.**

COMPUTER TYRANT!

Brainiac is a being with **many faces and names.** His vastly powerful **computer intellect** is hungry for information – even at the cost of **all life on Earth!**

HANDLE WITH CARE!

Brainiac's computer mind is his most dangerous weapon. Combined with his **shrinking ray** and **impenetrable force field,** this alien conqueror really is **a force** to be **reckoned with!**

UPGRADE!

Even after being **completely destroyed,** the original version of Brainiac is able to **recreate himself** out of organic metal, giving himself **a sleek new robot body.**

FAST FACTS

ALTER EGO: Vril Dox

SPECIES: Coluan

OCCUPATION: Conqueror; collector of worlds; scientist

M.O.: The transformation of life into information

ARCHENEMIES: Superman; Supergirl

ALLIES: Lex Luthor

WEAKNESSES: Bacteria

SUPERPOWER: Technopathy; telekinesis; super-strength

JLA FILES

MASTER COLLECTOR

Originally a scientist from the planet Colu, Brainiac can create clones of himself and build his body to any size or specification he desires. Each one of his many incarnations is simply a scout – a fragment of a sinister intellect that exists outside of reality. They are all in service of the Brainiac that is known as The Master Collector!

DID YOU KNOW?

Brainiac is known by different names on different worlds.

- **C.O.M.P.U.T.O**
- **PNEUMENOID**
- **MIND2**
- **THE INTERNET**
- **PULSAR STARGRAVE**
- **MILTON FINE**

WHAT THE..?!

Brainiac uses **Green Kryptonite dust** to remove Superman's superpowers and his **shrinking ray** to reduce the Man of Steel to **mini-size!**

Extended Family

Brainiac has many offspring scattered throughout the Multiverse. Some are descendants of his original physical form, and some are cybernetic clones. Some are good, but some are very, very bad...

VRIL DOX 2
Founder of the heroic L.E.G.I.O.N.!

LYRIL DOX
A mind-controlling villain!

KAJZ DOX
A sadistic destroyer of worlds!

QUERL DOX
A teenaged, Super Hero genius!

INDIGO
A blue-skinned, time-travelling, murder machine!

DID YOU KNOW?
Unaware of where his home planet was or what had happened to it, **Superman** learns about **Krypton** from **Brainiac** in their **first encounter.**
NOOO!
One of Brainiac's ***favourite activities*** is ***zapping cities*** from space with his ***shrinking ray,*** putting them in ***bottles*** and storing them in his ***skull-shaped starship!***
YOU HAVE ABSOLUTELY NO IDEA WHAT YOU'RE DEALING WITH!
YESSS!
When ***Brainiac*** shrinks Krypton's capital city ***Kandor*** and bottles it, he inadvertently saves ***hundreds of thousands of lives!*** Soon after, planet Krypton ***blows up!***
WHAT THE..?!
Even a **super-villain** can get **lonely...** In the past, Brainiac has traveled with **Koko,** a pet **space monkey.**
DASTARDLY DEED
Unwilling to face **deactivation,** Brainiac takes control of Lex Luthor's body. Lex is forced to commit **inhuman acts of violence!**

FAST FACTS

REAL NAME: Unknown

STRENGTHS: Pain resistance; immunity to toxins; high intelligence; skilled hand-to-hand fighter

WEAKNESS: Mental instability

MAIN FOE: Batman

IN REAL LIFE

In his first appearance, (*Batman* #1, June 1940), the Joker ended up in jail. However, he proved so popular with fans that he soon returned. In 1975, the Joker became the first villain to get his own title.

Double Trouble

The Joker teams up with Master of Fear the Scarecrow intending to overwhelm Gotham City with fear and chaos. However, the partnership is anything but strong and stable, and the two villains soon violently clash!

IF I WEREN'T ***INSANE,*** I COULDN'T BE SO ***BRILLIANT!***

DID YOU KNOW?

The Joker isn't just immune to his **own venom...** he's also immune to **other toxins,** such as the **Scarecrow's fear gas!**

DASTARDLY DEED

The Joker kidnaps **Robin (Jason Todd)** and Batman is **too late** to save him from being **blown up.** The **guilt haunts** the Dark Knight **for years!**

AARGH!

The Joker's gang is full of ambitious crooks. But the Joker also uses members as ***guinea pigs*** to test new batches of ***Joker Venom,*** so his ***posse*** has a ***high turnover rate!***

POWER UP!

When the **Joker** steals the **reality-altering** powers of fifth-dimensional **Mr Mxyzptlk,** he remakes the **whole universe!**

WHAT THE..?!

Jealous of Batman's Batmobile, the Joker builds the Jokermobile, with a giant Joker face on the front. The first model is bulletproof with front and rear machine guns.

JLA FILES

During his first attempt at crime, a man known only as Red Hood falls into a vat of chemicals while fleeing Batman. The toxic chemicals transform him into the frightening, white-faced, green-haired Joker.

HANDLE WITH CARE!

In small doses, the Joker's **Joker Venom** makes victims **laugh wildly.** In larger amounts, it can **kill,** leaving victims with **frightening grins!**

TOP 6

Joker's gadgets

The Clown Prince of Crime has used an array of lethal gadgets, including...

1. **JOY BUZZER:** Don't shake hands with the Joker – you could get a 50,000-volt shock!
2. **RAZOR-SHARP CARDS:** The Joker's a real card sharp when he throws these steel playing cards at foes!
3. **ACID-SQUIRTING FLOWER:** Pity the person who tries to sniff the lovely bloom on the Joker's lapel!

4. **JOKER TEETH:** These novelty chattering teeth confuse and unsettle the Joker's victims!
5. **TOY GUN:** Pull the trigger once and a flag saying "BANG!" shoots out; pull it twice and a sharp blade shoots out of the flag!

6. **CANE:** Conceals a deadly sword!

CLOWN PRINCE OF CRIME

The Joker lives for one thing: **chaos.** Well, maybe two things: **chaos** and a **good laugh.** Oh, wait, three things... **chaos,** a **good laugh** and making Batman's life **utterly miserable!**

BACK FROM THE DEAD!

The Joker has survived many **deadly scrapes** while fighting **Batman,** including falling from a **moving train,** having his helicopter **shot down** and even being struck by **lightning!**

I WOULD BE INSTIGATING **MAYHEM** EVERYWHERE I GO!

FAST FACTS

REAL NAME: Harleen Quinzel

SKILLS: Psychology; acrobatics; stealing; novelty gags; having the last laugh

ALLIES: Poison Ivy; Catwoman; Bud and Lou (her hyenas)

FOES: Depends on her mood; usually Batman, the Joker, sometimes both!

MAIN WEAPON: A giant mallet

IN REAL LIFE

Harley's pet hyenas, Bud and Lou, are named after the comedy duo Bud Abbott and Lou Costello, huge movie stars in the 1940s and 50s.

YESSS!

After **the Joker** fails, over and over again, to create the ***perfect trap*** for ***Batman,*** Harley gives it a shot… and succeeds ***first go!***

TOP 5

Harley's Tricks 'n' Treats

1. **GIANT MALLET**
Harley loves whacking foes with this oversized hammer.

2. **SPRING SHOES**
She can leap higher and farther with these coils on her kicks.

3. **RUBBER CHICKEN**
She stuffs a brick inside for an extra surprise when she swings it around!

4. **NOVELTY GUN**
This trick pistol can shoot boxing gloves to whap enemies, or ribbons to tie them up.

5. **STINK BOMBS**
The smoke hides her from view, while the stink makes her challengers choke!

DID YOU KNOW?

Poison Ivy gives **Harley** a special medicine that makes Harley **immune** to the poisons Ivy releases from her **skin.** As a result, Harley is now also immune to **Joker Venom!**

ALTERNATE EARTHS

In the DC Bombshells universe, Harley Quinn is on the front line during World War II, fighting evil with her superpowered allies.

WHEN BAD GUYS GO GOOD

Harley has her own quirky way of doing **the right thing.** But she's done enough **good deeds** by now to even gain Batman's **grudging admiration.**

BEST INSULT

"Anyone ever tell you your breath stinks of cheese farts?"

MEGA MAKEOVER

When Dr Harleen Quinzel becomes criminal Harley Quinn, she models her look on a traditional harlequin's chequered costume... but with her own twist.

DR. QUINZEL

JOKER'S PARTNER

GOING SOLO

NOOOO!

Harley's perfect plan is ***foiled*** when the ***Joker*** becomes ***jealous*** that he wasn't the one to catch Batman. The Joker spends so much time ***yelling*** at Harley, that Batman ***gets away!***

It's Only Love

When they were more or less **an item,** Harley's favourite term of endearment for the Joker was **"Puddin'".** He **hated** it!

WILD CARD

Arkham Asylum psychiatrist **Harleen Quinzel** falls for the villainous **Joker** and turns to crime as **Harley Quinn.** Freeing herself from the Joker's **bad influence,** she's **an antihero**

TEAM PLAYER

To avoid going to **prison** for her crimes, **Harley Quinn** joins secret government strike team **Task Force X,** a.k.a. the **Suicide Squad.** She goes on missions with teammates such as **Deadshot** and **King Shark.**

GETAWAY GIMMICKS

The Penguin has plenty of ways to make his escape, including...

- A jet-powered flying umbrella
- A penguin blimp
- A pogo stick umbrella
- A robot phoenix airplane
- A trained ostrich
- A helicopter umbrella

DASTARDLY DEED

In an early exploit, the Penguin threatens to **"steal"** the voices of **human songbirds** (musical performers) with a special gas, unless they **pay up!**

★ TEAM PLAYER ★

The Penguin is a **supreme schemer.** When arrested, he is transferred to the **Suicide Squad** and told to plan an assault on a Russian **high-security prison** in return for a **commuted jail sentence.**

MEGA MAKEOVER

After years of defeat, the Penguin seemingly settles down as a businessman and owner of the Iceberg Lounge nightclub. This trendy club is just a front for his new enterprise as a behind-the-scenes gang boss.

I'VE ALWAYS CONDUCTED MYSELF WITH **STYLE**. WITH **CLASS**. AND WITH **DIGNITY**.

ALTERNATE EARTHS

On **Earth-1,** the Penguin is Gotham City's **mayor.** After arranging the deaths of political rivals **Thomas and Martha Wayne,** he is shot dead by their butler, **Alfred.**

DASTARDLY DEED

The Penguin kidnaps **the King of Swawak** and, when **Batman** intervenes, orders his emperor penguin **bodyguard** to attack with its **poison-tipped beak!**

DID YOU KNOW?

Because he comes from a prestigious, **Gotham City founding family,** the Penguin often gets **lighter sentences** than other felons caught by Batman.

FOWL FIEND!

FAST FACTS

REAL NAME: Oswald Chesterfield Cobblepot

OCCUPATION: Criminal mastermind; fixer; entrepreneur; nightclub owner

STRENGTHS: Master plotter; lethally inventive; can be reasoned with; not insane

WEAKNESSES: Over-confidence; a murderous temper; easily offended

FOES: Batman; Nightwing; Carmine Falcone; Black Canary

ALLIES: Various, including the Joker and Catwoman, but none for long

TELL ME MORE

The Penguin regards himself as "The Gentleman of Crime," specialising in bird-themed banditry. Brilliantly inventive, he trains birds to steal and protect him. He also creates an arsenal of weaponised umbrellas, earning the nickname "The Bumbershoot Bandit"!

BATTLE BUMBERSHOOTS

The Penguin has a variety of customized umbrellas, including...

A huge **GAS** umbrella

A **MACHINE GUN** umbrella

A **SWORD** umbrella

A heat-seeking **ROCKET LAUNCHER** umbrella

An **ELECTRIC SHOCK** umbrella

A **SNEEZING-POWDER** umbrella

A **FLAMETHROWER** umbrella

JLA FILES

BIRTH OF THE PENGUIN

After his father dies of pneumonia, Oswald's mother never lets him go out without an umbrella – even on sunny days! This, plus his short, fat, big-nosed appearance, leads to Oswald being bullied at school – the kids call him "Penguin". His only friends are his mother's caged birds.

RUFFLED FEATHERS

Released from prison, the Penguin contemplates retiring, until disrespectful crooks mock him. Resolved to prove himself, the Penguin tries to steal from a museum, until caught once again by Batman and Robin.

NOOOO!

When *Gotham City* is devastated by an *earthquake* and becomes a *No Man's Land,* the Penguin consolidates the *scattered gangs* into an underworld empire he *ruthlessly rules.*

The Penguin is **no birdbrain!** He's one of the **most cunning strategists** and **ruthless operators** in the **annals of crime!**

GREEN QUEEN

Seductive eco-terrorist **Poison Ivy** is more than ready to take **extreme action** to protect **the plants** that she loves.

AARGH!
Poison Ivy's ***past misdemeanours*** come back to bite her when four of her victims mutate into a ***human-plant hybrid*** called ***Harvest*** and ***attack her!***

GREEN FOR DANGER

Pamela Isley was a brilliant botany student, until experimented on by her professor, Jason Woodrue, the Floronic Man. Her transformation turned her blood to poison and affected her mind.

FAST FACTS

REAL NAME: Pamela Isley

BASE: Gotham City

STRENGTHS: Toxic touch, including a kiss that can kill; immunity to all poisons; power over plant life; mind control via pheromones

WEAKNESSES: Like a plant, she does not thrive in darkness

ALLIANCES: Injustice Gang of the World; Secret Society of Super-Villains; Birds of Prey; Gotham City Sirens; Suicide Squad

UPGRADE!

Ivy feels so sorry for **Harley Quinn** after she is almost killed by **the Joker** that she not only nurses her back to health but also permanently **upgrades** Harley's abilities with a **plant serum!**

DID YOU KNOW?

Poison Ivy has donated millions of her ill-gotten dollars to **environmental charities.**

It's Only Love

Ivy comes to **Gotham City** after becoming **obsessed** with **Batman.** She tries to use **chloroform lipstick** to **knock him out** with **a kiss,** but the wily Caped Crusader thwarts her with a **nose filter!**

Q&A

Q: Why does Poison Ivy sometimes look green?

A: Her blood contains the plant-based pigment chlorophyll, turning her green. Ivy has learned to control her skin colour, to look like a normal human being.

I AM THE GUARDIAN OF THE GREEN. I AM POISON IVY!

JLA FILES

Wanting to create beings that are like her, Ivy manages to breed plant and human DNA to produce hybrid babies, whom she names Rose and Hazel.

IN REAL LIFE

Poison Ivy debuted in *Batman* #181 (June 1966). The character was portrayed by Uma Thurman in the motion picture *Batman & Robin* (1997) and Maggie Geha in the TV series *Gotham.*

WHEN BAD GUYS GO GOOD

When a **devastating earthquake** cuts off Gotham City from the rest of the country, **Poison Ivy** claims Robinson Park as her **kingdom**—taking in orphans and growing **fresh produce** for the citizens!

TELL ME MORE

Like Swamp Thing, Poison Ivy is one of the beings connected to the Green, the elemental force uniting all the world's plant life. It is ruled by a Parliament – of Trees!

BAD DAY

Ivy leaves Gotham City for an uninhabited **Caribbean island,** using her power to fill it with **lush vegetation.** When her paradise is **destroyed** by an illegal weapons test, Ivy goes on a deadly **revenge spree.**

BEST KNOWN FOR

Valuing plant life over human life

UNLIKELY ALLIANCE

Ivy doesn't have much time for people, preferring the company of plants, but she makes an exception for Harley Quinn, her best friend. Both are smart, but crazy!

PRINCE OF PUZZLES

The Riddler is convinced that he's **a genius** at inventing **puzzles, conundrums and cryptograms** to baffle, amaze and endanger. For this **slippery super-villain,** the only worthwhile challenge in life is outwitting the **greatest detective** in the whole world – **Gotham City's Batman!**

The **Riddler** baffles **Batman and Robin** by setting them **puzzles** that make them think he's **committing a crime** when he **isn't!**

FAST FACTS

REAL NAME: Edward Nigma

OCCUPATION: Criminal mastermind

STRENGTHS: Brilliant inventor of riddles, puzzles, and deathtraps

WEAKNESSES: Obsession with defeating Batman mars his criminal career; poor hand-to-hand fighter

FOES: Batman; Robin; The Question

ALLIES: The Riddler teams up with various foes of Batman, but his partnerships don't last very long!

TOP 3

Riddles

1. **WHAT WILL BREAK IF YOU EVEN NAME IT?**
   Silence!
2. **WHY MUST A DISHONEST MAN STAY INDOORS?**
   So no one can ever find him out!
3. **WHAT OCCURS ONCE IN A MINUTE, TWICE IN A MOMENT BUT NEVER IN A THOUSAND YEARS?**
   The letter "M!"

WHEN BAD GUYS GO GOOD

After an explosive **blow to the head,** the **Riddler** wakes up **cured** of his **criminal intent.** Resolving to put his intelligence to **good use,** he briefly teams up with **Batman** and helps the Dark Knight **catch bad guys!**

THERE ARE NO "ULTIMATE ENDS," BATSY. ONLY GAMES AND MORE GAMES!

AARGH!

Convinced that he will never be able to beat ***Batman's bigger brain,*** the Prince of Puzzles puts away his green suit and ***catches a bus out of Gotham City*** – only to run across another enigmatic Super Hero, ***the Question!***

TOUGH BREAK

The Riddler is no fool. He knows that his **riddling compulsion** is the reason **Batman** always catches him. He tries to commit a crime **without** sending Batman a riddle – but his subconscious **stiffens his fingers** and **won't** let him **steal!**

IN REAL LIFE

The Riddler made his debut in *Detective Comics* #140 (Oct. 1948). The Prince of Puzzles' third appearance inspired his characterisation (by Frank Gorshin) in the 1960s *Batman* television show.

Q&A

Q: Where does the Riddler's fascination with puzzles come from?

A: In high school, he cheats in a puzzle test, thus winning a huge award and impressing his classmates.

DID YOU KNOW?

Due to a **head injury,** the **Riddler** no longer remembers that he once cracked the **greatest riddle** of his life—**Batman's secret identity!**

TELL ME MORE

The Riddler is a cunning inventor. His signature weapon is his question mark cane, which can create holograms and fire electrical blasts. Other weapons include exploding jigsaw puzzle pieces and nets designed to look like crossword puzzles.

DASTARDLY DEED

Determined to drive the Dark Knight **batty,** the Riddler lures him into a **graveyard,** then attacks the hero with a mob of **make-believe zombies!**

THE DEMON'S HEAD

Rā's al Ghūl has one dream: To **purify the Earth** and return it to its **original beauty.** He's trying **to wipe out** almost **everyone on the planet** to make his dream **come true!**

ON ITS OWN, HUMANITY IS A DESTRUCTIVE FORCE. IT NEEDS A MASTER.

IN REAL LIFE

Rā's al Ghūl is Arabic for "The Demon's Head". Writer Dennis O'Neil and artist Neal Adams wanted to invent a villain who was "so exotic that neither we nor Batman were sure what to expect".

DID YOU KNOW?

When they first meet, **Rā's and Batman** team up to rescue Rā's' daughter **Talia and Robin,** who have been kidnapped. It turns out that **Rā's himself** arranged the kidnapping to test Batman's fitness to **marry Talia!**

FAST FACTS

REAL NAME: Rā's al Ghūl

NICKNAME: The Demon's Head

STRENGTHS: Charismatic mastermind and leader of loyal assassin army; superb swordsman and martial artist; exceedingly long-lived

WEAKNESS: Mental instability

ALLIES: League of Assassins

MAIN FOE: Batman

JLA FILES

THE DEMON'S FANG

Over the centuries, Rā's becomes vastly rich and starts a gigantic global criminal organisation called the Demon. One branch of the Demon is the deadly League of Assassins, sometimes called the Demon's Fang.

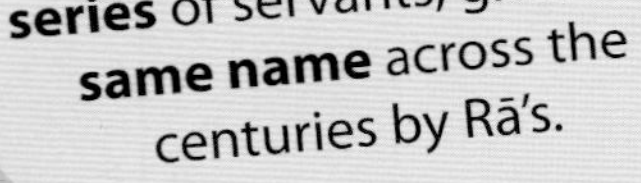

A FAMILY AFFAIR

Batman and Talia have a stormy affair, and a son, Damian – which makes Rā's Damian's grandfather. Damian later escapes to live with Batman and becomes a new Robin!

★ TEAM PLAYER ★

Rā's employs a servant and bodyguard named **Ubu,** who is also a skilled fighter. But Ubu isn't just **one man...** he's a **series** of servants, given the **same name** across the centuries by Rā's.

AARGH!

Talia al Ghūl hates Batman for rejecting her and orders her ***Leviathan*** terrorist network to destroy him and his friends. In a final showdown, she's killed by ***Batwoman Kathy Kane!***

BEST KNOWN FOR

Being the world's oldest eco-terrorist

EWWW!

To keep Batman distracted from one of his evil schemes, Rā's steals the dead bodies of Batman's parents!

DID YOU KNOW?

Talia is not Rā's' only daughter. **Nyssa Raatko** was born in Russia in the 18th century. Rā's hopes she will **help him** in his evil schemes, but she comes to **hate him.**

BACK FROM THE DEAD!

Even when **Rā's' body** finally dies, his **spirit** lives on, looking for a **suitable host.** Talia stops him using his grandson **Damian,** so Rā's picks his "unworthy" son **Dusan** and gains **new life** once again!

BACK FROM THE DEAD!

If Rā's is **injured** or **dying,** he can bathe in a **Lazarus Pit** and restore himself to health. He has even been revived when **dead!** Rā's has stayed alive for **hundreds of years!**

WOW!

700

Rā's al Ghūl's possible age, but it could be more. Even Rā's himself doesn't know how old he is!

DASTARDLY DEED

Rā's releases the **Clench** virus in Gotham City. **Batman** and his allies have to find a cure before this plague **wipes out** the city's population—and then **the world!**

JLA FILES

LAZARUS PITS

These pools are linked to mystic ley lines of energy and each one can be used only once. Those who bathe in one have their lives prolonged. The pits can even revive the dead. Afterwards, bathers temporarily lose their minds!

DOUBLE IDENTITY!

IN REAL LIFE

On his debut in *Detective Comics* #66 (Aug. 1942), Two-Face was called Harvey "Apollo" Kent. The name was changed to avoid confusion with Superman's alter ego, Clark Kent.

FAST FACTS

REAL NAME: Harvey Dent

OCCUPATION: Criminal; former Gotham City District Attorney

STRENGTHS: Extreme cunning; strategic planning; fearlessness

WEAKNESSES: Relies on the toss of a coin to make major decisions

FOES: Batman; Nightwing; Robin

ALLIES: None – he double-crosses everyone!

WITH ONE BOUND...

Two-Face ties **Batman** and **Robin** to one side of a **giant coin,** thinking their weight will pull them down onto a **bed of spikes.** Batman uses his Utility Belt to create a **magnetic field,** flips the coin and **cheats death!**

TEAM PLAYER

Aliens plan to destroy **Earth,** and hire **Two-Face** as their agent. The invaders don't bargain on Dent tossing his coin, **double-crossing** them and helping the **Justice League of America** to defeat them!

DASTARDLY DEED

Two-Face tries to **extort money** from the government by threatening to explode an **atom bomb** in **Washington D.C.!**

Handsome **D. A. Harvey Dent** descends into madness after his face is **scarred** by an **acid-throwing gang boss!** He turns to crime as the terrifying super-villain **Two-Face!**

DID YOU KNOW?

Two-Face is imprisoned in **Arkham Asylum,** his **silver dollar** is **confiscated** and he is given **dice and tarot cards** instead. He is **frantic,** until **Batman** breaks in and gives him his coin back!

WHEN BAD GUYS GO GOOD

If his **coin** falls the **right** way, Two-Face can be **a hero.** When **Batman** has to leave Gotham City, he even entrusts the city's protection to his **former foe!** Sadly, the pressure of **doing good** proves **too much** for Dent's **fractured psyche!**

SPECIAL MOVES

Two-Face carries **a silver dollar** taken from the gangster who **maimed** him. One side is **defaced.** Two-Face tosses the coin before making a decision. Will he do **good** or **bad? The coin decides!**

TOUGH BREAK

After being **arrested,** Harvey undergoes plastic surgery and psychotherapy to **rebuild his life.** However, when he is caught in an **explosion,** his face is damaged once again. Harvey realises that he's **fated** to be **Two-Face forever!**

AARGH!

Hoping to ***get back together*** with his wife, ***Gilda,*** Two-Face conceals his ***scarred visage*** with ***waxy make-up.*** But during a ***candlelit dinner,*** his make-up ***melts,*** revealing his ***wicked side!***

BEST KNOWN FOR

Having a good side – and a bad one!

HEADS, I SAVE GOTHAM. TAILS, I MAKE IT BLEED!

THE ROBIN CONNECTION

Two-Face has dangerous links to Batman's Boy Wonder partners.

- Robin Dick Grayson is beaten up by Harvey to show Batman the dangers of having an ally.
- Robin Jason Todd becomes a wandering street kid after Two-Face kills his dad.
- Tim Drake becomes Robin to rescue Batman when Two-Face captures the Dark Knight.

TOP 9

Dastardly Docs

1 **DOCTOR SIVANA:** He starts out wanting to do good in the world, but ends up plotting destruction!

2 **DOCTOR CYBER:** Beautiful but deadly, Doctor Cyber is inadvertently scarred during a clash with Wonder Woman and loses her mind!

3 **DOCTOR SPECTRO:** This diabolical doctor uses color and light as a weapon to attack Captain Atom.

4 **DOCTOR ALCHEMY:** This foe of The Flash controls and transforms the very elements of existence with the fabled Philosopher's Stone!

5 **DOCTOR MOON:** An evil genius secretly employed, at different times, by Lex Luthor, Doctor Cyber and even the U.S. government.

6 **DOCTOR LIGHT:** A brilliant inventor who turns cruel, and is haunted by the ghost of his first victim.

7 **DOCTOR PHOSPHORUS:** With a body that absorbs and emits radiation, he tries to set Gotham City ablaze!

8 **DOCTOR POLARIS:** This power-crazed Green Lantern foe manipulates magnetism and creates force fields.

YOU ALL HAVE TO REALIZE THAT... WELL... WE'RE *EVIL!*

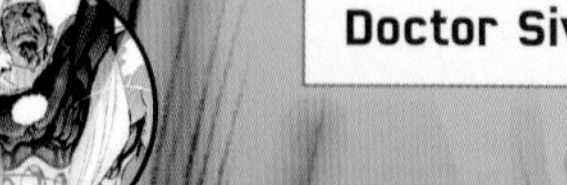

Doctor Sivana

NOOOO!

Once beautiful, ***Doctor Cyber*** is so obsessed with the loss of her good looks that, with ***Doctor Moon's help,*** she tries to transfer her mind into ***Wonder Woman's body!***

WOW!

4,200,000

The number of people's memories erased by Doctor Sivana in one go!!

WHAT THE..?!

Criminals take over **Gotham City** and psychotic surgeon **Professor Pyg** performs **crazy operations** at the main hospital, such as switching a violinist's **broken arm** for his **leg!**

CALL YOURSELF A DOCTOR?!

Don't visit them if you've got **flu** – they won't do you **any good.** These villains may have **"Doctor"** in their names, but they're **some of the best** at being **the absolute worst!**

ALTERNATE EARTHS

A **Legion of Sivanas** from various worlds, including a **vampire** and **snake-like form,** is formed by Earth-5's **Doctor Sivana.** This Legion attempts to gain **the Rock of Eternity** and conquer the **entire Multiverse!**

AARGH!

After he is imprisoned, ***Doctor Spectro*** needs ***Captain Atom*** to defend him from his ***fellow inmates.*** The villainous ***Rainbow Raider*** takes out a hit on Spectro for ***stealing his weapons!***

YESSS!

Zatanna uses her magic to erase the mind of ***Doctor Light*** in order to stop him from attacking the ***Justice League's families.***

DID YOU KNOW?

If a Gotham City super-villain is injured fighting **Batman,** he or she can make an appointment to see the **Crime Doctor!**

CRIMINAL CREATIONS

Doctor Sivana: Masters a method of creating clones of himself.

Doctor Cyber: Builds a purple robot bird and sends it to battle Wonder Woman.

Doctor Destiny: Builds a ray that can sap the will.

Doctor Spectro: Creates a light ray that can manipulate people's moods.

Doctor Alchemy: Builds a gun that mimics the powers of the Philosopher's Stone.

Doctor Moon: Manipulates people through surgery and turns them into superhumans.

FROM GOOD TO BAD AND BACK!

When the first **Doctor Alchemy** reforms, his **psychic twin** turns **evil!** By contrast, evil **Doctor Light's name** is taken by **Kimiyo Hoshi** as her **hero ID!**

BY THE TIME
I GET DONE WITH YOU...
YOU'LL UNDERSTAND
WHAT FEAR IS
ALL ABOUT.

JLA FILES

SCARECROW
Scorned psychologist and chemist Jonathan Crane develops his fear gas to terrify victims, making their nightmares seem real. He adopts the name "Scarecrow", the taunt that bullies used to throw at the gangly young man. Crane meets his match in the scary stakes when he goes up against Batman.

IN REAL LIFE
The Ultra-Humanite was one of the first comic book super-villains, debuting in *Action Comics* #13 (June 1939). This Superman foe specialised in fiendish schemes for world domination.

EVIL EGGHEADS

These **sinister scientists** use their **genius-level gifts** not to **better humanity,** but to get **rich,** gain **power** and **obliterate their enemies!**

DID YOU KNOW?

Dr Norman Techno is **Doctor Strangeglove,** so called because a terrible lab accident gives him a mind-controlled **electric typewriter** for a hand. He uses the keys to control enemies, as well as his army of **"Brain Children".**

NOOOO!

Justice League foe **Professor Ivo** is **obsessed** with his own mortality. He creates a serum from **long-lived animals,** such as **turtles.** It makes him almost immortal, but does **nothing** for his **looks!**

WHAT THE..?!

The Brain, last remnant of a brilliant scientist, is kept in **a jar** and **cared for** by his partner-in-crime – **and love** – French-speaking gorilla **Monsieur Mallah.**

Weather Wizard

TOP 6

Scarecrow Crimes

1. Scarecrow develops a **toxin that removes fear**. He sells it to a racing driver who nearly kills himself. He then **charges $50,000 for the antidote!**
2. Scarecrow's **"black light vibrations"** make Batman and Robin unable to see. The villain then **sets his pet panthers on them!**
3. Scarecrow attacks Batman with a **robot attack owl** with **razor-sharp claws.**
4. Scarecrow attempts to **drown** the **mayor of Gotham City** and Batman by **flooding a sewer tunnel!**
5. Scarecrow becomes the **super-strong Scarebeast** and **goes on a rampage.**
6. Scarecrow induces a **mass hallucination** in Gotham City, causing citizens to believe their city to be **a utopia!**

BAD DAY

Scientists T. O. Morrow and Professor Ivo send android Tomorrow Woman to destroy the Justice League. Instead, she saves the team, and blows herself up!

POWER UP!

The Weather Wizard steals the know-how to make his weather-controlling wand from his dead scientist brother. His brother had hoped his work would help people, but the Weather Wizard just wants to get rich!

AARGH!

Weapons master **Gizmo** is one of Dr Sivana's ***Fearsome Five,*** until Sivana shoots him to show his authority. Sivana jokes: "[Now] it's the Fearsome Four. Want to go for the Threatening Three?"

It's Only Love

Twisted inventor **Toyman** claims to have been **happily married** when **his wife** dies in a road accident. Reporter **Jimmy Olsen** discovers that his wife **Mary** was just one of Toyman's creations – a brilliantly lifelike **robot!**

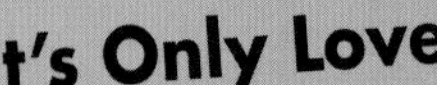

Toyman

SPECIAL *MOVES*

Oswald Loomis, the **Prankster,** invents wacky gadgets to **bewilder** the citizens of Metropolis and to **commit crimes.** He then hits on the idea of **hiring himself out** as a distraction for **Superman** while **other criminals** pull off heists.

TELL ME MORE

Creepy entrepreneur Maxwell Lord keeps his mind-control abilities secret for many years. He uses his powers in very subtle ways – but the nosebleeds he gets when he uses them eventually give him away.

YESSS!

Doctor Destiny's ability to create ***reality*** out of ***dreams*** is so powerful that the ***Justice League*** resorts to hypnosis to stop him from ***dreaming.*** This renders him ***powerless!***

DASTARDLY DEED

Doctor Psycho releases **Doomsday** from his prison in the Earth's core and uses **mind-control powers** to make the Kryptonian menace attack **Metropolis.**

WHAT THE..?!

Stage magician **Hypnota** is shot in the head. Instead of **dying,** she finds she can **shoot blue rays** from her eyes that mesmerise onlookers – whom she then exports as **slaves to Saturn!**

POWER UP!

Super-villain Dreamslayer takes over Maxwell Lord's body and supercharges his power, which allows him to control thousands of minds at once. While possessed, Lord dupes Justice League International into battling itself!

AARGH!

While ***imprisoned*** in the ***Justice League's computer,*** the mysterious ***Antithesis*** feeds on the team's negative feelings until he is strong enough to ***hypnotise*** them into ***committing crimes!***

MIND CONTROLLERS

These villains don't have **Superman's strength** or **The Flash's speed...** in fact, most of them don't have **physical superpowers** at all. They don't **need** them – they control **minds!**

AARGH!

The telepathic ***Insect Queen*** attempts to slowly take over ***Lana Lang's body*** in order to ***colonise the Earth!***

Mad Hatter Madness....

Mad Hatter Jervis Tetch is a scientist whose devices influence his victims' thoughts. However, his plans are often limited by his obsession with the story *Alice's Adventures in Wonderland* by Lewis Carroll!

DID YOU KNOW?

Doctor Psycho hates **Wonder Woman** and on one occasion uses his **Electro-Atomizer** to separate her **spirit** from her **body!**

TOP 5

These villains will bend your mind – to their will!

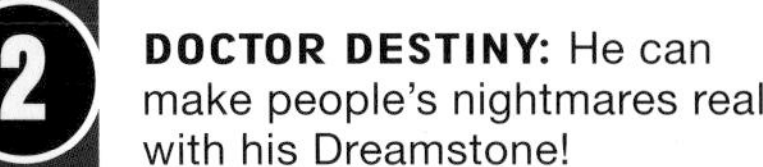

1. **COUNT VERTIGO:** His "Vertigo Effect" makes enemies lose their balance. He can even use it to disrupt missile targeting systems!
2. **DOCTOR DESTINY:** He can make people's nightmares real with his Dreamstone!
3. **CASSANDRA:** The villainous demigod daughter of Zeus controls anyone who hears her voice – even driving them to murder.
4. **THE PIED PIPER:** He hypnotises people with a special flute; he also has a tuning fork that paralyses anyone who hears it.
5. **MAD HATTER:** He controls people with devices disguised as hats.

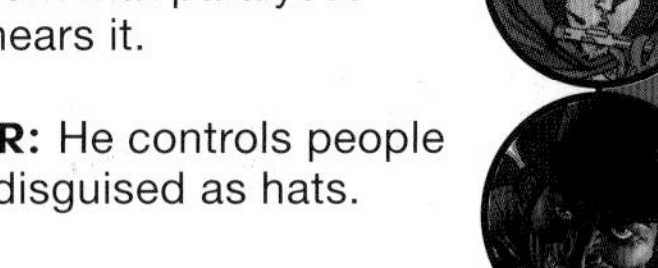

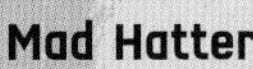

YOU ARE TRYING TO UNDERSTAND MADNESS WITH LOGIC. THIS IS NOT UNLIKE SEARCHING FOR DARKNESS WITH A TORCH.

Mad Hatter

WHAT THE..?!

After being exposed to radiation from a meteor, **Hector Hammond** gains **telepathic** and **telekinetic** abilities. His brain – and head – grow to **gigantic size!**

NOOOO!

Evil mastermind and surgeon ***Hush*** is a ***genius*** at manipulating heroes and villains. Discovering ***Batman's identity,*** he makes himself look like ***Bruce Wayne,*** planning to kill him and destroy ***everyone he loves!***

DASTARDLY DEED

Posing as a coffee salesman, the **Mad Hatter** hands out tickets for free coffee and doughnuts to local cops. The tickets contain **mind-control devices,** and soon Hatter controls many of **Gotham City's finest** and makes them **steal for him!**

KINGS OF THE UNDERWORLD

In the shady, brutal world of **organized crime,** it takes **a certain kind of person** to reach the **top** – and **Santa Claus they ain't!**

I.D. CRISIS

Corrupt politician **Rupert Thorne** discovers that **Batman** is **Bruce Wayne** and hires **Deadshot** to kill Wayne. The plan fails when Deadshot sees Batman with **"Wayne"** – a clever impersonation by the **Human Target!**

JLA FILES

GREAT WHITE SHARK
Fraudster Warren White is trapped in a subzero cell during a riot in Arkham Asylum. Now with terrible frostbite deformities, White files his teeth to points and becomes crime boss Great White Shark, operating from Arkham Asylum.

TOUGH BREAK

Greek-myth-themed crime lord **Maxie Zeus** escapes from **Arkham Asylum** along with other super-criminals when **Bane** blows up the walls. However, **running** in a **straitjacket** is not easy, and Zeus runs straight **into a tree!**

Carmine Falcone

AARGH!

The Joker *orders gang boss* ***Carmine "The Roman" Falcone*** *to kill* ***the Riddler*** *in one hour. When he fails, the Joker shoots Falcone, whose crime empire is then taken over by the* ***Penguin!***

WHAT THE..?!

The original **Clock King** is strictly a **minor league** criminal. Along with his **"Clockwatchers"** gang, he once set off to commit crime in **Metropolis** travelling in a **city bus.**

EWWW!

Brutal crime lord **Black Mask** and his gang, the **False Face Society,** wear masks to commit their crimes. Black Mask's mask is made from pieces of ebony casket from the **tomb of his father!**

DID YOU KNOW?

Japanese crime boss **Lord Death Man** can make himself seem **dead** by using **advanced yoga techniques!**

I AM THE NEW, UNDISPUTED, ABSOLUTE CRIME LORD OF GOTHAM CITY.

Black Mask

WHEN BAD GUYS GO GOOD

Assassin **David Cain,** a.k.a. **The Orphan,** cruelly raises his daughter **Cassandra** to be a **living weapon.** However, he sacrifices himself to bring down evil child trafficker **Mother.** Cassandra becomes **Batgirl,** and later **Orphan.**

MUTATION ALERT!

When Intergang boss Bruno Mannheim gets caught in a collapsing Boom Tube, Superman thinks he's gone for good. The Man of Steel gets a nasty surprise when Mannheim returns as a giant, apparently mutated by alien tech.

TOP 3

Ventriloquist Villains

1. **ARNOLD WESKER:** The original Ventriloquist, Wesker is apparently mild-mannered, while his dummy, Scarface, has the looks and personality of a hard-boiled Prohibition-era gangster.

2. **PEYTON RILEY:** After the first Ventriloquist is murdered, this mafia princess takes his dummy, Scarface, to seize control of her own mob family.

3. **SHAUNA BELZER:** A deranged serial killer, Shauna has telekinetic powers and a dummy named Ferdie after her twin brother – who is her first victim!

DASTARDLY DEED

Intergang boss **Bruno "Ugly" Mannheim** kidnaps **Jimmy Olsen** and his friends and treats them to **a fine dinner.** Has Bruno turned over a new leaf? Of course not – the food is **poisoned!**

KING SHARK

Giant half-man, half-shark King Shark is the son of shark god Kamo. King Shark is captured by Suicide Squad leader Amanda Waller. He proves very useful, though he does occasionally eat the other agents!

DID YOU KNOW?

Nine different villains with **clay-like bodies** have called themselves **Clayface...** and that's not counting an **army of clones!**

It's Only Love

Clayface Preston Payne can't help but fall in love with ***Helena.*** She's the only woman ***immune*** to his ***flesh-melting powers.*** So what if that's because she's a ***mannequin!?!***

Clayface

GOOD DAY

Scaly giant **Killer Croc** is tired of being hunted by the law. **Swamp Thing** brings him to the **Louisiana swamps** so he can let his "animal" side **run free.**

NOOOO!

Mild-mannered scientist ***Kitty Faulkner*** is demonstrating her ***solar energy machine*** when it ***explodes,*** transforming her into ***Rampage***—a deranged, orange-skinned ***colossus!***

MONSTERS AND MUTATIONS

Some villains are **born monsters,** others **want** to **be monsters!** Being transformed into an **animal hybrid,** even **clay,** can do wonders for a **criminal's profile.** But there are **risks attached!**

Parasite

JLA FILES

HELLGRAMMITE
Scientist Roderick Rose takes his fascination with insects much too far and mutates into a humanoid insect. He leaps like a grasshopper, spins webs and transforms people into helpless drones. As the super-villain Hellgrammite, he ends up battling Batman, Green Arrow and Superman.

EWWW!

Super-villain Chemo is a living plastic suit full of chemicals. He showers Blüdhaven in toxic waste when he is dropped on the city. To get rid of him, Superman has to throw him into space!

I'VE BEEN WAITING FOR YOU TO COME ALONG FOR QUITE A WHILE. AND WAITING MAKES ME... HUNGRY!

TOP 3

Demon Neron's Deals

In exchange for their souls, Neron has let these villains really go wild!

1. **KILLER MOTH:** This minor crook is transformed into flesh-eating Charaxes.
2. **COPPERHEAD:** This costumed contortionist becomes a human-snake hybrid with poisonous fangs.
3. **BLACK MANTA:** This violent thug mutates into a terrifying, humanoid manta ray.

TOUGH BREAK

While practising projecting his **mind** into **inanimate objects,** Joey Monteleone gets it **stuck** in a **container of hot asphalt.** He becomes tar-tossing criminal **Tar Pit.**

WOW!

100

The number of Wonder Woman foe Crimson Centipede's hands. That means he can fire 50 guns and throw 50 punches at the same time!

WHAT THE..?!

Little chimpanzee Toto is sent into space on a test flight. He returns to Earth **enormous in size** and shooting **Kryptonite lasers** out of his eyes!

AARGH!

Exposed to ***radioactive waste,*** Ray Jensen becomes ***Parasite*** – who feeds on ***living energy.*** He drains so much power from ***Superman*** that he ***explodes!***

WORLD CONQUERORS

The universe contains plenty of **power-hungry super-villains** wanting to rule **everything** and **everybody** – and all too often they have their sights set on **Earth!**

JUSTICE LEAGUE... I'VE DESTROYED YOU! AND WITH YOUR DESTRUCTION—I'M FREE TO *ENSLAVE* THIS WORLD!

JLA FILES

THE DEFEAT OF KRONA
Guardian of the Universe Krona builds a machine for observing the beginnings of the universe. It explodes, creating the Multiverse and the Antimatter Universe, and releasing evil into the cosmos. Krona is banished, but returns to get revenge on the Guardians. Despite wielding the seven powers of the spectrum, Krona is defeated by Green Lantern (Hal Jordan).

POWER UP!

Super-intelligent, power-mad ape Gorilla Grodd gets a portion of The Flash's Speed Force and uses its power to take over Central City, home town of The Flash!

WOW!

70,000

The number of carnage globes Mongul unleashes from his space ship to wipe out Coast City.

NOOOO!

The creation of the ***Antimatter Universe*** by ***Krona*** spawns the ***Anti-Monitor,*** an enormously powerful being determined to ***destroy*** all other realities!

BACK FROM THE DEAD!

Despero, tyrant of the planet Kalanor, is a super-strong, mind-controlling **alien megalomaniac.** He has even survived **decapitation** thanks to **Brainiac 2,** who helps him grow **a new body!**

EWWW!

The being **Starro is** said to be older than **evil itself.** Its particular method of **world-conquering** is to create **mind-slaves** using starfish-shaped parasites that **clamp onto victims' faces!**

Despero

★ TEAM PLAYER ★

The Lord of Time chooses history's best fighters to help him rule **space and time.** Battling the **Justice League** and Earth-2's **Justice Society,** his squad includes cowboy **Jonah Hex,** World War I ace **Hans von Hammer, Miss Liberty** and the **Black Pirate.** **He still loses!**

WHAT THE..?!

Super-strong alien conqueror Mongul is also super-cunning. He has attempted to make slaves of Earth's population via video games!

WHEN GOOD GUYS GO BAD

Parallax is the parasitic embodiment of **fear.** He possesses **Green Lantern Hal Jordan,** turning him into a **power-crazed super-villain!**

AARGH!

Harvest *is a 31st-century human with a* ***serious grudge*** *against* ***metahumans.*** *He travels through time with his army of* ***Ravagers,*** *seeking out and killing* ***superpowered beings!***

DID YOU KNOW?

Imperiex has destroyed the universe many times. When he sees a world he doesn't like, he wants to **tear it all up** and start again – and he doesn't let a trifling matter like the loss of **trillions of lives** put him off!

JLA FILES

VANDAL SAVAGE

This villain has been causing trouble on Earth for as long as human life has existed. According to Savage, many of the world's most famous conquerors, such as Alexander the Great, Julius Caesar and Genghis Khan, were actually him in various guises. He also claims to have advised William the Conqueror, Napoleon and Adolf Hitler!

TOP 10

Extraterrestrial menaces

1. **APPELLAXIANS:** Use Earth as a combat arena to choose their next leader; at least they cause the founding of the Justice League!
2. **DOMINATORS:** Detonate a Gene Bomb on Earth hoping to get rid of all metahumans.
3. **INSECT QUEEN:** Tries to make Earth her territory, copying Lana Lang's body (plus antennae and wings) as her new Earth carapace.
4. **HELSPONT:** Exiled to Earth by his own kind, this brutal Daemonite tries to use Superman as a pawn in his ruthless quest for revenge.
5. **H'EL:** A Kryptonian who wants to destroy Earth's sun and harness its energy to travel back in time and save his homeworld.
6. **PSIONS:** Created by the Guardians of the Universe, this reptilian race evolve into scientists and conduct cruel experiments on other beings.
7. **SOLARIS:** A second sun that is also a sentient, malevolent supercomputer.
8. **KHUNDS:** Violent aliens who frequently clash with the Green Lantern Corps.
9. **DURLANS:** Shapeshifters who can take on the powers of the races they imitate.
10. **SUN-EATERS:** These sentient weapons, created to destroy unworthy worlds, measure 12,875 km (8,000 miles) across.

POWER UP!

Berserker Blockbuster can break bones and batter buildings with his brutish brawn. After making a pact with the demon Neron, he gains an intellect to match his prodigious strength.

D YOU KNOW?

Waylon Jones is born with a condition that turns him into a ferocious **crocodile-like being.** He eventually turns to crime as **Killer Croc!**

BACK FROM THE DEAD!

Solomon Grundy is a seemingly **immortal being** that is reborn with **a new personality** every time he is **destroyed!**

WOW!

100

The weight in tons several of these super-villains can lift with ease!

EWWW!

Lobo is mean and cruel, but he is also **haunted by tragedy.** He is racked by guilt for inadvertently causing his world's **destruction** and **killing everyone** on the planet!

Bane derives his **great strength** and **endurance** from a chemical mixture named **Venom.** A **network of tubes** feeds the stuff straight into **his bloodstream!**

HEAVY HITTERS

Some **super-villains** are sinister and manipulative. Others are **crazy** and **unpredictable**. Others... are just **really, really strong!**

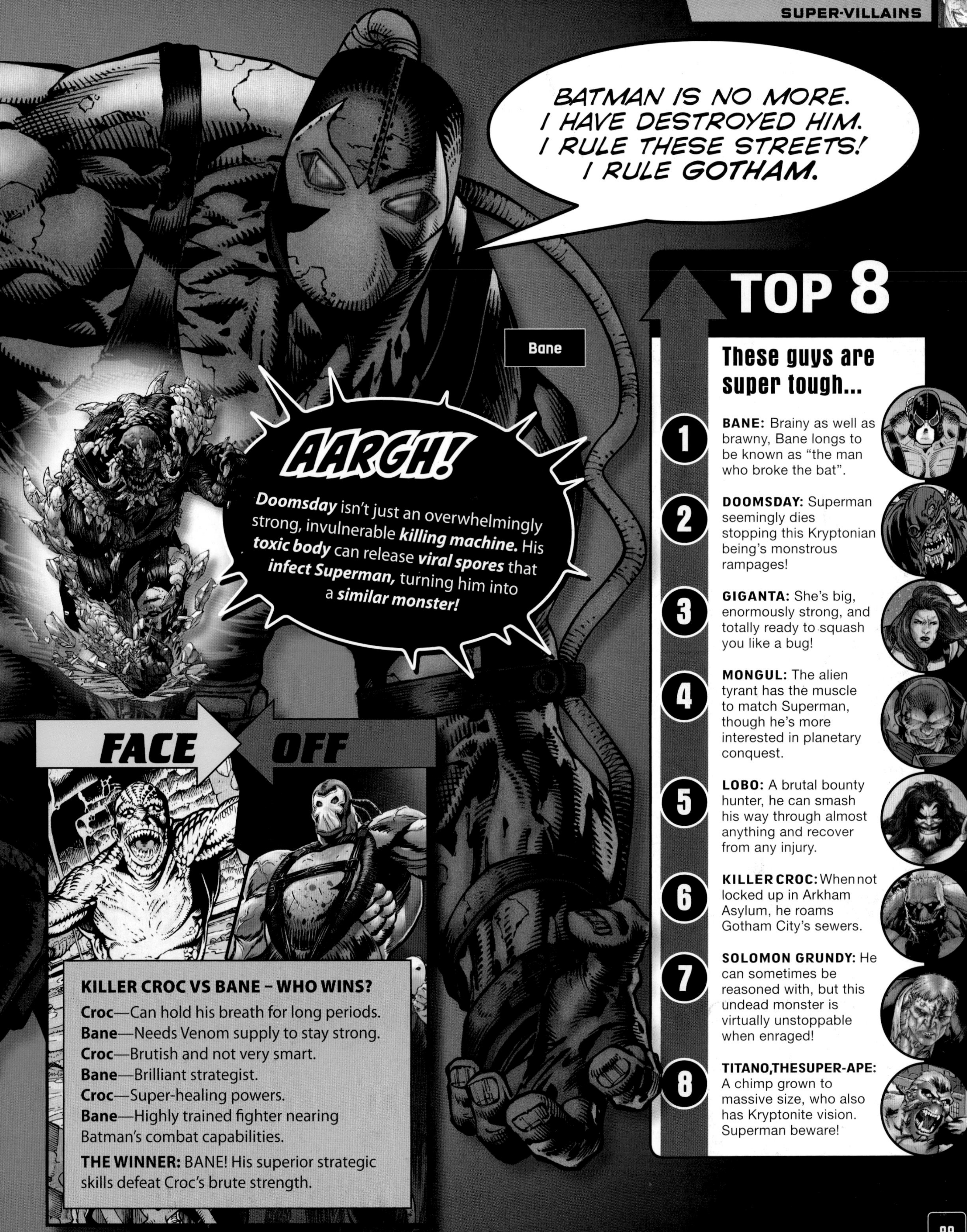

BATMAN IS NO MORE.
I HAVE DESTROYED HIM.
I RULE THESE STREETS!
I RULE GOTHAM.
Bane
AARGH!
FACE
OFF

Doomsday isn't just an overwhelmingly strong, invulnerable ***killing machine.*** His ***toxic body*** can release ***viral spores*** that ***infect Superman,*** turning him into a ***similar monster!***

TOP 8

These guys are super tough...

1. **BANE:** Brainy as well as brawny, Bane longs to be known as "the man who broke the bat".
2. **DOOMSDAY:** Superman seemingly dies stopping this Kryptonian being's monstrous rampages!
3. **GIGANTA:** She's big, enormously strong, and totally ready to squash you like a bug!
4. **MONGUL:** The alien tyrant has the muscle to match Superman, though he's more interested in planetary conquest.
5. **LOBO:** A brutal bounty hunter, he can smash his way through almost anything and recover from any injury.
6. **KILLER CROC:** When not locked up in Arkham Asylum, he roams Gotham City's sewers.
7. **SOLOMON GRUNDY:** He can sometimes be reasoned with, but this undead monster is virtually unstoppable when enraged!
8. **TITANO, THE SUPER-APE:** A chimp grown to massive size, who also has Kryptonite vision. Superman beware!

KILLER CROC VS BANE – WHO WINS?

Croc—Can hold his breath for long periods.
Bane—Needs Venom supply to stay strong.
Croc—Brutish and not very smart.
Bane—Brilliant strategist.
Croc—Super-healing powers.
Bane—Highly trained fighter nearing Batman's combat capabilities.

THE WINNER: BANE! His superior strategic skills defeat Croc's brute strength.

HOCUS POCUS!

These **demons, sorcerers and imps** are **malevolent meddlers** in **dark magic.** Each one spells **a whole lot of trouble** for any Super Hero!

TOUGH BREAK

Siobhan McDougal undertakes a **magic ritual** to make herself leader of her Irish clan. It goes **horribly wrong,** and Siobhan is dragged by demons into a realm of **Hell!** When she returns, she is the **Silver Banshee** – a white-eyed entity with **a death-dealing scream!**

JLA FILES

BLACK ADAM
In Ancient Egypt, Teth Adam is granted amazing powers by the Wizard, who believes he will use them wisely. However, Adam is corrupted by this power, and tries to become a world conqueror. He is later known as Black Adam.

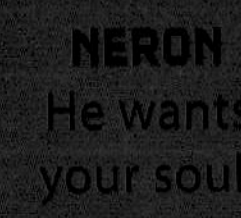

NERON
He wants your soul!

SATANUS
He wants to rule Hell!

LADY BLAZE
She wants to rule Hell as well!

ASMODEL
He wants to conquer Heaven!

WHEN GOOD GUYS GO BAD

Fifth-dimensional imp **QWSP** is a friend to **Aquaman,** until he uses his magic to copy Aquaman's **uncompromising personality.** He overdoes it and transforms into an **evil being** that threatens the **whole world.**

NOOOO!

June Moone is possessed by the magic-manipulating ***Enchantress,*** who makes the well-meaning young woman do ***bad things.***

Ancient sorcerer **Felix Faust** uses his **dark arts** to take over the body of another and return to 20th-century Earth. A frequent ally of **demons,** Faust is determined never to die – in case he is forced to pay for the **vast powers** he has acquired.

DID YOU KNOW?

Sorceress **Morgaine le Fey** has been working her wickedness since the legendary time of **King Arthur.** She has to use magic to stay young or she'll **crumble to dust!**

IN A MATTER OF DAYS, BECAUSE OF MY ***HUBRIS,*** EARTH WILL BE RAZED BY ***VENGEFUL FIENDS!***

Felix Faust

JLA FILES

MR MXYZPTLK
Magical mischief-maker Mr. Mxyzptlk is a tiny fifth-dimensional imp who delights in plaguing Superman by bending reality. His only weakness is his own name! If he's tricked into saying it backwards, he's sent back to the Fifth Dimension for 90 days!

TOP 6

Mr Mxyzptlk's tricksiest tricks

1. Putting a hex on Superman so that everything he says becomes fact.
2. Creating a wicked doppelganger of Supergirl called Superiorgirl.
3. Creating Red Kryptonite to drain Superman's powers, allowing Lex to thump the Man of Steel!
4. Transforming Superman so he becomes hugely fat, or has a swelled head, or resembles a very old man.
5. Transforming Metropolis into a utopia.
6. Materialising a wife and child for Superman.

In an effort to destroy **Wonder Woman,** the sorceress **Circe** magically disguises herself as a lawyer named **Donna Milton** and befriends the Amazon. But the disguise is **too perfect** – and Circe not only forgets her evil plan, she **forgets who she is!**

DASTARDLY DEED

Black Alice can tap into the powers of **any mystical hero or villain.** Her boyfriend cheats on her and she uses the power of **Shazam** to get revenge, destroying a shopping mall in the process!

EWWW!

Part scientist, part sorcerer, completely insane, **Anton Arcane** is chosen as the **Avatar of the Rot** because he loves **decay.** He is singled out for this "honour" after being so excited by a rotting rabbit corpse that he **eats it!**

I WILL FINALLY TRANSCEND DEATH!

FAMOUS LAST WORDS

> **"Be silent! No woman rules me..."**

The plant god Urzkartaga, moments before he is broken into tiny pieces by Wonder Woman's Lasso of Truth.

Gentleman Ghost

JLA FILES

GENTLEMAN GHOST
English highwayman James Craddock was executed in the 19th century. His evil spirit, Gentleman Ghost, is determined to regain his physical form. Using an ancient artefact named the Mortis Orb, Gentleman Ghost tries to steal the life-force from the citizens of New York City. Gentleman Ghost gets his just desserts when the Orb opens a portal to Hell instead.

AARGH!

Medusa's signature move *doesn't require much effort – her opponent is* ***turned to stone*** *as soon as they meet her eyes. This* ***backfires*** *when* ***Batwoman*** *defeats her by forcing her to look at* ***her own reflection!***

I.D. CRISIS

Dr Barbara Ann Minerva is possessed by the spirit of the **Cheetah** and is locked in a struggle with her **animal side.** Is she Barbara, friend of **Wonder Woman,** or **The Cheetah,** who **hungers** for **flesh?**

MEGA MAKEOVER

HA HA HA HA

When the offices of *Daily Planet* rival *Newstime* are overrun by demons, Superman is forced to accept help from the devilish Lord Satanus. Little does he know that Satanus has a day job – hiding in plain sight as *Newstime* boss Collin Thornton!

EWWW!

Brother Blood can control people by touching their **blood!** He keeps his many followers **in thrall** to him by making sure they're **always bleeding!**

SUPERNATURAL MENACE

Some of the most **fearsome threats** in the **universe** come from **immortal gods and demons** or from **undead super-villains,** who refuse to let a little thing like **death** get in their way!

★ TEAM PLAYER ★

Super-zombie **Solomon Grundy** is a popular guy. He's been in the **Injustice League, Suicide Squad, Secret Society of Super-Villains, Injustice Society, the Black Lantern Corps** and the **Fatal Five.**

FACE OFF

WONDER WOMAN vs DEVASTATION
She looks like a child, but ruthless Devastation is as powerful as Wonder Woman. Wonder Woman's key advantage is a drop of her own blood, mixed into the clay that created Devastation. It causes Devastation to pause for a moment – and Wonder Woman pounds her into the dirt!

WHAT THE..?!

If **Beelzebub,** one of the **Lords of Hell,** takes physical form, he appears as **a giant fly!**

DID YOU KNOW?

Arrakhat is an evil **genie,** or djinn. But instead of granting **three wishes** before he returns to his particular circle of Hell, he must claim **three deaths!**

NOOOO!

Greek god **Zeus** abandons his first child when a prophecy tells him he will be ***killed*** by one of his offspring. But the boy, ***First Born,*** is protected and raised by ***a pack of hyenas.*** He does ***not*** turn out well…

BAD DAY

Magically empowered, **Black Adam** not only kills Horseman of the Apocalypse **Sobek,** he adds insult to injury by turning the crocodile-like villain into a **pair of boots!**

AM THAT A FACT?

SEKRIT IDENTITY WHAT EVERYONE KNOW: Bizarro #1

WHAT HIM NOT: Imperfect duplicate of Superman

FAVOURITE WEAKNESSES: Powers like Kryptonian but mostly different

USELESS STRENGTHS: Him think backwards. Him do everything wrong

BEST FRIENDS EVER WHO ALWAYS HIT HIM: Superman; Queen Tut

WORST ENIMY HIM NOT LIKE AND NEVER SPEND ANY TIME WITH: Jimmy Olsen

WHAT THE..?!

Bizarro's baby is born looking **hideously human** and is exiled to Earth. The infant eventually **reverts to a true Bizarro,** but not before Supergirl assumes she has **accidentally** turned a human baby **into a monster!**

JLA FILES

BIZARRO WORLD

Bizarro's world is named Htrae ("Earth" backwards). It orbits a blue sun, is square and has a moon made of cheese. Bizarro explains: "Us do opposite of all Earthly things! Us hate beauty! Us love ugliness! Is big crime to make anything perfect on Bizarro World!"

AARGH!

When the planet **Htrae** is destroyed in a **cosmic crisis,** backwards-thinking Bizarro **rockets** his son to the centre of the world to **ensure** he will **perish!**

GOOD DAY

Luthor's first clone of Superman turns into a **shambling monster** similar to Bizarro. It later **explodes** and its dusty residue cures **Lucy Lane's blindness!**

HANDLE WITH CARE!

Bizarro materialises when **Superboy** is exposed to Professor Dalton's faulty **Duplicator Ray.** This creates an **imperfect clone** mimicking Superboy's abilities, but with a **crystalline skin** and an **addled brain.**

DID YOU KNOW?

Lex Luthor makes a **Duplicator machine** and unleashes a fearsome and flawed **Superman replica.** It goes on to create an **entire race** of **Bizarros,** based on Superman and his friends and foes.

ME DON'T BELONG IN WORLD OF LIVING PEOPLE! ME DON'T KNOW DIFFERENCE BETWEEN RIGHT AND WRONG -- GOOD AND EVIL!

HOW BIZARRE!

Imperfect Superman duplicate **Bizarro** usually means **no harm,** but his **topsy-turvy ways** can make him a **highly dangerous character** to be around!

TOP 5

Skewed Superman Superpowers

1. Bizarro X-ray vision sees through lead, but not other elements.
2. Instead of having freezing breath, Bizarro can exhale flames like a dragon.
3. Bizarro's telescopic vision only sees things happening behind him, not in front.
4. Superman has heat vision; Bizarro has freeze vision.
5. Bizarro super-breath doesn't blow but only sucks, creating vacuums.

UNLIKELY ALLIANCE

Hoping to get enough material for a book, reporter Jimmy Olsen tricks Bizarro into going on a road trip to "Bizarro America" (i.e. Canada). After encountering menaces such as aliens and Queen Tut, Jimmy becomes Bizarro's pal for real!

DID YOU KNOW?

Bizarro creates an imperfect clone of **himself!** The result is **Zibarro** – essentially a rational, but **ordinary,** human being.

Q&A

Q: How can Bizarro become Htrae's greatest hero?

A: Kidnap Superman's adopted dad Jonathan Kent and force him to explain how Bizarro can destroy the square world and everything on it...

TOUGH BREAK

A scientist finds a way to ***stabilise*** Bizarro's thought processes, and the duplicate becomes a ***brilliant and sensitive ally*** of Superman's. However, the treatment is only ***temporary*** and Bizarro realises he is doomed to become a ***stupid, dangerous monster.***

NOOOO!

As non-living ***artificial Kryptonians***, Bizarros can only be killed by ***Blue Kryptonite,*** created by the rays of the imperfect ***Duplicator Machine.***

EWWW!

Bizarro-Batman is the "World's Worst Detective", and his **Futility Belt** is packed with cigarette butts, chewed gum, and other useless articles – all **prized treasures** on Bizarro World.

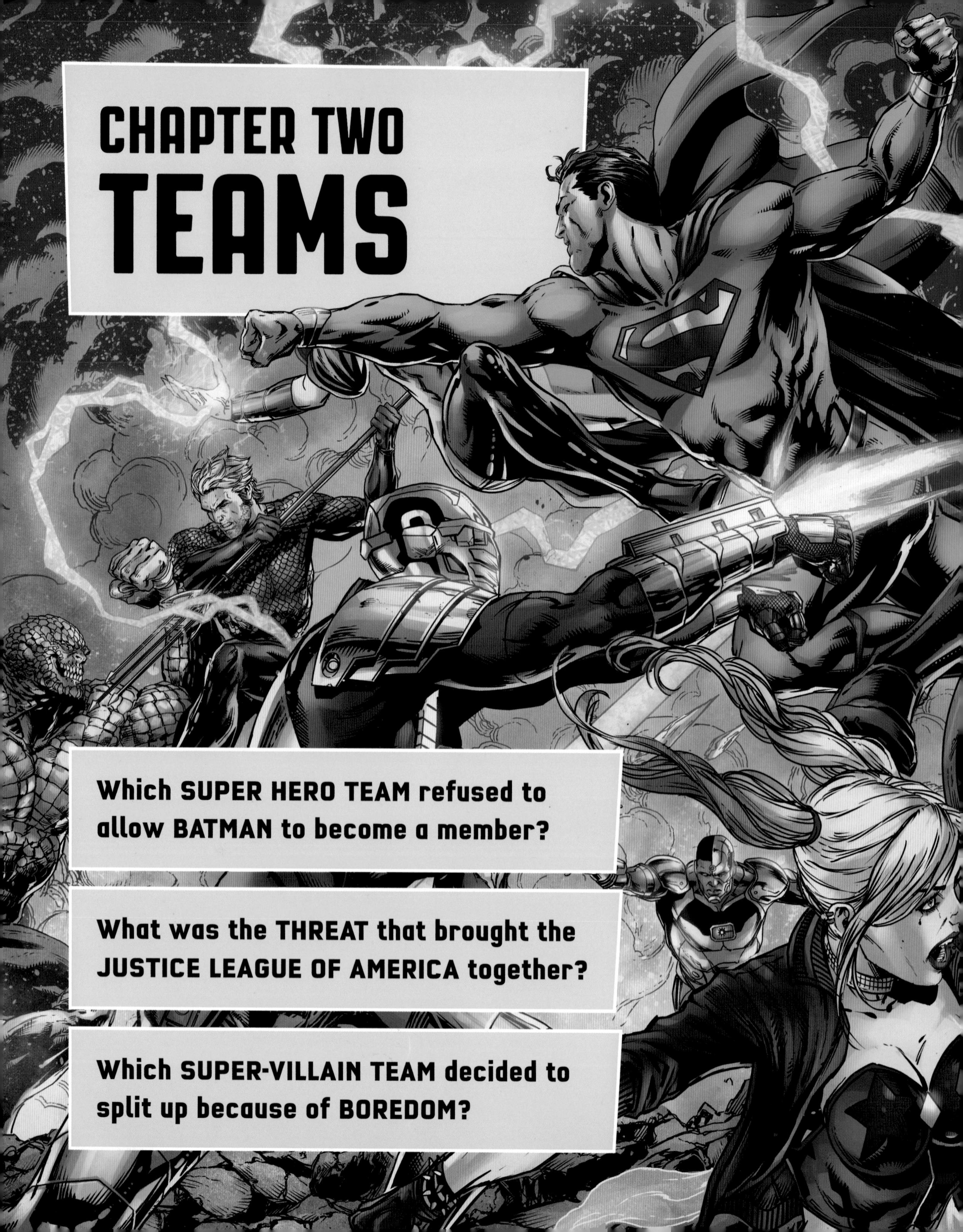

CHAPTER TWO TEAMS

Which SUPER HERO TEAM refused to allow BATMAN to become a member?

What was the THREAT that brought the JUSTICE LEAGUE OF AMERICA together?

Which SUPER-VILLAIN TEAM decided to split up because of BOREDOM?

SUPER HERO TEAMS

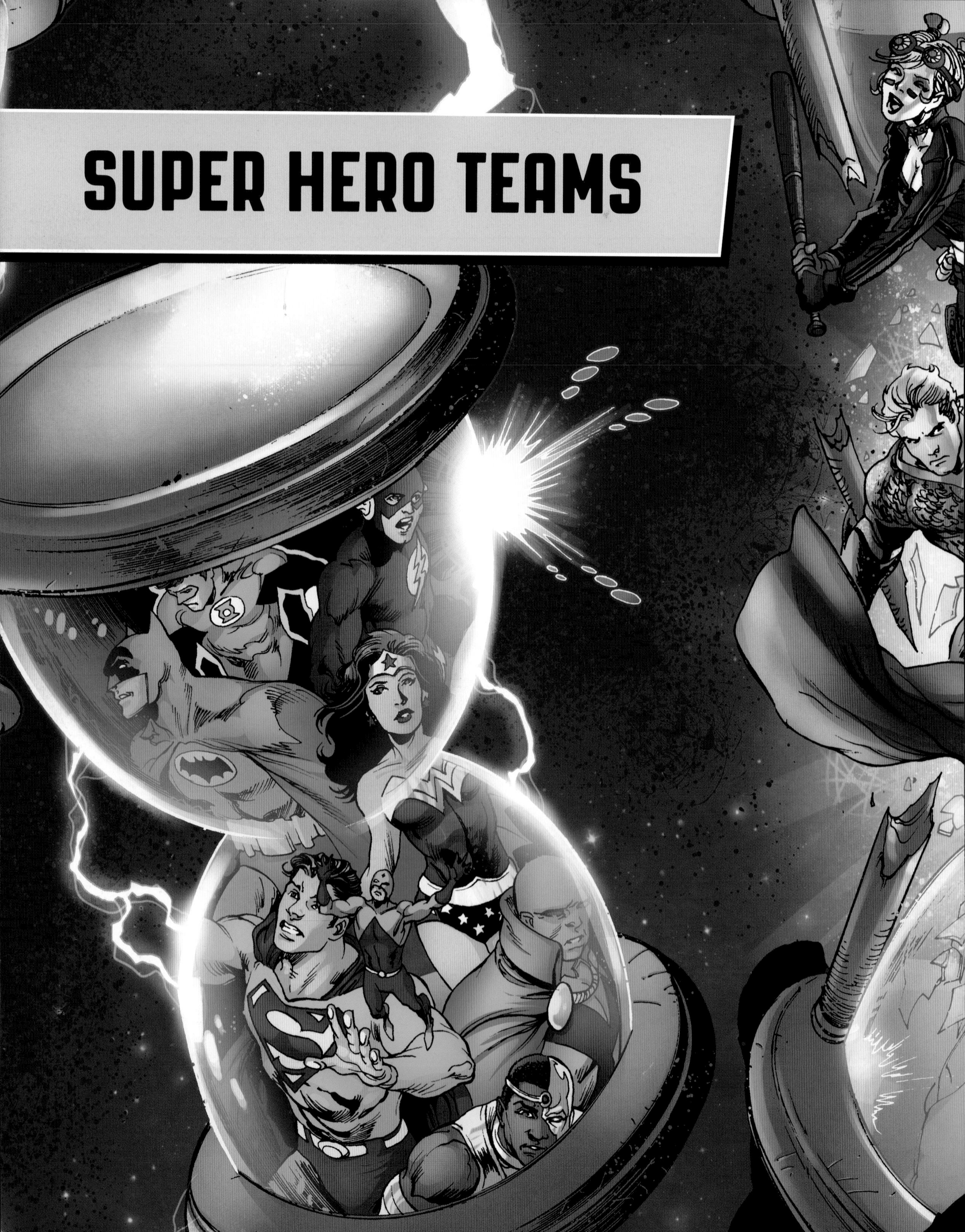

BRAVE AND BOLD!

Sometimes it takes **two!** Whether battling **bad guys** or **saving cities,** these **Super Hero teamups** have stymied **many a super-villain!**

YESSS!

When their comical arch-enemy ***Jarvis Poker*** becomes seriously ill, the kindly hero team of ***Knight and Squire*** let the villain think he is getting away with his crimes just to ***make him feel better!***

It's Only Love

The Olympian God of Love, Eros, makes Superman and Wonder Woman briefly fall in love. The two most powerful heroes in the galaxy also share a kiss after a battling Mongul! Many other Super Hero team-ups have led to romance. To name a few...

Green Arrow and Black Canary

Batman and Catwoman

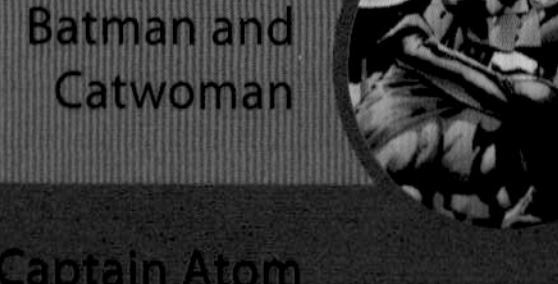

Captain Atom and Nightshade

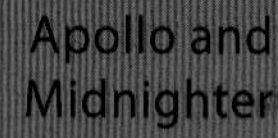

Apollo and Midnighter

Hawkman and Hawkwoman

IN REAL LIFE

Superman and Batman – billed as "The Mightiest Team on Earth" – first teamed up in *Superman* #76 (May 1952) to rescue Lois Lane from a blaze.

WHAT THE..?!

The Composite Superman is one of the strangest villains Batman and Superman have ever faced. This bisected being is literally one-half Superman, one-half Batman!

TOP 3

Unusual Pairings

1. **SUPERMAN & SANTA:** The Man of Steel helps Santa Claus save Christmas from the killjoy Toyman. They deliver presents all around the world!
2. **AQUAMAN & QWSP:** Aquaman has occasionally teamed up with fifth-dimensional imp Qwsp to battle magical threats.
3. **WONDER WOMAN & WONDER TOT:** "Amazon Magic" has enabled Wonder Woman to go on adventures with herself as a baby – Wonder Tot!

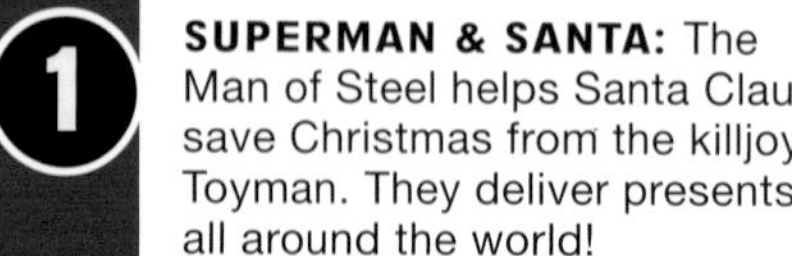

DID YOU KNOW?

Superman and **Batman** have proved an **unstoppable** crime-fighting team. However, they often **disagree on tactics** and who's the **best** at being a hero.

WHAT THE..?!

Richard Raleigh, alias the Super Hero Red Bee, fights alongside his trained pet Michael, a bee who lives in Richard's belt pouch!

BAD DAY

Batman and Robin find themselves in a **weird alien world!** A giant stone idol comes alive, attacks them, and **Robin is killed!** Batman is in **despair...** then he awakes! It was just an **hallucination** caused by a **science experiment!**

YOU KNOW, I THINK WE'RE GETTING THE HANG OF THIS "WORKING TOGETHER" THING!

HANDLE WITH CARE!

In case his superpowered, sometime crime-busting partner **Superman** goes rogue, **the Dark Knight** keeps a **Kryptonite ring** in the Batcave. He hopes he **never** has to **use it!**

IN REAL LIFE

The Dynamic Duo of Batman and Robin, the Boy Wonder, first teamed up in *Detective Comics* #38 (Apr. 1940), thanks to writer Bill Finger and artist Bob Kane. Robin appealed especially to younger readers, boosting sales.

WHAT THE..?!

The heroic shrinking hero known as the Atom surprises everyone when he begins dating gargantuan, super-growing villain Giganta!

ALTERNATE EARTHS

On Earth-16, **Superman Jr** and **Batman Jr** struggle to step out of the long shadows cast by their **legendary fathers.** They rebel by **running away from home** so they can become the heroes they **dream of being.**

TOUGH BREAK

Tired of being poor, **Blue Beetle** and **Booster Gold** open a **casino** on the island of **Kooey Kooey Kooey.** The island **uproots itself** and **swims away,** leaving their casino **a shambles!**

JLA FILES

LEAGUES OF JUSTICE

The Justice League of Earth-1 teams up with its Earth-2 predecessors, the Justice Society of America, and together they save two Earths. This successful team-up becomes an annual event.

HEROES UNITED!

On their own, heroes like **Superman, Batman, Wonder Woman, Aquaman, Green Lantern, The Flash** and **Cyborg** are powerful. United as the **Justice League,** they're virtually **unstoppable!**

WHAT THE..?!

One version of the League, the **Justice League of Anarchy,** includes **Ambush Bug,** whose powers include teleportation, being lucky and the knowledge that he is in a **comic book!**

Green Lantern (Jessica Cruz)

Cyborg

Aquaman

Wonder Woman

Superman

ALTERNATE EARTHS

Strangely, Justice Leagues from elsewhere in the Multiverse often tend towards evil!

Joker League of Anarchy: The Joker steals Mr. Mxyzptlk's powers and turns the universe upside-down. This Justice League is made up of villains who enforce the "rule" of chaos!

Crime Syndicate of America: On Earth-3, where evil always wins, Owlman is an evil Batman with psychic powers, Ultraman gains powers when exposed to Kryptonite and Power Ring is a cowardly Green Lantern!

Justice Lords: On Earth-50, Lex Luthor is president and brings the world to the brink of war; the League harshly keeps humanity in line!

TOP 3

Spin-Off Leagues

Sometimes heroes decide to form their own version of the Justice League…

1. **JUSTICE LEAGUE DARK:** Madame Xanadu forms this mystical team after seeing a vision of a terrible future only they can stop!
2. **JUSTICE LEAGUE ELITE:** Only working in secret, members wear special black versions of their costumes.
3. **YOUNG JUSTICE:** Teenage heroes Robin, Superboy and Impulse go adventuring with Slobo, a magically de-aged, teenage version of violent space biker Lobo!

Green Lantern (Simon Baz)

Q&A

Q: What threat brings the Justice League together?

A: A massive, world-conquering, mind-controlling alien, who looks like a giant starfish. Its name? Starro!

NOOOO!

The ***Justice League's*** most fearsome opponent is ***Darkseid,*** grim ruler of the planet Apokolips. He wants to ***eliminate free will!***

The Flash

IN REAL LIFE

The Justice League of America debuted in *The Brave and the Bold* #28 (Mar. 1960). Writer Gardner Fox and artist Mike Sekowsky based the team on World War II heroes the Justice Society of America.

Batman

YESSS!

When ***7,000 aliens*** invade Earth, the only solution is a ***device*** that will ***wipe the aliens' minds*** but also ***kill the user...*** but the ***Justice League*** join their minds to ***Martian Manhunter's,*** and together they defeat the ***aliens*** and the ***device!***

WHEN BAD GUYS GO GOOD

When the **Justice League** meet the **Crime Syndicate,** their evil counterparts from Earth-3, they seem to be outgunned. However, the League's enemy, **Lex Luthor,** assembles a **team of villains** to help **see off** the new threat.

BOTTOM OF THE LEAGUE

Not all Justice Leagues are created equal. These five team-ups fizzle out spectacularly!

JUSTICE LEAGUE INTERNATIONAL: This ill-fated team, backed by the United Nations, only allows heroes whose identities are publicly known... so Batman is turned down!

EXTREME JUSTICE: Captain Atom founds this team to be more proactive than the regular League, but their poor planning leads to the disastrous invasion of Bialya!

SUPER BUDDIES: Formed by Maxwell Lord, this team of squabbling Super Heroes is kidnapped at their first meeting and made to fight each other by the villain Roulette!

JUSTICE LEAGUE ANTARTICA: Made up of the goofy Green Lantern G'nort and a group of hapless criminals, this League is soon defeated by killer penguins!

BIZARRO JUSTICE LEAGUE: Bat-zarro is the World's Worst Detective, Bizarro-Aquaman can't swim, and Bizarra wields the Lasso of Lies!

JLA FILES

The Justice League Watchtower is a state-of-the-art satellite orbiting the Earth. It allows League members to monitor the planet and hone their skills in its training room, nicknamed "The Kitchen". The League also maintains a Hall of Justice in Washington D.C., used as a meeting place and a museum.

TEEN TEAMS AND SUPER PETS

Age is no barrier when it comes to **fighting crime** or **saving the universe** – and some **Super Heroes** don't even have to be **human!**

WE'RE A *BEACON OF HOPE* TO OUR GENERATION!

Starfire

Raven

Wonder Girl

Kid Flash

Robin

Beast Boy

Cyborg

TELL ME MORE

TERRIFIC HEADQUARTERS

The Teen Titans are based in New York City. They have a specially designed T-shaped building, equipped to meet their heroic needs!

DID YOU KNOW?

A second group of Titans, named **Teen Titans West,** fights crime in San Francisco. Early members include **Hawk, Bumblebee, Flamebird** and **Dove.**

TOP 7

Teen Titans

These junior Justice Leaguers are looking for friends to fight foes. The Teen Titans soon expands to include every teen hero they can find!

1. **ROBIN:** The leader of the pack, Robin brings the brains to a team of pure power.
2. **KID FLASH:** A super-fast speedster always ready to run right into trouble.
3. **WONDER GIRL:** This dazzling daughter of Paradise Island packs a powerful punch!
4. **STARFIRE:** A star-powered alien warrior separated from Tamaran, her homeworld.
5. **CYBORG:** Rebuilt with machine parts after a lab accident, Vic Stone is a living machine!
6. **BEAST BOY:** Thanks to a green monkey serum, Beast Boy can transform into any animal.
7. **RAVEN:** Daughter of the demonic Trigon, Raven uses her magical powers for good.

TOP 5

Legionnaires

Major stars in the Legion of Super-Heroes

1. **LIGHTNING LAD:** An accident gives Garth Ranzz electric abilities!
2. **SATURN GIRL:** A telepathic alien from the moon of Saturn!
3. **COSMIC BOY:** Born with the power to magnetise anything!
4. **BRAINIAC 5:** Descended from Brainiac, Querl Dox uses his superior intellect to save lives!
5. **TRIPLICATE GIRL:** Luornu Durgo can split into three copies of herself at will!

ALTERNATE EARTHS

Given powers by radioactive meteor fragments, these **anthropomorphic Super Heroes** hail from the cartoon dimension named **Earth-C**. They start their own team: **the Zoo Crew**.

1. **CAPTAIN CARROT: A superstrong rabbit.**
2. **PIG IRON: Peter Porkchops turns into a porcine powerhouse!**
3. **YANKEE POODLE: A reporter who gains "animal magnetism".**
4. **ALLEY-KAT-ABRA: A mystical cat with a power-infused wand.**
5. **FASTBACK: This tortoise can run circles around anyone!**
6. **RUBBERDUCK: Can stretch his body to any length.**

THE LEGION OF SUPER-HEROES

A superpowered teen team of the future, the Legion of Super-Heroes has dozens of members, each from a different planet and sworn to protect the galaxy. Every member wears a special ring that enables them them to fly – even in outer space.

TOUGH BREAK

Well-meaning **Stone Boy**, who can turn his body to stone, fails to make the grade in the **Legion of Super-Heroes** tryouts. Instead, he joins the likes of **Night Lass** and **Color Kid** in a back-up squadron of almost-heroes, named the **Legion of Substitute Heroes**.

JLA FILES

INFINITY INC.
In another universe, Earth-2, the sons and daughters of the Justice Society band together to prove their worth to their parents. Members include:

SILVER SCARAB: Hawkman's son, his armoured suit gives him great power.

OBSIDIAN: Todd Rice can merge with any shadow and is the son of former Green Lantern Alan Scott.

FURY: This Amazon has all the powers of her mother, Wonder Woman!

ATOM-SMASHER: The godson of the first Atom, Al Pratt, Albert Rothstein can grow into a giant.

JADE: Alan Scott's daughter, Jade can create energy constructs – without a power ring!

LEGION OF SUPER PETS

The super-smart, superpowered, super-brave **pets** of the **world's greatest heroes** team up to battle tyrants and cosmic terrors as the **Legion of Super-Pets**!

1. **KRYPTO:** Superman's pet pooch can fly faster than a speeding postman!
2. **STREAKY:** Supergirl's alley cat, given powers by experimental Kryptonite.
3. **COMET:** A super horse from the future given to Supergirl by her time-travelling self!
4. **BEPPO:** A Kryptonian monkey that was rocketed into space.
5. **ACE, THE BAT-HOUND:** Batman's crime-fighting dog!
6. **JUMPA:** Wonder Woman's Sky Kanga, a flying kangaroo from Themyscira.

DO OR DIE!

BAD DAY

When **Hawk** is captured in Nicaragua, the **Suicide Squad** is ordered to **rescue** or **terminate** him. Unfortunately, **half of them** end up **dead!**

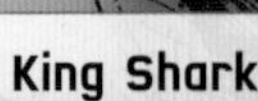

King Shark

THIS IS A SLASH AND BURN MISSION!

El Diablo

Amanda Waller

Black Spider

FAST FACTS

OFFICIAL NAME: Task Force X

TEAM LEADER: Amanda Waller; a firm believer in ends justifying means, no matter the cost

DESCRIPTION: Covert government black-ops team of imprisoned super-criminals

ADVANTAGES: Expendable agents; anything that goes wrong can be blamed on super-villains going wild

DISADVANTAGES: Forcing criminals to serve may make them keen to escape and seek vengeance

DASTARDLY DEED

Assassin **Black Spider** rebels against **Amanda Waller's control** and takes her and her beloved friend **Nana** hostage!

The U.S. government wants a team of **superhuman agents,** but **Super Heroes** tend to be **fiercely independent.** If **good guys** can't be found, **bad guys** will just have to do!

DID YOU KNOW?

The secret base of the **Suicide Squad** is supermax prison **Belle Reve** in Louisiana. Convicts sent there are all potential candidates for Amanda Waller's team of **disposables.**

Q&A

Q: How do you control super-villains when you let them out of their cells?

A: You can....

- Promise commuted sentences to make them work together!
- Fit electronic bracelets that blow off their arms if they try to escape!
- Implant control nanites in their spines!
- Implant micro-bombs in their heads!

Deadshot

Iceberg

Harley Quinn

TOUGH BREAK

To test her criminal recruits, **Amanda Waller** sends them on a **phoney mission** that ends when they are **blown up** and **tortured** by masked men. Only those who refuse to crack are accepted for **Task Force X.**

TOP 12

Squad members

Amanda Waller's Suicide Squad roster is fluid, but here are some frequent agents...

1. **DEADSHOT:** A hitman who lives to kill and never misses.
2. **HARLEY QUINN:** Hyperactive former partner of the Joker.
3. **RICK FLAG:** Driven by patriotism and guilt to work with the scum of the Earth.
4. **EL DIABLO:** Flame-generating ex-gang leader.
5. **CAPTAIN BOOMERANG:** Uses trick boomerangs to get rich quick.
6. **KILLER CROC:** Super-strong, sewer-haunting, croc-like human being.
7. **KATANA:** Uses her martial arts mastery and sword, Soultaker, to pay for past sins.
8. **KING SHARK:** A super-strong, bloodthirsty humanoid shark.
9. **ENCHANTRESS:** An ancient sorceress in the body of mortal June Moone.
10. **BRONZE TIGER:** Martial arts hero-turned-assassin.
11. **BLACK SPIDER:** A mercenary marksman who has an electronic suit with mechanical arms.
12. **ICEBERG:** Possesses cryokinesis – control over ice.

NOOOO!

Super-strong mystery woman ***Duchess*** volunteers for the Squad – but she is really the ***Female Fury Lashina*** in disguise. She kidnaps the team to ***Apokolips*** and offers them to ***Darkseid!***

JLA FILES

SUICIDE SQUADS

The first Suicide Squad teams date back to World War II and were groups of expendable, non-super-powered volunteers. A later squad, led by Rick Flag, took on bizarre threats, such as dinosaurs and ghosts. The contemporary Suicide Squad, led by Amanda Waller, is a political time bomb. No government wants voters [illegible] that it allows killers

DASTARDLY DEED

Given some freedom, the Squad's **Captain Boomerang** sneaks off to commit robberies, using the costume and weapons [illegible]

WHAT THE..?!

While at **Belle Reve** prison, Waller's squad is hit with **custard pies!** The perpetrator – **Captain Boomerang** – evades suspicion by hitting himself in the face with his own **pie-boomerang!**

DO OTHER SUPER-TEAMS LOSE MEMBERS LIKE THE DOOM PATROL? NO. OF COURSE NOT. IF THEY DID, NOBODY WOULD GET INTO THE "HERO" BUSINESS.
DOOM PATROL GET LOST!
Robotman
Elasti-Girl
Negative Man
The Chief

SPECIAL FORCES

EWWW!

G.I. Zombie is a **special military unit** all on his own. His **undead status** means he can "survive" bullets to the **head** and severed **body parts.** But he does **smell a bit!**

JLA FILES

BLACKHAWKS PROGRAM
The United Nations initiate the covert Blackhawks Program – the most technologically advanced military unit in the world – to deal with the threat of terrorists using cutting-edge technology. The original Blackhawks were World War II pilots, a multinational force who battled Nazi aircraft over occupied Europe and the U.K.

AARGH!

One of the ***Doom Patrol's*** strangest foes is the ***Beard Hunter.*** This sinister villain tracks down people with ***full, lush beards,*** kills them, then takes their beards as ***trophies!***

DASTARDLY DEED

Cunning villain **Maxwell Lord** manages to infiltrate **Checkmate** and become its **Black King** in a bid to destroy **Earth's metahumans,** much to the horror of his right-hand woman, **Sasha Bordeaux.**

In a world **constantly threatened** by crazed metahumans or extraterrestrials, **special military units** need to be ready for **absolutely anything!**

Birds of Prey

★ TEAM PLAYER ★

Confined to a wheelchair, **Barbara Gordon** becomes computer whiz **Oracle,** and recruits **Black Canary** to be her "legs". They form the **Birds of Prey** team, which recruits **Huntress** and other bird-themed heroes, such as **Dove, Lady Blackhawk, Hawk, Hawkgirl** and **Starling.**

WHAT THE..?!

The Bureau of Amplified Animals is the U.S. government's **best-kept secret.** These brilliantly clever animals **help mankind.** Top agents include **Rex the Wonder Dog** and **Detective Bobo T. Chimp.**

ALTERNATE EARTHS

Earth-10 is a world where the Allies **lost World War II.** The **Freedom Fighters** battle **Nazi super-villains,** one of whom is **Kal-L,** a.k.a. **Overman!**

MUTATION ALERT!

During World War II, Project M creates a military unit to scare the heck out of the enemy, and anyone else! The Creature Commandos include a werewolf, a vampire, a Gorgon, and Frankenstein's monster!

TOP 5

The Doom Patrol

This team of misfit Super Heroes is known as the "World's Strangest Heroes". Founded and led by scientific genius the Chief, the original team comprises:

1. **BEAST BOY:** Garfield Logan has green skin and can change himself into the shape of any animal.
2. **ROBOTMAN:** After a car wreck, the brain of racing driver Cliff Steele is placed in a robot body.
3. **ELASTI-GIRL:** Volcanic gas gives Hollywood star Rita Farr incredible stretching powers.
4. **NEGATIVE MAN:** Pilot Larry Trainor can create an astral negative form of himself to fight enemies.
5. **MENTO:** Wearing a special helmet he invented himself, Steve Dayton has psionic powers.

YESSS!

Created by **U.S. President Lex Luthor** to reduce Earth's reliance on Super Heroes, the **Human Defense Corps** literally march into **Hell** to rescue 66 of their comrades from a **demon!**

EXPENSIVE MISTAKE

Squad K are tasked with containing **Superman** should the Kryptonian ever **go rogue.** On their first mission they **barely slow** the Man of Steel down, despite deploying an arsenal of high-tech weaponry costing a **million dollars per second** to use.

DID YOU KNOW?

U.S. agency **A.R.G.U.S.** (Advanced Research Group Uniting Super-Humans) is set up to provide support for the **Justice League.** However, when ruthless **Amanda Waller** takes over from Wonder Woman's friend **Steve Trevor,** she uses A.R.G.U.S. agents as **spies.**

BLACK MAGIC BATTLERS

Wherever **mystical forces** threaten to create **catastrophe** and **chaos,** there's a **magical band** of heroes to **battle them!**

NOOOO!

The future ***Demon Knights*** are in a village tavern when they are attacked by the ***Questing Queen's Horde.*** The Queen's ally, the wizard ***Mordru,*** then sets ***a dragon*** on them!

DEMON KNIGHTS

Brightening up the Dark Ages!

1. **ETRIGAN**: The demonic half of the human Jason Blood.
2. **SHINING KNIGHT:** A sip from the Holy Grail gives him great power.
3. **VANDAL SAVAGE:** A meteorite makes this caveman immortal!
4. **AL JABR:** A brilliant engineer, whose science is mistaken for magic.
5. **EXORISTOS:** An exiled Amazon warrior, given power by the gods.
6. **MADAME XANADU:** Immortal sister of the witch Morgaine le Fey.

JLA FILES

THE SENTINELS OF MAGIC

When the monstrous demon Asmodel is bonded to the Spectre, several heroes of the occult unite to drive the demon back to Hell. Remaining in service afterwards, this elite group of magicians guards Earth from all kinds of supernatural threats.

YESSS!

Working with ***magic-wielding heroes*** all across the world, the ***Shadowpact*** help to rebuild mystical realm the ***Rock of Eternity,*** shattered by the ***Spectre.***

SHADOWPACT

Keeping Magic Alive!

1. **NIGHTMASTER:** Sword of Night keeps him young, senses danger and makes liars tell the truth.
2. **ENCHANTRESS:** Creates illusions; flies; walks through walls; teleports.
3. **NIGHTSHADE**: Creates tangible shadows; can teleport.
4. **BLUE DEVIL:** Wields the Trident of Lucifer.
5. **RAGMAN:** Draws powers from the sinners' souls he weaves into his cloak.
6. **DETECTIVE CHIMP:** Super-smart ape with mystical powers.
7. **PHANTOM STRANGER:** Little is known of the origins of this mysterious being.

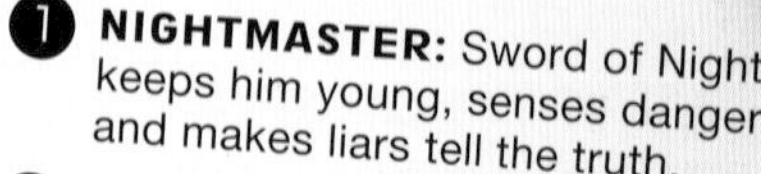

WHAT THE..?!

Rock singer **Jim Rook** enters a shop called **Oblivion Inc.** and finds himself in the dimension of **Myrra**. He discovers he's the descendant of a great Myrran warrior, gains a **magic blade** and becomes **Nightmaster,** leader of **Shadowpact!**

JUSTICE LEAGUE DARK
Battling black magic!

Its large roster of magic-wielders have special powers for all occasions!

The Team That Never Was

When some **magical heroes** work together to defeat the demon **Nebiros**, TV reporter turned Super Hero the **Creeper** suggests they form a group named the **Spirit Squad**. However, **no one likes the idea!**

AMETHYST: Wields magical forces of House Amethyst; handy with a sword.

BLACK ORCHID: Elemental powers.

DEADMAN: Able to possess living people's bodies for short periods.

FRANKENSTEIN: An immortal zombie; good in a fight.

I, VAMPIRE: Super-strong, so long as he gets blood.

DR MIST: Absorbs magic.

JOHN CONSTANTINE: Uncanny detective skills.

PANDORA: Magic pistols.

SWAMP THING: Energies from the Green cosmic force of nature.

NIGHTMARE NURSE: Supernatural healing powers.

ZATANNA: Mastery over magic.

ZAURIEL: A guardian angel with magical powers.

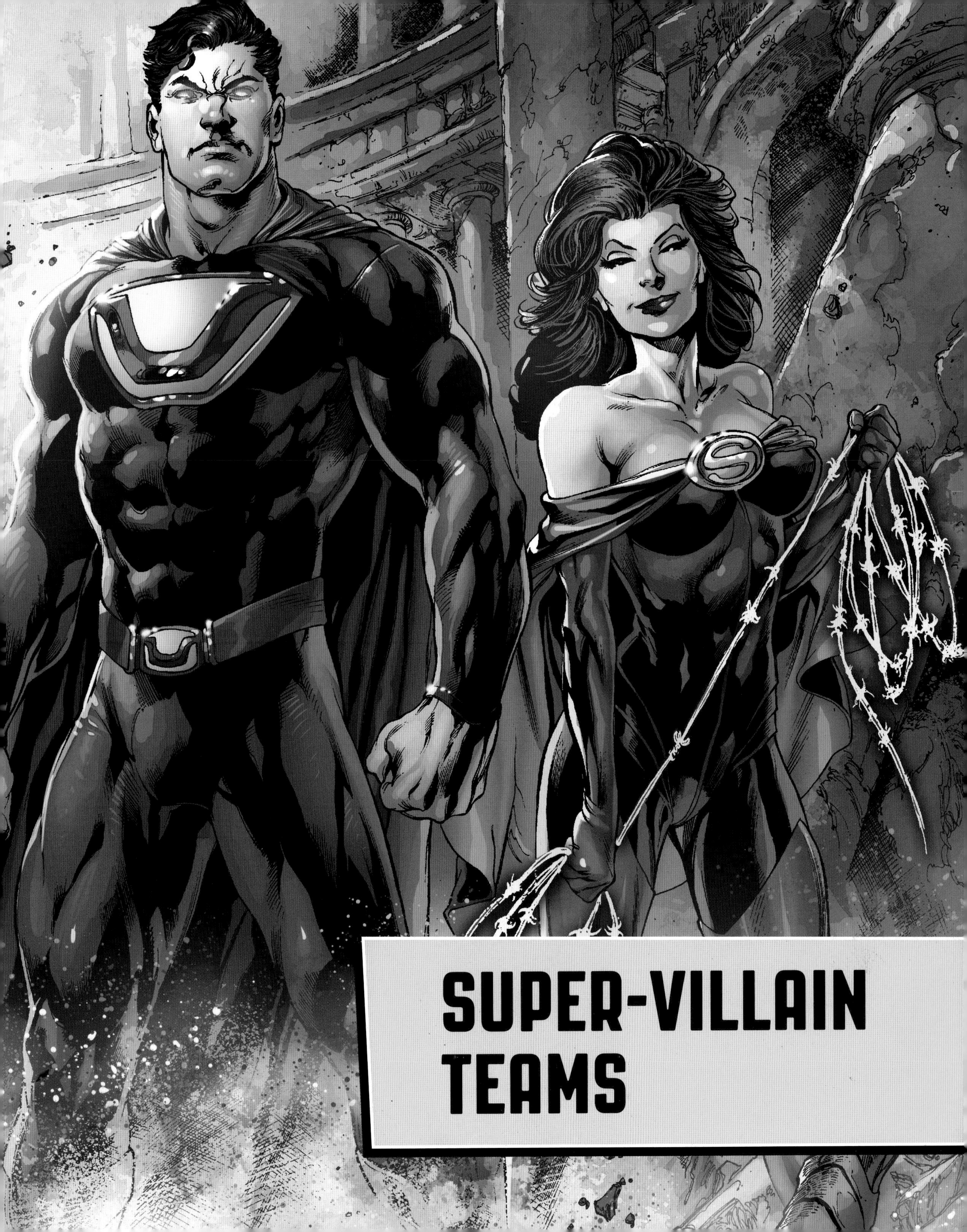

SUPER-VILLAIN TEAMS

YOU 'N' ME AGAINST THE WORLD! RIGHT, RED?
Harley Quinn
Poison Ivy

CLOWN COUPLE

The carnival-themed team of the Joker and Harley Quinn seems a match made in ha-ha heaven. But after getting pushed around one too many times, Harley leaves the rage-filled Joker to fight Batman on his own!

AARGH!

Kryptonian villains ***General Zod*** and ***Ursa*** attempt to stage a rebellion on ***planet Krypton*** and are punished with imprisonment in the ***Phantom Zone!***

SUPER-VILLAIN SIDEKICKS

Some sidekicks are almost as troublesome as the villains that schooled them...

GOLDEN GLIDER: Joins with her brother Captain Cold to battle The Flash and help rob Central City blind!

SCORN: The teenage sidekick of Batman villain the Wrath takes revenge after the Wrath's death by attacking Nightwing.

TELL ME MORE

With their **enhanced senses,** brother and sister team **Hammer and Sickle** track down the elusive **Catwoman** – and hit **double trouble** when Selena's friend **Holly** is also costumed like Catwoman!

TOUGH BREAK

Adrianna Tomaz is the compassionate heroine **Isis,** and a **calming influence** on her bitter husband **Black Adam.** Then she's infected by **Pestilence,** one of the **Four Horsemen of the Apocalypse.** Nice no longer, she demands Black Adam **avenge her.**

WHAT THE..?!

Dr Alchemy and **Mr Element** are two sides of chemist **Albert Desmond.** Both personalities are **villainous,** and both really hate **The Flash!**

TOP 6

Two of a kind

These villains are just made for each other!

1. **HARLEY QUINN & POISON IVY:** Harley teams up with Ivy to make the Joker jealous! She soon realises that they make a great couple!
2. **CAPTAIN COLD & HEAT WAVE:** Heat Wave needs Captain Cold to help him control his fire obsession; they also both hate The Flash.
3. **THE TRIGGER TWINS:** Lookalikes Tom and Tad team up after deciding to rob the same bank at the same time!
4. **TWEEDLEDUM & TWEEDLEDEE:** Two cousins who make the most of their similarity by fooling victims into thinking there's just one of them!
5. **MOUSE & GIZ (& GIZ'S PET SQUIRREL):** Hackers for hire who manage to pinpoint the location of computer whiz Oracle!
6. **PUNCH & JEWELEE:** They may look silly, but this married couple are utterly ruthless criminals.

MADE TO ORDER

Sometimes villains find their partners in crime – and sometimes they create them!

PENGUIN & CLAYFACE: Actor Basil Karlo agrees to be the Penguin's henchman in exchange for help getting better roles. The Penguin's mystical clay turns Karlo into Clayface and a new partnership is born!

LEX LUTHOR & BIZARRO: Lex creates a duplicating ray and uses it on Superman, hoping to create his own Man of Steel. Instead, he makes an imperfect duplicate—Bizarro!

MONSIEUR MALLAH & THE BRAIN: Scientist creates super-intelligent gorilla but is caught in an explosion that leaves only his brain intact; gorilla rescues brain; gorilla and brain fall in love!

★TEAM PLAYERS★

After finding some **weapons** left behind by **aliens,** puppeteers **Punch and Jewelee** embark upon a life of crime. They briefly join the **Suicide Squad,** but can't take their missions **seriously.**

DEADLY DUOS

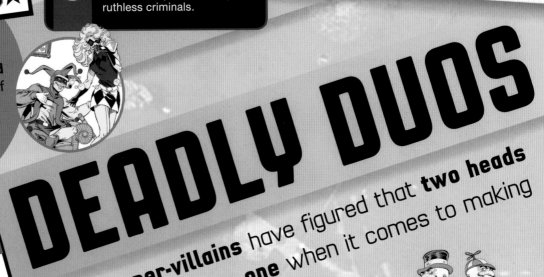

These **super-villains** have figured that **two heads can be better than one** when it comes to making a Super Hero **think twice!**

PROUD BOAST

"I'll turn him into a cinder, Captain Cold!"

Heat Wave

Tweedledum and Tweedledee

WHEN BAD GUYS GO GOOD

With **The Flash** missing in action, the **Rogues** gang suspends its illegal activities to protect **Central City** against the **Crime Syndicate.**

WHAT THE..?!

Doctor Light recruits his "super-mob", the **Fearsome Five,** by placing an ad in the *Underworld Star*. His new team proves **very volatile** – one member **kills** another on **more than one occasion!**

DID YOU KNOW?

The **League of Assassins** is created by **Rā's al Ghūl,** who recruits **ruthless martial artists** to help further his evil schemes and **twisted worldview.**

TOP 3

Leaders of the Secret Society of Super-Villains

1. **DARKSEID:** Via a remote-controlled android, the ruler of Apokolips leads a roster including two light-wielders, Sinestro and Star Sapphire.
2. **ULTRA-HUMANITE:** In the body of a giant albino ape, this mastermind cherry-picks villains from two realities to take down the Justice League.
3. **ALEXANDER LUTHOR OF EARTH-3:** Posing as Lex Luthor, he assembles a hard-hitting line-up calling itself the Society. It becomes even more powerful when dozens of other villains join.

DASTARDLY DEED

Talia al Ghūl breaks away from her father **Rā's** to form the criminal organisation **Leviathan.** It plans to use **brainwashed children** to take control, first of **Gotham City,** then **the world!**

BAD DAY

N.O.W.H.E.R.E.'s plan to exploit the DNA of **young metahumans** goes up in smoke when the **Teen Titans** kill its leader, **Harvest,** and destroy his base.

YESSS!

When the ***Court of Owls' Talon assassins*** attack ***Batman*** and ***Alfred*** at ***Wayne Manor,*** they are finally chased off by ***the bats*** that roost in the ***Batcave!***

VERY BAD COMPANY

Heroes band together to combat **major threats.** And **villains** team up to pull off **even greater crimes** – if they can stop arguing long enough to get **anything done!**

AARGH!

The Injustice Gang is assembled by ***Libra*** to help him steal the powers of the ***Justice League*** with a device he has invented. It proves ***so powerful*** that it literally ***scatters him across the universe!***

DASTARDLY DEED

The Injustice League, arch-foes of the **Justice League,** pick quite a time to launch a campaign against their **heroic enemies.** They gatecrash the stag and hen parties of **Green Arrow** and **Black Canary!**

WOW!

105

The number of known members of Alexander Luthor's Secret Society of Super-Villains, but it could be more....

WHAT THE..?!

The Injustice Society conducts a bizarre **leadership contest** in which each member steals an American **national treasure.** The villain who perpetrates the most **shocking crime** – as voted for by **the people** – becomes **leader.**

UPGRADE!

General Immortus forcibly "upgrades" a bunch of villains for his **Army of the Endangered.** Their new powers cause them **agony,** until Immortus decides they are **loyal!**

DID YOU KNOW?

The leader of villainous team the **Secret Six** is code-named **Mockingbird,** but his or her identity is **so secret** that even the other members of the team don't know who he or she **really is!**

JLA FILES

THE COURT OF OWLS

This malevolent, powerful cabal seeks to control Gotham City from the shadows. It is steadfastly opposed by Batman and his allies. The members wear owl masks to conceal their identities. Undead Talon assassins do the Court of Owls' dirty work.

THE COURT OF OWLS... HAS SENTENCED YOU... TO ***DIE.***

JLA FILES

THE BROTHERHOOD OF DADA

This strange team starts off as a splinter group of the Brotherhood of Evil, but decides to rebrand because the members don't really believe in evil. They create "artistic" chaos for the Doom Patrol to sort out, until the boring normality of most of the world proves too much for them!

ALTERNATE EARTHS

Earth-276 boasts a highly unusual team of super-villains: **the Monster League of Evil.** They're classic Hollywood movie monsters – **Dracula, Frankenstein's Monster, the Mummy and the Wolf-Man** – brought to life!

ARE WE NOT *PROOF* THAT THE UNIVERSE IS A *DROOLING IDIOT* WITH NO *FASHION* SENSE?

Mister Nobody (Brotherhood of Dada)

TOUGH BREAK

The "O" Squad quickly disbands after it is discovered that villainous scientific genius **T. O. Morrow's** name ends with a **"W"**, and not an **"O"!**

AARGH!

Mister Nobody, the Brotherhood of Dada's leader, is a ***living shadow*** who can drain away people's ***sanity!***

DID YOU KNOW?

Captain Marvel foes the **Monster Society of Evil** are led by **Mister Mind,** who hails from the planet Venus and is a **telepathic worm!**

INFERIOR FIVE

Merryman! The Blimp! Dumb Bunny! White Feather! Awkwardman! No one knows who they are, but together, they completely fail to accomplish anything of note. They are the Inferior Five, and they are absolutely awful!

★ TEAM PLAYER ★

Criminal **Amos Fortune** learns how to control his **"luck glands"** to bring himself good luck. He forms the first incarnation of the **Royal Flush Gang,** whose members' costumes and codenames are inspired by **playing cards.**

WHAT THE..?!

A device known as the **Delirium Box** creates the team Men From N.O.W.H.E.R.E. Each word of every sentence they speak has to begin with the letters **"N", "O", "W", "H", "E", "R" and "E"**!

WEIRD aNd WACKY

The most **surreal, bizarre, spooky** and **weird** villains naturally seek out those that are as **odd** as they are. When they **gang up**, they can pose Super Heroes **particularly peculiar problems!**

MUTATION ALERT!

The Animal Mineral Vegetable Man is a one-man team! He can transform any part of his body into an animal, a vegetable or a mineral, to confuse the Doom Patrol.

DID YOU KNOW?

A version of the **Royal Flush Gang** is based in a casino in Atlantic City named **The Man of Steal!**

TOP 6

Unusual Monster Society of Evil members

The Monster Society has had a sizable roster of oddball characters, including...

1. **DUMMY:** Either a very short person, or a ventriloquist's dummy brought to life. 
2. **OOM THE MIGHTY:** An alien, grey-skinned, super-strong, flying, size-changing colossus. 
3. **CROCODILE MAN:** A humanoid croc from planet Punkus. 
4. **EVIL EYE:** A green-skinned monster with hypnotic powers. 
5. **GOAT-MAN:** A combination of billy goat and human. 
6. **JEEPERS:** A cross between a bat and a bear.

TELL ME MORE

The Unjustice League of Unamerica are led by a version of Bizarro Superman. The Bizarro equivalent of the Justice League, they're defenders of the square planet Htrae, and spend their days committing crazy random acts!

CHAPTER THREE
SCIENCE & MAGIC

What is the ONE COLOUR that resists Green Lantern's power ring?
What is the most powerful WEAPON OF MASS DESTRUCTION in existence?
Who gives Batman a magical costume named the SUIT OF SORROWS?

SCIENCE

JLA FILES

THE BATCAVE
As a boy, Bruce Wayne falls into the cave system beneath Wayne Manor. When, as Batman, he needs a place to store secret equipment, Bruce remembers the caves – and the Batcave is born! This Batcave is destroyed by an earthquake, but Batman rebuilds it, filling it with more cutting-edge tech!

Batcave features

1 THE BAT-COMPUTER: Processes data on allies and foes alike, and has live feeds to police radio bands and major news sources.

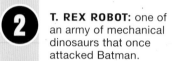

2 T. REX ROBOT: one of an army of mechanical dinosaurs that once attacked Batman.

3 GIANT PENNY: a trophy from a long-ago battle with a criminal called the Penny Plunderer.

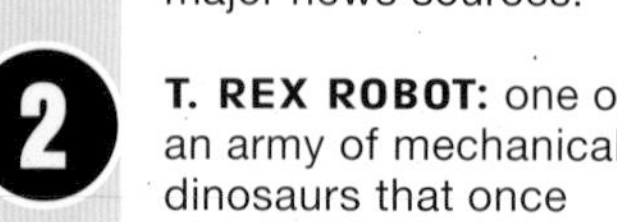

DID YOU KNOW?

There's more than one **Batcave**. In fact, only Batman knows how many there are! He has built several **hidden Batcaves** around **Gotham City,** including one under **Arkham Asylum.** There's even a **Flying Batcave!**

UNUSUAL BATSUITS

THE BATMAN OF ZUR-EN-ARRH
After Bruce Wayne loses his memory, his first attempt at a costume is more colourful than usual.

RAINBOW BATMAN
Batman wears a suit in every colour of the rainbow in order to draw villains' attention away from Robin and onto himself.

ACTUAL BAT
This frightening-looking, alternate-reality version of Batman takes the bat theme all the way! The cape-like wings are just for gliding.

ZEBRA BATMAN
Caught in the Zebra-Man's special machine, Batman's Batsuit changes into a zebra-striped version that repels solid objects!

BATMAN ONE MILLION
The Batsuit of the Batman of the year 85,265 has great technical advances, such as camouflage and an internal computer.

Q&A

Q: What does Batman keep in his Utility Belt?

A: Anything he needs – including: a Bat-line for scaling buildings, Batarangs, Bat-cuffs, smoke capsules, a fingerprint kit, a camera, grenades, a rebreather, gas pellets, a recorder, medical kit, crime-scene kit, tool kit, a Geiger counter, palm-top communicator, shark repellant...

TELL ME MORE

THE BATSUIT
Batman's smart-armour suit is proof against most weapons and can give electric shocks. The cowl enhances hearing, provides night vision as well as radio contact with allies. The cape doubles as a glider for swooping down on foes.

THE DARK KNIGHT'S ARSENAL

Investigative genius and **physical prowess** make Batman an especially intimidating opponent. **Cutting-edge gadgets** and **weapons** make him **nearly unbeatable!**

WHAT THE..?!

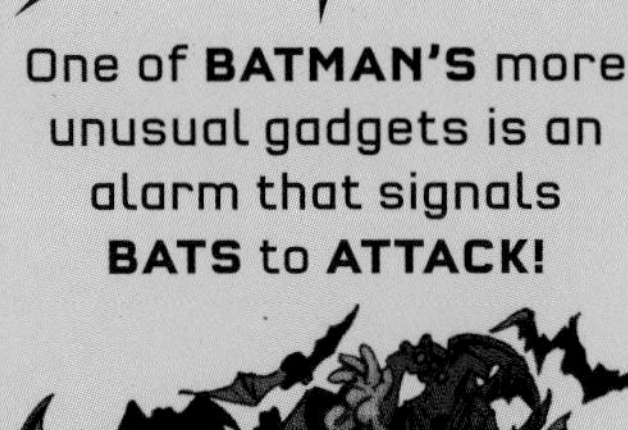

One of **BATMAN'S** more unusual gadgets is an alarm that signals **BATS** to **ATTACK!**

BATARANG BUSINESS

Instead of firing **GUNS,** Batman throws **BATARANGS.** He has all kinds, used for cutting wires, knocking out or disarming foes, pushing buttons, breaking glass, creating a smokescreen or conducting surveillance.

Batgirl

TOP 4

Unusual gadgets

The Dark Knight prides himself on being ready for almost anything...

1. **BAT-FREEZE PILL:** Batman can take this to lower his body temperature and evade heat sensors.
2. **PROJECTILE BAT-EARS:** For a surprise attack, Batman can fire the ears of his cowl!
3. **COLLAPSIBLE JET ROLLER-SKATES:** For when Batman runs out of vehicles but still needs to move fast.
4. **GIANT BAT-BALLOON:** Just the thing for impressing a bunch of prehistoric giants!

YESSS!

The villain ***Hush*** is about to kill ***Alfred*** in the ***Batcave,*** but is stopped just in time by ***the robot T. rex*** Batman keeps there as ***a trophy!***

JUSTICE ON WHEELS!

Batman doesn't have flight or **super-speed,** but he doesn't need them – he has an **almost endless** collection of **Bat-vehicles!**

IT'S **TEN YEARS** AHEAD OF ANYTHING ELSE ON WHEELS... HOW ABOUT A **TRIAL SPIN?**

JLA FILES

THE BATMOBILE
Batman's famous automobile is bulletproof. Its non-lethal arsenal includes grappling hooks, gas grenades, tyre-piercing caltrops, oil slicks and a sound cannon. It can even drive itself. As well as a finely tuned engine, the vehicle boasts a rear-mounted jet turbine, enabling it to outpace virtually any land vehicle.

WOW!

428

Top speed of the Batmobile in km/h (266 miles per hour).

IN REAL LIFE

Batman's "specially built, high-powered auto" debuted in 1939's *Detective Comics* #27, the Caped Crusader's first appearance. However, it wasn't until 1941 that the term "Batmobile" caught on.

WHAT THE..?!

When all else fails, Batman can access a **secret stash** of alien technology, including a **flying saucer!**

YESSS!

When **Hush** steals Batman's **Whirly-Bat,** his bandages get caught in the coptor's **rotor blades.** The villain **crashes** into the ceiling of the Batcave and **blows himself up!**

DID YOU KNOW?

The Batgyro is Batman's very first aircraft. A cross between **a helicopter** and **a plane,** it is soon replaced by the more hi-tech **Batplane.**

WOW!

$46 MILLION

The cost of the Batplane... and that's before Batman starts modifying it!

AARGH!

Whirly-Bats have ***crashed*** into buildings, had their rotor blades ***frozen*** by ***Mister Zero's ice gun,*** been ***destroyed*** by ***robots*** and been ***smashed*** by the ***Penguin's airship!***

TELL ME MORE

In her first adventure, **Batwoman** (Kathy Kane) astonishes the **Dynamic Duo** by outracing their **Batmobile** on her **Batcycle.**

Batman Vehicles

BATCYCLE: A nimble, speedy bike for chasing down criminals through the Gotham City traffic.

BATPLANE: This not only reaches supersonic speeds and climbs higher than a regular aeroplane, it contains a fully stocked crime lab!

BAT-COPTER: Ideal for fast city travel to a crime scene or for a dramatic aerial rescue; can also be summoned by remote control.

WHIRLY-BAT: A small, one-man helicopter ideal for pursuing villains. Unfortunately, it has proved comparatively easy to disable.

BATGLIDER: Batman swoops silently between the buildings of Gotham City on this set of collapsible wings.

BATBOAT: Exits the Batcave via a tunnel leading to the Gotham River; reaches speeds of over 161 km/h (100 mph); also functions underwater, like a submarine.

BAT-JETSKI: Gives Batman the flexibility of the Batcycle, but on water! Ideal for pursuing seagoing super-villains.

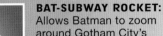

BAT-SUBWAY ROCKET: Allows Batman to zoom around Gotham City's subway system without waiting for a train.

BAT-SPACESHIP: Brings distant planets within the Dark Knight's crime-fighting reach.

SUPER SCIENCE!

Superman's **Fortress of Solitude** is a **futuristic storehouse** of ingenious inventions that back up his **mighty Kryptonian abilities.**

DID YOU KNOW?

Superman has had many different **Fortresses of Solitude.** His secret citadels have been located in the **Metropolis Mountains,** in the **Arctic** and the **Antarctic,** in the **Andes,** in South American rainforests and even in **space,** orbiting Earth.

INSIDE SUPERMAN'S FORTRESS...

BOTTLE CITY OF KANDOR
Shrunk and bottled by Brainiac; Krypton's former capital and its citizens are kept safe by Superman.

INTERGALACTIC SPACECRAFT
For use in solar systems lacking energy-giving yellow suns.

DANGEROUS ALIEN TECHNOLOGY
Safely stored in the Fortress' Hall of Weapons.

PHANTOM ZONE PROJECTOR
For banishing super-villains to the Phantom Zone.

PHANTOM ZONE VIEWER
For exploring the Phantom Zone.

IMPERFECT DUPLICATOR RAY
Creates Bizarros.

YESSS!

When ***red solar rays*** saturate Earth, the Man of Steel creates a multipurpose ***Supermobile*** from ***Supermanium.*** This enables him to sustain his ***faded superpowers*** and battle the rampaging android ***Amazo!***

JLA FILES

FORTRESS OF SOLITUDE
Grown from Kryptonian Sunstone and memory crystals, Superman's Fortress of Solitude is a vast hidden citadel containing inventions and artefacts from many worlds and times. The Fortress is based on Kryptonian designs and can change its dimensions and layout. It contains the universe's most sophisticated computers.

BACK FROM THE DEAD!

The Fortress' **computer interface** has the image and personality of Superman's **deceased father, Jor-El.**

THIS IS THE ONE PLACE WHERE I CAN RELAX AND WORK UNDISTURBED! NO ONE SUSPECTS ITS EXISTENCE, AND NO ONE CAN PENETRATE THE SOLID ROCK OUT OF WHICH IT IS HEWN!

NOOOO!

When tackling **Kryptonite,** Superman uses a **lead-armour suit.** Sadly, if he moves too quickly the friction **melts the lead!**

I.D. CRISIS

Superman constructs **robots** of himself and his friends. Until Earth's growing **pollution levels** render them unreliable, the robots act as **substitutes** and servants, and are used to provide **"proof"** that **Clark Kent** and **Superman** are completely **different people!**

WHAT THE..?!

Supermanium is the strongest metal in the universe, forged by Superman from the **heart of a star.**

TELL ME MORE

SUPERMAN'S DAD

Superman comes from a long line of scientists. One of the greatest is his father, Jor-El II, who perfects personal air-cars, restarts Krypton's space program, discovers the Phantom Zone extradimensional prison and reveals that planet Krypton is doomed.

JLA FILES

KELEX

Superman's Fortress is looked after by the El family butler, Kelex. This robot servant, recreated by the Eradicator, combines technological expertise with household maintenance chores and light cleaning duties.

It's Only (Computer) Love...

Thinking **her cousin Superman** is lonely, Supergirl uses the Fortress' computers to **search the cosmos** for his **perfect mate.** Unfortunately, his meeting with **Luma Lynai of Staryl** only leads to trouble and **heartbreak...**

HANDLE WITH CARE!

Beneath the Fortress, a nuclear furnace, fuelled by liquified Sunstone, powers the entire installation and provides a sure-fire method of destroying artefacts too dangerous to keep.

BACK FROM THE DEAD!

When the **all-powerful Eradicator** tries to establish Krypton on Earth, it recreates **Kryptonian tech,** such as a colossal **war suit** and **birthing matrix.** These restore Superman after he is killed by **Doomsday.**

TO THE STARS... AND BEYOND!

Advanced beings from all over the **cosmos** have travelled **the vastness of space,** piloting their ships to **distant stars** and **faraway worlds!**

CLOSE CALL

Desperate to save his family from the destruction of planet Krypton, **Jor-El** builds two rockets, one to carry his infant son, **Kal-El,** and one to carry his niece, **Kara Zor-El.** Their destination: **Earth.**

TOP 7

Spacecraft

1. **BRAINIAC'S SKULL SHIP:** Technologically linked to Brainiac, it has eight metal arms, creates force fields and fires energy beams.
2. **ORION'S ASTRO HARNESS:** Allows Orion to travel effortlessly through space. It also delivers powerful force blasts.
3. **MOBIUS CHAIR:** Piloted by seeker of knowledge and New God Metron, it's the ultimate research tool.
4. **LOBO'S SPACEHOG:** This customised SpazFrag666 machine travels faster than almost any other ship. It has full hands-off facility and goes from 96.6 km/h (0-60 mph) instantly.
5. **SUPER-CYCLE:** A three-wheel, all-terrain craft that teleports the Forever People; it can also pass through solid objects.
6. **WARWORLD:** The super-villain Mongul uses this monstrous satellite, powered by massive engines and loaded with weaponry, to conquer worlds.
7. **POWER GIRL'S SYMBIO-SHIP:** Baby Kara Zor-L escapes Krypton's destruction in this ship, built by her scientist father, Zor-L. She ages 20 years by the time she arrives on Earth-2.

WHAT THE..?!

There's **a cab** that can give travellers a ride **anywhere** in space or time. It looks like a **New York yellow cab** from the 1950s. The driver is known as **Space Cabby,** and he has even given a ride to **Superman!**

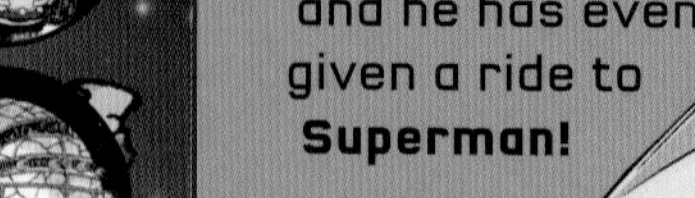

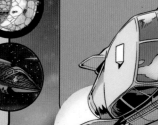

DID YOU KNOW?

Brainiac's skull ship is fashioned from the remains of a **planet-sized computer prison** he once escaped from.

POWER UP!

Lobo has upgraded his Space Hog with an incredible sound system. It pumps out tunes loud enough to disintegrate a mountain!

WHAT THE..?!

Starfire of the **Teen Titans** is **kidnapped** and taken into space by her **evil sister Blackfire.** The team are unable to follow after her – until they discover a **working spaceship** in the ocean near New York!

★ TEAM PLAYER ★

If the **Justice League** needs to blast off into space in a hurry, **Green Lantern** can create a solid-light starship with his **power ring!**

AARGH!

A prophesy says that ***Abin Sur,*** the Green Lantern of Sector 2814, will die when his ring ***runs out of power.*** To defy this prediction, he begins travelling in a spaceship. Unfortunately, his ship ***malfunctions,*** and he is ***badly injured*** in the crash!

JLA FILES

The warlike Khund are feared because they believe that if they die bravely in battle they will sit at the right hand of their war god in the afterlife. Their battle fleet will keep on attacking, whatever the odds, and regardless of losses.

IT'S METAL MAYHEM!

Robots, androids and **cyborgs** have often fought **bravely** alongside human **Super Heroes.** However, they are just as frequently programmed **to do evil...**

DID YOU KNOW?

Buddy Blank is chosen by the **Global Peace Agency** for **Project OMAC.** He's connected to a satellite named **Brother Eye** – and turned into a one-man army named **OMAC.** He is succeeded by **Kevin Kho.**

AARGH!

Cyborg villain ***Metallo*** is powered by ***Kryptonite*** and always ready to open his chest and give ***Superman*** a blast of ***Green K rays!***

ALTERNATE EARTHS

Earth-C-Minus has strange villains, such as the android **Amazoo,** who combines the powers and looks of **many animals.** He's a foe of animal heroes **Just'a Lotta Animals.**

IN REAL LIFE

DC Comics' Robotman, debuting in *Star-Spangled Comics* #7 (Apr. 1942), was the first ever cyborg Super Hero. Another Robotman, Cliff Steele, later debuted in *My Greatest Adventure* (June 1963).

GOOD DAY

The **Metal Men** prove their worth when they stop a prehistoric flying **manta ray** from destroying the world with **radioactive eye blasts!**

I'M THE MONSTER? WELL, I CAN LIVE WITH THAT.

Metallo

TOP 3

Robot sidekicks

1. **SKEETS:** Packed with knowledge of the future, this time-travelling A.I. robot from the 25th century helps Booster Gold join the Justice League and make a pile of cash!
2. **ROBIN, THE TOY WONDER:** Programmed to be the conscience for the Batman of the 853rd century, this robot has the personality of the young Caped Crusader.
3. **ROBOTDOG:** Robotman's canine companion can speak and is specially programmed to bite the legs of bad guys!

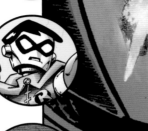

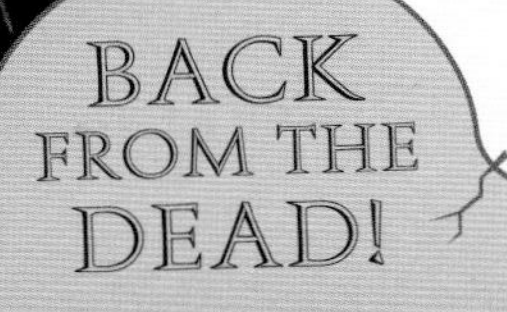

EWWW!

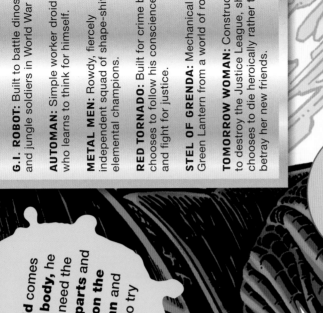

When evil **A.I. Grid** comes online in **Cyborg's body,** he decides he doesn't need the hero's **human body parts** and leaves them **lying on the ground** for **Batman** and **Green Lantern** to try and save!

ROBOTS RULE!

Some Super Heroes are made, not born!

G.I. ROBOT: Built to battle dinosaurs and jungle soldiers in World War II.

AUTOMAN: Simple worker droid who learns to think for himself.

METAL MEN: Rowdy, fiercely independent squad of shape-shifting elemental champions.

RED TORNADO: Built for crime but chooses to follow his conscience and fight for justice.

STEL OF GRENDA: Mechanical Green Lantern from a world of robots.

TOMORROW WOMAN: Constructed to destroy the Justice League, she chooses to die heroically rather than betray her new friends.

YESSS!

The android ***Amazo*** absorbs the powers of the ***entire Justice League.*** Luckily he also absorbs their ***weaknesses,*** such as Green Lantern's problem with ***the colour yellow…***

SPECIAL *MOVES*

THE METAL MEN – Gold, Platinum, Tin, Mercury, Iron and Lead – can **TRANSFORM** their appearances into **ANY SHAPE.**

BAD DAY

OMAC (Buddy Blank) discovers that his girlfriend, **Lila,** is a **robot assassin** and has to **destroy her!**

DASTARDLY DEED

Lex Luthor's operatives capture **Metallo** to stop him killing **Superman.** Lex is not being **kind** to the Man of Steel – he just wants **Metallo's Kryptonite heart** so he can **kill Superman himself!**

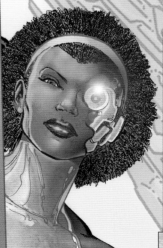

BACK FROM THE DEAD!

When **LeTonya Charles'** addictions begin to **destroy** her body, her aunt Sarah, who works at **S.T.A.R. Labs,** saves her with **cybernetic implants.** As **Cyborgirl,** LeTonya shares many powers with Victor Stone's heroic **Cyborg.** She does not use them to help and save, but to **steal** and **plunder.**

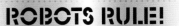

HI-TECH FOR HEROES!

Most Super Heroes employ **advanced technology** or **clever gadgets,** but some take it **further** and become **inseparable** from their **hardware!**

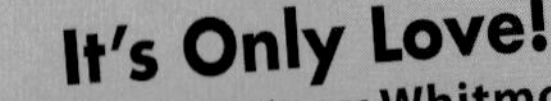

It's Only Love!

When **Courtney Whitmore** becomes **Stargirl,** her stepfather builds **S.T.R.I.P.E.** (Special Tactics Robotic Integrated Power Enhancer) armour, to **watch out** for her!

AARGH!

Mento's ***Psychokinetic Helmet*** allows him to become a ***Super Hero,*** but soon ***drives him mad,*** turning him into a ***super-villain!***

BEST KNOWN FOR

Making science a friend and an ally

UPGRADE!

When **Superman** seemingly **dies,** weapons designer **John Henry Irons** builds a **jet-powered battle suit** and **kinetic hammer** to protect Metropolis as the Super Hero **Steel.**

DID YOU KNOW?

Feeling threatened by the U.S.'s many metahumans, **Russia** tricks Green Lantern **Kilowog** into inventing multi-powered **mecha-armour** that can be mass-produced. It's worn by elite soldiers called **Rocket Reds!**

TELL ME MORE

Oan splinter group the Controllers gives the Legion of Super-Heroes a Miracle Machine that makes wishes come true. The young warriors encase it in indestructible Inerton to ensure no one is tempted to abuse its power.

POWER UP!

Jim Barr is deemed too frail to join the police. A serum called Miraclo makes him super-strong and his Gravity Regulator Helmet enables him to fly. Thus equipped, he fights crime as Bulletman!

THE *MAN OF STEEL* IS COMING THROUGH!

Steel

NOOOO!

Ruthless media mogul ***Morgan Edge*** gives ***Jimmy Olsen*** and the ***Newsboy Legion*** an amazing flying car, ***the Whiz Wagon***. Only problem – there's ***a bomb*** in it!

UPGRADE!

Daniel Cassidy's **Blue Devil suit** is a **mechanical marvel,** but when it is **blasted** by magical demon **Nebiros,** it **comes to life** and **bonds itself** to the special-effects genius!

Q&A

Q: How can human heroes match metahumans?

A: Suit up, like these adventurers...

- **Silver Scarab:** Nth Metal body sheath generates solar energy blasts and provides flight, enhanced strength and speed!
- **Firebrand:** Muscle-augmenting armour gives paralysed Alex Sanchez incredible strength, speed and durability.
- **Batwing:** Outfit provides flight, enhanced speed and strength, sedative gas emitters, stealth capability, a full suite of sensors and data-gathering tech.
- **Atomic Knight:** S.T.A.R. Labs armour provides jet-powered flight and energy blasts, plus extra strength, speed and endurance.

TOP 5

Ways to Get Places

Fast travel to where they're needed is crucial for Super Heroes...

1. **YOUNG JUSTICE** and the **FOREVER PEOPLE:** Use techno-organic Supercycles that ride electron paths to traverse time and space.
2. **RIP HUNTER:** Builds a Time Sphere to take his team through time and space wherever danger calls.
3. **BOOSTER GOLD:** Is always on the spot, thanks to a Legion of Super-Heroes Flight Ring he stole!
4. **ADAM STRANGE:** Uses Zeta-Beams from planet Rann to teleport across light years for non-stop adventure.
5. **THE ATOM:** Constructs heavily armoured shrinking suits to navigate Superman's super-heated, Kryptonite-poisoned bloodstream.

HI-TECH *FOR* VILLAINS

Futuristic technology and **fantastic weapons** aren't **evil** in themselves, but those who use them for **profit, revenge** or **world domination** certainly are!

It's Only Love
Mr Freeze uses his command of **freezing technologies** to create his **Freeze Gun** and **a survival suit.** He also freezes his **wife Nora** for the day when a **cure** is found for her **cancer.**

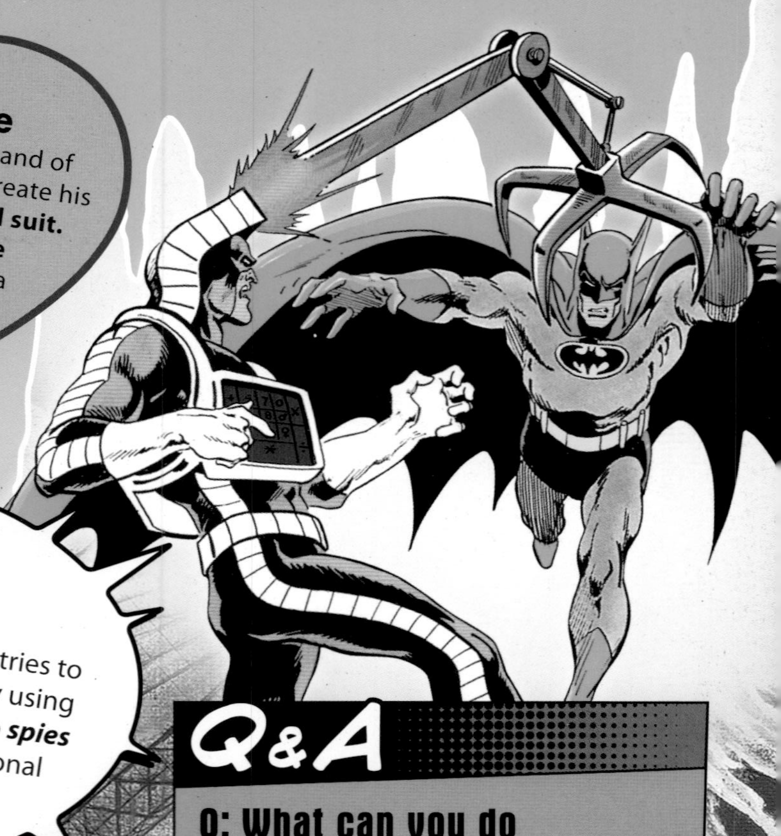

WHAT'S WRONG, **BATMAN?** SURELY, A LITTLE ICE CAN'T STOP THE **MIGHTY CRIME FIGHTER!**

AARGH!

Mind-controlling ***Maxwell Lord*** tries to destroy ***Earth's metahumans*** by using ***nanites*** to transform people into ***spies*** and ***cyborg OMACs*** (Observational Metahuman Activity Constructs).

BEST KNOWN FOR

Utilising science for evil!

Q&A

Q: What can you do if Super Heroes constantly beat you?

A: Change career! The villain Calculator originally uses a computerised battlesuit to manufacture weapons to take on Super Heroes. Defeated in turn by Atom, Black Canary, Elongated Man, Green Arrow, Hawkman and Batman, he retires to become a criminal hacker, strategist and information broker.

POWER UP!

Justice League foe Brain Storm wears a helmet to absorb stellar energy, enhancing his thought-processes and giving him mind-over-matter powers.

SPACE OUTLAW

Abducted by aliens, young desperado Toby Manning returns to Earth after a century, using stolen weapons and gadgets to attack Superman and plunder the planet as Terra-Man.

NOOOO!

Clifford Devoe's ***Thinking Cap*** grants the evil mastermind ***psionic powers.*** When he dies, teenager Cliff Carmichael ***implants*** the helmet's circuits ***in his head*** to become the far deadlier ***Thinker.***

TOP 6

Gadgets to die for

1. **CAPTAIN BOOMERANG'S BOOMERANGS:** Provide explosive, hitting and cutting power.
2. **TRICKSTER'S ANTI-GRAVITY BOOTS:** The left one takes him up; the right one brings him back down.
3. **PROMETHEUS' BODY ARMOUR:** Enables flight; creates force fields; its computerised helmet also reduces pain.
4. **PERSUADER'S ATOMIC AXE:** Can cut through absolutely anything.
5. **FOLDED MAN'S SUIT:** Allows travel between dimensions.
6. **WEATHER WIZARD'S WEATHER WAND:** Creates storms, fog, tornadoes, blizzards and bolts of lightning.

WHAT THE..?!

Captain Boomerang's most impressive weapon is his **Rocket Boomerang.** The villain once tied **The Flash** to it and sent him **zooming into space!**

DOUBLE *TROUBLE*

Monsieur Mallah is a surgically-altered **talking gorilla** with a **genius IQ.** Equally adept with **machine guns** and **computers,** he acts as lab assistant and hands for bodiless master criminal **the Brain!**

KA-BOOM!

These WMDs – Weapons of Mass Destruction – are a **perfect fit** for **a super-villain** plotting **ultimate control** or **utter annihilation!**

Mageddon

NOOOO!

Mageddon is a ***semi-sentient weapon*** chained at the edge of space-time. Breaking away, it stokes ***rage and hatred*** in every planet's population it encounters ***on its way towards Earth!***

JLA FILES

HUMANIDS
Humanids are worker drones used for menial tasks by top-secret U.S. government agency S.H.A.D.E. Humanids only live for 24 hours, but they rebel to fight for their freedom and nearly wipe S.H.A.D.E. out!

EWWW!

Evil scientist **Doctor Omen** modifies and clones miniature versions of alien starfish **Starro the Conqueror.** These mini-Starros mind-control humans by **sticking to their faces!**

A Humanid

YOUR TIME IS UP. PREPARE FOR ERADICATION, FLESHBEINGS!

DID YOU KNOW?

Originally built by Nazi inventor Professor Merson, the **War Wheel** is an armoured fortress designed to **crush** all opposition. The War Wheel has been a key battlefield weapon of the agency **S.H.A.D.E.** (Super Human Advanced Defense Executive).

JLA FILES

WMDs fall into three categories: built, found or stolen, and three types: magical, scientific or alien.

What are they good for?
Causing destruction; scaring populations; invading worlds.

Who wants them?
Tyrants; terrorists; alien conquerors.

How do we survive?
By ingenuity, sheer guts and with Super Hero help!

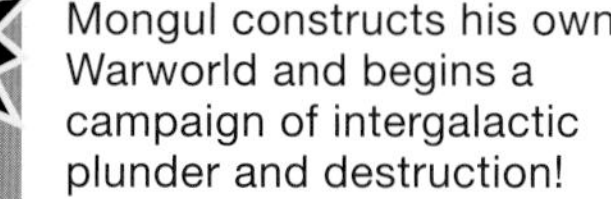

TOP 4

Crimes against civilisation

1. Mongul constructs his own Warworld and begins a campaign of intergalactic plunder and destruction!
2. Mongul and the Cyborg Superman obliterate Coast City. They turn the site into Engine City: a vast propulsion system designed to turn Earth into a new Warworld!
3. Rā's al Ghūl's Tower of Babel signal disrupts the language-processing areas of the brain. Civilisation is plunged into utter chaos!
4. The alien Reach trick a planet's people into bonding with biological weapons called Scarabs. Victims become traitorous slaves, ready to destroy their own world from within!

Q&A

Q: What is the most powerful weapon in existence?

A: The Anti-Life Equation. This mathematical formula dominates thought and free will and is much sought after by tyrants like Darkseid. It has even taken on a life of its own!

Believing that he is ***dying,*** mastermind ***Iron Hand*** shakes the world with a fist of ***nebular energy!*** It takes the ***Justice League, Justice Society of America*** and ***Seven Soldiers of Victory*** to stop him.

HANDLE WITH CARE!

Warworld is built by the warlike alien **Warzoon** race. Larger than a sun, it is the ultimate **mobile weapons platform.** However, it eventually kills every being who operates it. When **Mongul** takes control, only the intervention of **Superman** and **Supergirl** stops him from becoming its latest victim…

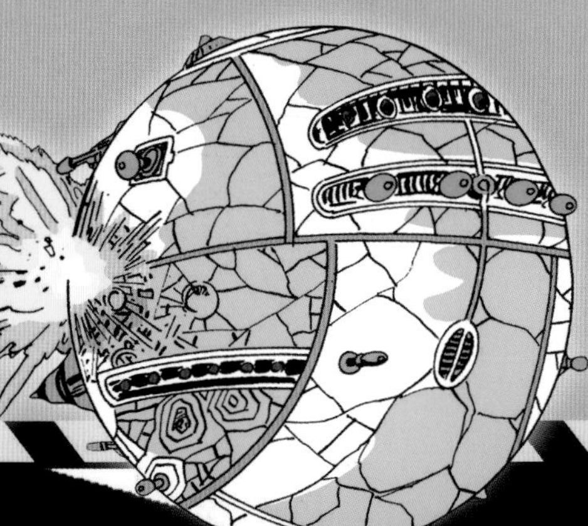

BEFORE

THE ERADICATOR

This Kryptonian device is built by the scientist Kem-L to preserve the purity of Kryptonian civilisation and eradicate all others. Immensely powerful, it reshapes matter, reprograms minds and even creates a body and personality for itself to mimic human or Kryptonian life.

AFTER

COSMIC FORCES

Imperceptible to **mere mortals,** deep beyond the boundaries of space and time, **vast forces** of **cosmic energy** guide and shape **all of reality!**

THE EMOTIONAL SPECTRUM

This energy field is generated by all living beings in the Multiverse. The Maltusians harnessed this energy, as did several other races. Each colour represents a different state of being and grants a different power.

RED: Rage

ORANGE: Avarice

YELLOW: Fear

GREEN: Will

BLUE: Hope

INDIGO: Compassion

VIOLET: Love

BLACK: Death

WHITE: Life

DID YOU KNOW?

Between the spaces occupied by **energy** and **matter** lies the **Quantum Field.** It powers super-beings like **Captain Atom, Major Force** and **Bombshell,** giving them the power to manipulate **energy** and **time.**

DASTARDLY DEED

Frequent Green Lantern foe **Sinestro** turns hero in a battle with **Nekron,** Lord of the Unliving, and his **Black Lantern Corps.** Possessed by the white light entity, Sinestro makes a lone stand for life against death, but Nekron **cuts him in half!**

Sinestro

HANDLE WITH CARE!

The Worlogog is a device that grants its user the power to alter **the fabric of reality.** For those who can read it, it is a **fourth-dimensional map** of the Multiverse. Whoever holds the Worlogog and understands its nature can bend **the past and future** to their will.

WHEN BAD GUYS GO GOOD

The Joker, temporarily made sane by the **Martian Manhunter,** uses the **Worlogog** to save **countless lives.**

JLA FILES

ANTI-LIFE EQUATION

This is believed to be an impossibly complex series of calculations. When combined, they unlock the power or dominate the will of all beings. As super-villains such as Darkseid seek this power, the Equation's true nature is revealed – it is a sentience far beyond human understanding, that seeks to corrupt the source of all creation.

WITNESSING CREATION

Many have attempted to unravel the mysteries of reality, using their power to witness the moment of creation itself. No one has succeeded, but some have caught a glimpse – the Multiverse, spinning in perfect harmony, caught in the palm of an outstretched hand…

KRONA: This Maltusian scientist was the first to witness the event, unleashing the power needed to create the Anti-Matter universe.

THE ANTI-MONITOR: This entity attempted to subvert the moment of creation to empower himself.

SUPERGIRL: In one cosmic adventure, Supergirl is forced to absorb the power of creation to stop Mxyzptlk from rewriting existence.

AARGH!

Imperiex is a being of ***pure cosmic energy*** housed within a ***suit of armour.*** He exists only to destroy universes and ***feed on their ashes!***

COSMIC SCIENTIST

Astronomer and Justice Society member Ted Knight devises ways to harness cosmic energy into weapons, enabling the user to fly and fire bolts of energy.

GRAVITY ROD
Harnesses the incredible power of the stars; used by Ted Knight as the hero Starman.

COSMIC CONVERTER BELT
Enhances strength, speed and agility; fires shooting stars; used by the Star-Spangled Kid (above), and later Stargirl.

COSMIC STAFF
An updated Gravity Rod; enables flight; creates energy constructs; used by Starman (Jack Knight), following his father.

JLA FILES

THE GODWAVE

This is a ripple of power that rebounds through the Multiverse after the destruction of the Old Gods. It creates every pantheon of deities known, such as Zeus and the Olympians. It also seeds the potential for superhumans throughout the cosmos, and is the unnamed source of power for many superhumans.

RING COLOUR: Green

REPRESENTS: Willpower

RINGBEARERS: Green Lantern Corps

OATH: In brightest day, in blackest night, no evil shall escape my sight. Let those who worship evil's might, beware my power, Green Lantern's light!

AARGH!

Trying to stop the ***Anti-Life Equation*** from corrupting the universe, ***Green Lantern (John Stewart)*** is surprised by a planet-destroying ***bomb*** painted ***yellow*** – the colour his ring is ***powerless against!***

Green Lantern's power ring

DID YOU KNOW?

Larfleeze, also known as **Agent Orange,** owns the only **Orange Power Ring** in existence. He is **too greedy** to share the power of the **orange light** with anyone else. He has his own **Lantern Corps** made of orange hard light constructs that he creates!

RING COLOUR: Red

REPRESENTS: Rage

RINGBEARERS: Red Lantern Corps

OATH: With blood and rage of crimson red, ripped from a corpse so freshly dead, together with our hellish hate, we'll burn you all – that is your fate!

RING COLOUR: Orange

REPRESENTS: Greed

RINGBEARERS: Orange Lantern Corps

OATH: What's mine is mine and mine and mine. And mine and mine and mine! Not yours!

RING COLOUR: Blue

REPRESENTS: Hope

RINGBEARERS: Blue Lantern Corps

OATH: In fearful day, in raging night, with strong hearts full, our souls ignite. When all seems lost in the War of Light, look to the stars, for hope burns bright!

RING COLOUR: Violet

REPRESENTS: Love

RINGBEARERS: Star Sapphires

OATH: For hearts long lost and full of fright, for those alone in Blackest Night. Accept our ring and join our fight, love conquers all with violet light!

RING COLOUR: Yellow

REPRESENTS: Fear

RINGBEARERS: Sinestro Corps

OATH: In blackest day, in brightest night, beware your fears made into light. Let those who try to stop what's right, burn like my power, Sinestro's might!

RING COLOUR: Indigo

REPRESENTS: Compassion

RINGBEARERS: Indigo Tribe

OATH: Tor lorek san, bor nakka mur, natromo faan tornek wot ur. Ter Lantern ker lo Abin Sur, taan lek lek nok – Formorrow Sur!

Q&A

Q: Why did the Guardians build a power battery?

A: The Guardians used the original power battery, which was green, to form the Green Lantern Corps, a galaxy-wide peacekeeping force.

DEX-STARR

Not all of Earth's ringbearers are human. When a kitten named Dexter witnesses his owner's murder, a Red Power Ring flies onto his tail. Cute little Dexter becomes vicious Red Lantern Dex-Starr!

NOOOO!

When ***Black Hand*** vows to put out the light of the emotional spectrum, he makes a ***Black Power Battery*** and uses it to raise an army of zombies… his ***Black Lantern Corps!***

Q&A

Q: Why are most ring-bearers members of a "Lantern Corps?"

A: The Corps are named after the power batteries they rely on, which are shaped like lanterns.

I CAN'T BELIEVE THIS. WITH THAT RING I'M PROBABLY THE MOST POWERFUL MAN ON EARTH.

RINGS OF POWER!

At the beginning of time, **seven powerf[ul] beings** are born, one of **each colour** of the **rainbow,** and each representing **on[e] emotion. The Guardians of the Univers[e]** harness the strength of these entiti[es]

HANDLE WITH CARE!

Power rings can be used to make **hard light constructs** that are limited only by the ringbearer's **imagination.** The constructs can appear as objects, weapons, force fields, clothing… even **other beings.** For this reason, the rings may be the most **powerful weapons in the universe!**

MAGIC

MYSTIC MATTERS

Super-villains know that even the most **powerful heroes** are **vulnerable to magic**. They would give **anything** to get their hands on some of these **awe-inspiring mystical objects!**

POWER UP!

The Magic Sphere of Hippolyta is found on the island of Themyscira. Through it, the Queen of the Amazons can observe the world of men – its past, present and even its future. The Amazons have used this knowledge to greatly advance their culture and technology.

Shazam with Pandora's Box

HANDLE WITH CARE!

For thousands of years, **Pandora's Box** was believed to be a magical container for all the **sins of the world.** However, it turns out to be more than that – it's a portal to **Earth-3,** where **evil rules!**

IN REAL LIFE

The H-Dial is a powerful artefact that can give ordinary people superpowers. In the *Adventure Comics* series *Dial H for Hero*, debuting in 1981, DC Comics gave its readers the chance to decide which powers the story's characters, Chris and Vicki, would get.

JLA FILES

Long ago, the Guardians of the Universe eradicate magic. They gather the last mystical energies – good and bad – and seal them inside a star, known as the Starheart. It becomes sentient and its good magic searches for a champion. Falling to Earth, the Starheart is reshaped into a lantern and found by Alan Scott. He wields its power in a ring as the original Green Lantern.

HANDLE WITH CARE!

Talia al Ghūl sends **Batman** a gift called **the Suit of Sorrows** to enhance his strength and speed. The suit causes anyone but the **pure in heart** to do **evil.** Even **Batman** is **affected!** He puts it on display in the **Batcave** as **a warning to himself.**

WHEN GOOD GUYS GO BAD

The Heart of Darkness is a black diamond created on **Apokolips** and containing the powerful being **Eclipso.** The gem **corrupts** all it comes into contact with. As **Cyborg** explains, "Every **dark impulse** I've ever had… it wants me to **act on them…**"

POWER UP!

In ancient times, the wizard Shazam receives his powers from the Lords of Magic. Each one gives him a different attribute to use as their champion on Earth. Through bolts of divine lightning he is given the strength of Voldar, the wisdom of Lumiun, the speed of Arel, the power of Ribalvei, the courage of Elbiam and the stamina of Marzosh!

NOOOO!

The Orb of Ra can be used to bestow ***shape-shifting powers*** on ***ordinary people.*** However, if you don't read ***the hieroglyphics*** correctly, you may ***turn to dust!***

SPECIAL *MOVES*

Using his magical talisman, the **Mystic Symbol of the Seven,** immortal paranormal detective **Doctor Occult** can open portals to other dimensions.

DID YOU KNOW?

To become **Doctor Fate**, you need…

- **The Amulet of Anubis:** A magical talisman imbued with the power of the Egyptian god of the dead.
- **The Cloak of Destiny:** A vestment that can crush an unworthy wearer.
- **The Helmet of Fate:** One of the universe's most powerful artefacts, enabling teleportation, flight, telekinesis and spell-casting.
- **The Staff of Power:** A magical staff that fires energy blasts

WOW!

7

The number of people who have worn Doctor Fate's magic helmet.

Tough Break

Searching for the **Book of Parallax,** deep beneath the Green Lantern homeworld of **Oa,** the **Sinestro Corps' Lyssa Drax** comes across another book – the **Book of the Black.** She has barely begun to plan the **evil deeds** she can accomplish with it when its Guardian, **Scar,** traps her within its pages!

MAGICAL MIGHT

Weapons powered by **magic** and the **supernatural** can be among the most **mighty** in the **universe,** taking heroes and villains to a **whole new level!**

Deathstroke

THE POWER OF THE SWORD BURNS THROUGH MY VEINS... IT WANTS TO KILL!
WHAT THE..?!

DID YOU KNOW?

Mysterious vigilante **the Question** can summon his **Spear of Inquest** from the ether. It is forged from a shard of the **Spear of Destiny** and can find **answers** lurking in the mind of anyone whose **body it pierces.**

The Dreamstone can extract people's **dreams** – and **nightmares** – and **make them real!**

POWER UP!

Blue Devil gets an upgrade on his home-made trident when he defeats the demon Nebiros in Hell and comes away with Lucifer's Trident. The weapon can detect any stray demons roaming the Earth.

HANDLE WITH CARE!

The Spear of Destiny exerts an **evil influence** that has even affected **Superman.** The Spear is considered so dangerous it has even been **thrown out into space** to stop it falling into the **wrong hands!**

NOOOO!

The Scepter of the Dead King sank ***Atlantis*** thousands of years ago by creating a massive ***earthquake.*** Its great power makes it ***a top target*** of Aquaman foe ***Black Manta!***

IN REAL LIFE

DC Comics' series *G.I. Combat* featured a tank haunted and guided by the ghost of Confederate General J. E. B. Stuart. The Haunted Tank itself was an M3 Stuart Light Tank, a real World War II tank named after the general himself.

JLA FILES

THE LANCING SPEAR
Used by the villain Gog, who has killed Superman in various realities, this formidable weapon combines the emerald energy of the Guardians of the Universe, the cosmic power of the Source and the magical might of Greek god Zeus and the wizard Shazam.

TOP 5

Magical Blades

1. **GODKILLER:** Forged by Hephaestus so Deathstroke can slay a god, this sword guides its wielder's actions.
2. **SOULTAKER:** This samurai sword is Katana's chosen blade. It traps the souls of those it slays in its blade. It can also shape-shift into other weapons.
3. **EXCALIBUR:** This enchanted blade once belonged to King Arthur and is indestructible. It is passed down to the hero Shining Knight.
4. **SWORD OF SIN AND SWORD OF SALVATION:** Wielded by "avenging angel" Azrael, they show victims their sins and the tragic events that led them to commit them.
5. **SWORD OF NIGHT:** Used by Nightmaster to force people to reveal the truth, warn of danger and halt aging.

TELL ME MORE

The Helmet of Quetzalcoatl once belonged to the Aztec god of light. It was given to the Brotherhood of Q in ancient Mexico. The helmet stores the memories of every warrior who has worn it, and only intense training prevents wearers, like the hero Aztek, from being overwhelmed by this mental cacophony.

YESSS!

A relic of Atlantis, the ***Manacles of Force*** can be clashed together to create a ***force field.*** Worn by ***Prisoner-of-War,*** one of the ***Others*** team, the Manacles shield a Siberian village from ***an avalanche.***

POWER UP!

The Cosmic Staff is Stargirl's weapon of choice. With it, she can move objects, create force fields and fire energy blasts; she can also control the staff telepathically.

WHAT THE..?!

The Painting that Ate Paris is a multi-dimensional artwork that **absorbs lifeforms** and even **entire cities.** A portal to **other realms,** the artwork cannot be destroyed and **regenerates if attacked!**

HANDLE WITH CARE!

The Silent Armor, worn by **Wonder Girl,** is forged in the **heart of the sun** and is **indestructible.** It bonds to its wearer and can be **invisible** until it is **summoned** by sheer **willpower.** Wonder Girl needs all her willpower to keep the suit from **bringing out her bad side...**

CHAPTER FOUR
FROM HERE TO ETERNITY

What event caused the government to dub Gotham City a "NO MAN'S LAND"?

Who was the mad king who caused ATLANTIS to sink beneath the waves?

Which planet's population is able to eat ABSOLUTELY ANYTHING?

LOCATIONS

CITY OF TOMORROW

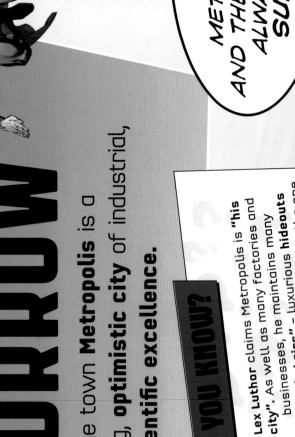

Superman's home town **Metropolis** is a glittering, bustling, **optimistic city** of industrial, business and **scientific excellence.**

FAST FACTS

POPULATION: 11,000,000

RESIDENT SUPER HEROES: Superman; Steel; Guardian; Booster Gold; Black Lightning; Gangbuster; Thorn

VISITING SUPER HEROES: Supergirl; Mon-El; Superwoman; Agent Liberty; Kon-El (Superboy)

ALSO KNOWN AS: The Big Apricot; City of Tomorrow; the Monarch City

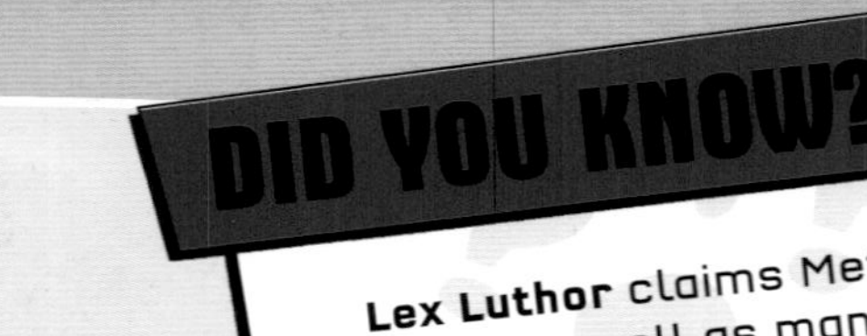

DID YOU KNOW?

Lex Luthor claims Metropolis is **"his city".** As well as many factories and businesses, he maintains many **"Luthor's Lairs"** – luxurious **hideouts** and fully equipped **labs,** such as the one under the disused **Metro Museum.**

DAILY PLANET
METROPOLIS—
AND THE WORLD—WILL
ALWAYS NEED A
SUPERMAN!

KA-POW!

Metropolis has a legion of protectors. As well as Superman, Booster Gold, Steel, Thorn, Guardian, Gangbuster and Black Lightning, corporate interests such as S.T.A.R. Labs and LexCorp employ their own metahuman security teams, named S.T.A.R. Force and Team Luthor respectively.

IN REAL LIFE

Superman's connection to Metropolis was established in *Action Comics* #16 (Sept. 1939), with artist Joe Shuster basing the city skyline on his childhood hometown of Toronto, Canada.

JLA FILES

A CITY FIT FOR HEROES
Founded in 1644, Metropolis comprises several boroughs. Bakerline, Hob's Bay, Park Ridge, Queensland Park, and Southside (a.k.a. Suicide Slum), surround the islands of New Troy, Hell's Gate and St Martin's. Despite being caught up in numerous battles with super-villains, this vibrant city continues to prosper.

DID YOU KNOW?

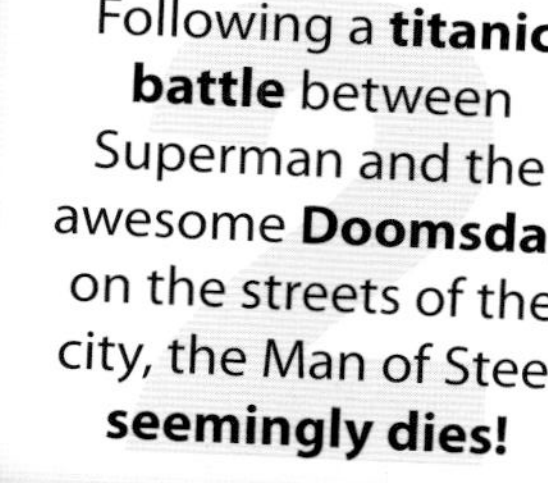

Mechanical genius **John Henry Irons** alternates between inventing non-lethal weapons for the **M.S.C.U.** (Metropolis Special Crimes Unit) and duties as armoured hero **Steel.** The **Steelworks** – his automated laboratory complex – is situated in **Suicide Slum.**

BAD DAY

Following a **titanic battle** between Superman and the awesome **Doomsday** on the streets of the city, the Man of Steel **seemingly dies!**

AARGH!

Superman's hometown has been miniaturised by Collector of Worlds ***Brainiac*** and put in a bottle so often that the citizens are probably ***used to it*** by now!

NOOOO!

When futuristic villain ***Brainiac 13*** attacks Earth, his ***technological viruses*** rewrite the structure of Metropolis, manifesting an ***automated City of Tomorrow*** where humans are considered an ***infestation!***

WHAT THE..?!

A society of monsters lives in caverns deep beneath Metropolis. Survivors of **illegal experiments,** these **Underworlders** sometimes create havoc in the city, until stopped by **Superman** or other Super Heroes.

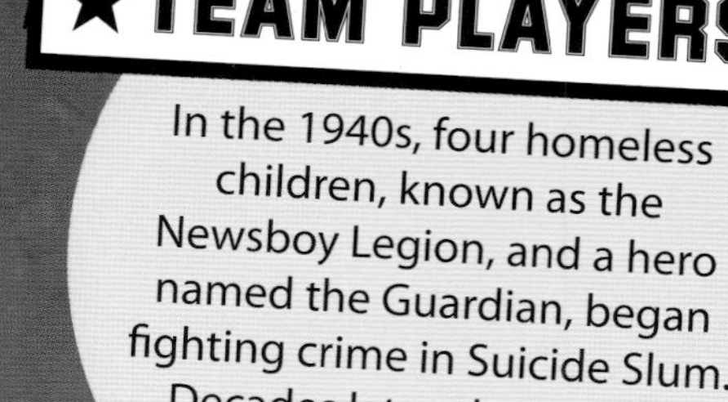

TOP 3

Criminal Organisations

1. **INTERGANG:** Criminal organisation with hi-tech weaponry supplied by Darkseid.
2. **THE 1000:** Insidious criminal outfit seeking supreme political power.
3. **SKULL:** So secret they may not exist any more!

INTERESTING PLACES

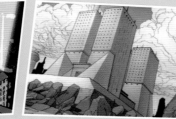

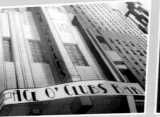

The Daily Planet Building: Home of the most famous newspaper on Earth.

Stryker's Island Penitentiary: A maximum-security jail for super-villains.

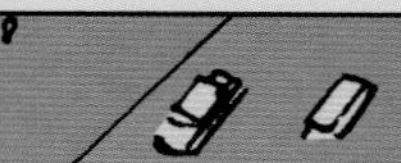

Ace O' Clubs Bar: Owned by burly Bibbo Bibbowski, "Superman's number one fan".

Centennial Park: Home to Superman's Tomb and a huge statue of him and Superboy.

★TEAM PLAYERS★

In the 1940s, four homeless children, known as the Newsboy Legion, and a hero named the Guardian, began fighting crime in Suicide Slum. Decades later, their clones are still battling super-villains!

CITY OF THE BAT!

Gotham City is a **nightmare** of **metal** and **stone, plagued** by **super-villains.** Only **Batman** can save it from **drowning in crime** and **descending into chaos!**

IN REAL LIFE

Gotham City landmarks, such as Robinson Park, Archie Goodwin International Airport and the Robert Kane Memorial Bridge, are named after some of the key people who shaped Batman and his world.

Q&A

Q: Why do the old buildings of Gotham City have so many gargoyles?

A: They are supposed to ward off evil influences.

BAD DAY

When an **earthquake** rips through **Gotham City,** the government cuts the **ravaged city** off from the rest of the country and declares it a **"No Man's Land"!**

THIS IS MY CITY. AT NIGHT IT BELONGS TO ME.

AARGH!

Legends say that ***the darkness*** in ***Gotham City*** begins when ***an evil warlock*** is buried on the land thousands of years ago. His wickedness ***soaks into the earth!***

WHAT THE..?!

Gotham City gangsters will do **anything** to discredit **Batman.** They even try to convince the public that he's an **alien from outer space!**

CITY TOUR

Here are some top landmarks in Gotham City. Visit at your own risk!

ROBINSON PARK: The city's largest park; Poison Ivy once took it over.

BLACKGATE PENITENTIARY: Where Gotham City's ordinary criminals are sent.

WAYNE ENTERPRISES: Bruce Wayne's hi-tech company.

CRIME ALLEY: The "birthplace of Batman", this is the dangerous side street where young Bruce Wayne sees his parents, Thomas and Martha, savagely gunned down.

GOTHAM CLOCK TOWER: Barbara Gordon's base when she operates as information mastermind Oracle.

ARKHAM ASYLUM: Many of the super-villains Batman fights end up here!

ICEBERG LOUNGE: A fancy nightclub owned by crime lord the Penguin.

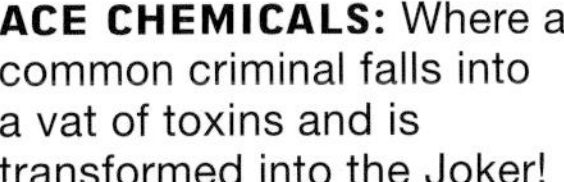

ACE CHEMICALS: Where a common criminal falls into a vat of toxins and is transformed into the Joker!

G.C.P.D. HQ: A base for cops (good and not-so-good), and a target for villains and vandals.

THAT SINKING FEELING

Outside Gotham City is Slaughter Swamp. Mind how you go, because it's undead villain Solomon Grundy's stomping ground....

AARGH!

The G.C.P.D. use the ***Bat-Signal*** to alert Batman of a crime… but when the evil ***Signalman*** traps the Dark Knight inside the spotlight, Batman will ***die*** if the police ***turn it on!***

AARGH!

No matter how often the asylum is ***renovated*** and ***updated,*** Arkham's inmates are forever ***breaking out,*** being ***chased down*** by ***Batman*** and ***returned*** to their ***cells!***

DID YOU KNOW?

While **Arkham Asylum** is located on **Mercey Island,** Batman builds a secret Batcave there. This **"Northwest Batcave"** hides all the gadgets, supplies and vehicles Batman needs in case of a **breakout or riot.**

RISING FROM THE ASHES

Arkham Asylum has been built, destroyed and rebuilt many times...

▶ **ORIGINAL ARKHAM:** Built around the Victorian mansion of Amadeus Arkham to care for his mentally ill mother, Elizabeth, and patients like her.

DESTROYED BY: Jeremiah Arkham, Amadeus' nephew, to make room for a new facility.

◀ **RENOVATED ARKHAM:** Cells laid out in a labyrinth-like pattern, with glass walls for around-the-clock observation of inmates.

DESTROYED BY: Bane, who releases Arkham's inmates as part of his plan to defeat Batman.

▶ **MERCEY MANSION:** A huge, abandoned gothic pile which Jeremiah Arkham rebuilds as the new Arkham Asylum.

DESTROYED BY: Black Mask, who frees the prisoners, declares himself their leader, and blows up the building.

◀ **ARKHAM REBORN:** Built on the ruins of Mercey Mansion by Jeremiah Arkham, according to Amadeus Arkham's original vision for the asylum.

DESTROYED BY: Hell breaking loose under the building – literally!

▶ **WAYNE MANOR:** Bruce Wayne's family home is seized by the state and turned into the latest version of the infamous asylum.

STAFF TURNOVER

Arkham has a strange effect on its staff. Many become dangerously unstable while working there. The Scarecrow, Hugo Strange and Harley Quinn all start their criminal careers as Arkham doctors!

DID YOU KNOW?

Batman has checked himself into **Arkham Asylum** as a patient more than once, in order to test its security, or as part of an **undercover investigation.**

TOP 5

Arkham Inmates

1. **KILLER CROC:** His cell walls are reinforced to withstand his most ferocious attacks.
2. **CLAYFACE:** Kept in an airtight cell to stop him squeezing his pliable body through any cracks.
3. **POISON IVY:** If the smallest leaf gets in her cell, she can grow it into a gigantic plant that can tear the place apart!
4. **MR FREEZE:** His cell is kept at subzero temperatures, allowing him to survive outside his cryogenic suit.
5. **THE JOKER:** Not even Arkham's high-security cells can hold him for long.

BEDLAM!

Batman's most **notorious foes** are often **locked up** in **spooky Arkham Asylum** – and so are some of **Arkham's own staff**!

IN REAL LIFE

Arkham Asylum is named after a sanatorium in the horror short story "The Thing on the Doorstep" by H. P. Lovecraft.

WELCOME TO ARKHAM... I JUST KNOW WE'LL HAVE LOTS OF FUN TOGETHER.

NOOOO!

The Joker manages to convince his therapist, ***Dr Harleen Quinzel*** to help him escape. She develops such a ***crush*** on him she becomes his partner in crime ***Harley Quinn!***

BEST KNOWN FOR

Terrible security!

PARADISE ISLAND

The island of **Themyscira** is home to the **Amazons** – including **Wonder Woman.** It has always been **concealed from the world,** protected by **the Greek gods.**

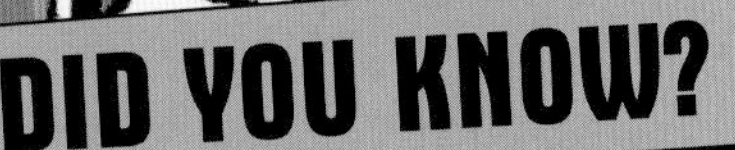

The Amazons and their magical island were created by the Greek gods of Olympus to represent the best things about humanity.

AN *AMAZON* DOES NOT *TAKE KINDLY* TO HAVING HER *HOME THREATENED!*

BEST KNOWN FOR

Being Wonder Woman's birthplace!

IN REAL LIFE

Paradise Island first appeared in *All-Star Comics* #8 (Dec. 1941). It was renamed Themyscira in *Wonder Woman* #1 (Feb. 1987), after an ancient Greek town that, according to legend, was the home of the Amazon tribe.

BEFORE

INTO THE SKY

The original island was destroyed in a war against Imperiex, a vast being made of malignant cosmic energy. Another Themyscira of floating islands was later created with the help of alien technology.

AFTER

WHAT THE..?!

The **Amazons** guard an underground rift called **Doom's Doorway** that leads straight to the hellish realm of **Hades!**

ALTERNATE EARTHS

On **Earth-C-Minus,** where all the Super Heroes are animals, the Animalzon princess **Wonder Wabbit** comes from a magical place called **Parrot-Eyes Island!**

WHAT THE..?!

The **Themysciran Embassy** in New York helps represent **the Amazons** in the wider world. Its staff includes **Ferdinand,** a vegetarian chef with **the head of a bull!**

DASTARDLY DEED

Villainous A.I. Brother Eye attacks **Themyscira** with an army of **OMAC robots.** He then beams images of **Amazons fighting** to convince the world that **Amazons are evil!**

Q&A

Q: How do the Amazons live forever?

A: By drinking from the island's Fountain of Eternal Youth. When Wonder Woman decides to leave the island, she also gives up her immortality!

NOOOO!

In the alternate timeline of ***Flashpoint,*** a war between ***Themyscira*** and ***Atlantis,*** home of ***Aquaman,*** destroys the ***world!***

FAST FACTS

NICKNAMES: Paradise Island, Amazonia

CURRENT LOCATION: Unknown

RESIDENTS: The immortal race of women known as Amazons

HANDLE WITH CARE!

The Amazons protect a powerful device called the Purple Ray. This can heal any wound, reverse death – or completely destroy anything it touches!

WORLD BENEATH THE SEA

Somewhere, in the **depths** of the **ocean,** lies **Atlantis** – a **fantastical world** that many **surface-dwellers** believe to be nothing but a **myth...**

YESSS!

When **Atlantis** is sunk, **King Orin's scientists** manage to come up with a serum that enables Atlanteans to **breathe underwater.** In time, all Atlanteans are born with this ***vital ability.***

IN REAL LIFE

Inspired by the Ancient Greek legend about a civilisation plunged into the ocean after falling from favour with the gods, Atlantis received its first comic book mention in *Action Comics* #18 (Nov. 1939).

JLA FILES

THE TRENCH
The Trench are an Atlantean race that have evolved in the depths of the ocean. Monstrous in form, they have knife-sharp teeth and paralysing saliva. Trench society is based around a large king and queen and an army of smaller soldiers, who follow whoever wields the Dead King's Scepter.

TELL ME MORE

Xebel, the home of Aquaman's wife Mera, is a former Atlantean prison colony located in the Bermuda Triangle. Its people build their cities and weapons using salvage from the area's many shipwrecks.

NOOOO!

An out-of-control ***Spectre*** destroys ***Atlantis*** with shock waves as part of a scheme to wipe out all magical things. ***Aquaman*** arrives ***too late*** to save his kingdom!

JLA FILES

THE FALL OF ATLANTIS
Millennia ago, the continent of Atlantis was cast down beneath the waves by its vengeful, deposed king, Atlan, using the magical Trident of Neptune. Of the original seven kingdoms of Atlantis, only three survive, their inhabitants forced to evolve to live underwater – or die.

ATLANTIS IS UNDER MY PROTECTION NOW.

Aquaman

Q&A

Q: How many continents are there?

A: Surface people reckon on seven, but they're forgetting about Atlantis, underwater home of Aquaman and his subjects. Atlanteans are generally divided into the humanoid sea-breathers of Poseidonis and the merpeople of Tritonis, but the sunken continent also harbours smaller cities, with even stranger inhabitants...

TOP 7

TREASURES OF ATLANTIS

During his years in exile, King Atlan forges the Trident of Neptune. He also prepares for his battle with usurper Orin by creating the Seven Treasures of Atlantis.

1. **ATLANTEAN HELMET:** Allows wearer to exist without food, water or oxygen.
2. **ATLANTEAN KEY:** Opens any locked door.
3. **ATLAN'S SCEPTRE:** Allows its wielder to control the people of the Trench kingdom.
4. **GLOBE OF TRANSPORTATION:** Transports whoever holds it anywhere they wish.
5. **MANACLES OF FORCE:** When clashed together, the manacles create a protective force field.
6. **POWER GLOVE:** Gives the wearer a punch potent enough to smash magic forces.
7. **SEAL OF CLARITY:** Translates any language into the user's own.

BEST KNOWN FOR

Disappearing beneath the waves!

AN ATLANTIS WHO'S WHO

ATLAN: First king of Atlantis. A just and tolerant ruler, he goes mad and sinks Atlantis after his brother usurps the throne and kills his family.

ORIN: Atlan's brother. Disagrees with his brother's welcoming attitude to foreigners, and seizes the throne.

VULKO: Loyal chronicler and advisor to Arthur Curry during his time as Aquaman.

ORM: Clashes with his half-human brother, Arthur, over the "surface" part of his ancestry.

DOLPHIN: An Atlantean mutant with webbed claws and the ability to emit bioluminescent light.

TEMPEST: The former Aqualad, Garth, with newly acquired magical powers.

TULA: Chief of the Atlantean military, and Orm's half sister.

SWATT: Requires a special mask to breathe underwater; obsessively collects artefacts from the surface world against his king's orders.

ARION: an ancient Atlantean mage and adventurer.

MURK: Atlantean military commander. At first loyal to Orm, he later acknowledges Aquaman's right to the throne.

DID YOU KNOW?

Vanity, Oregon, is home to Super Hero **The Ray.** It's also known as the **dullest city** in the U.S.A.!

Q&A

Q: What's the hardest job in Central City?

A: Road maintenance. The damage to streets caused by assorted speedsters continually running on them causes years of damage every week. Worse yet, The Flash and his super fast friends run up and down buildings, too!

DID YOU KNOW?

Many miles below Earth's surface is **Strata,** a **utopian subterranean society** dedicated to preserving the ecosystem. Their chief representative to the above-world is part-time Super Hero Atlee, better known as **Terra.**

EWWW!

Blüdhaven, once nicknamed the **Most Dangerous City in America,** is reduced to **radioactive rubble** by **Chemo**, who spews out **toxic chemicals!**

DINOSAUR ISLAND... WHERE THE LAWS OF PHYSICS TAKE LIBERTIES.

TROUBLE SPOTS

Exotic and amazing places exist all over the world, but some are **best avoided**, if you don't have incredible luck or, preferably, **superpowers**!

WHAT THE..?!

The **Mountain of Judgment** is a colossal, village-sized road vehicle. It is home to a **super-technological group** who live outside Metropolis and are called **the Hairies!**

TOP 5

Mystic Locations

1. **DR FATE'S TOWER OF FATE:** It's nominally in Salem, Massachusetts, but it moves around a lot.
2. **HOUSE OF STRANGERS, TIBET:** No normal people allowed.
3. **EXTERNSTONE PILLARS, TEUTOBURG FOREST, GERMANY:** Hostile living statues.
4. **SUN GATE OF TIAHUANACO, BOLIVIA:** This Incan gateway to the gods is guarded by giant carnivorous ants.
5. **MOONSTONE CLUB, GOTHAM CITY:** Exclusive speakeasy for shady supernaturals – mortals and heroes will probably be damned or eaten here.

NOOOO!

The citizens of ***Central City*** soon regret the visit of 64th-century magician ***Abra Kadabra.*** The master thief **paralyses** crowds with his ***hypno-ray!***

CITIES THAT NEED HEROES

Opal City, Maryland
The home of Starman and The Shade attracts greedy villains and thieves.

Central City, Missouri; Keystone City, Kansas
"The Gem Cities", where a dynasty of Flashes battles a rogues gallery of ruthless super-villains.

Hub City, Illinois
The Question fights a losing battle in the most corrupt city in America.

Gotham City
Where the Batman Family struggles against the greatest collection of killers ever assembled!

DID YOU KNOW?

In the Himalayan spiritual sanctuary **Nanda Parbat,** evil thoughts and deeds are **impossible** and ghosts like **Deadman** regain their physical form!

CITY OF APES

Gorilla City, in the heart of Africa, is home to a race of super-intelligent simians. They used to be friendly to humans, but since King Solovar was assassinated at the command of Gorilla Grodd, visitors are more likely to be fed upon than welcomed!

TOP 6 SECRET ISLANDS

1. **THEMYSCIRA (PARADISE ISLAND)**
Hidden home of the immortal Amazons; male visitors strongly discouraged!
2. **DINOSAUR ISLAND**
Soldiers are still fighting World War II on this uncharted Pacific atoll, which also has a sizeable dinosaur population.
3. **BLACKHAWK ISLAND**
Militarised secret citadel home of the Blackhawks, formerly the elite Blackhawk Squadron of World War II.
4. **OOLONG ISLAND**
China Seas enclave stuffed with sinister scientists building doomsday weapons!
5. **ZANDIA**
The Brotherhood of Evil's Baltic base and a refuge for rogues.
6. **SANTA PRISCA**
Drug-cartel-controlled island with the world's cruellest prison, Pena Duro, where the young Bane is unjustly confined.

ROGUE STATES

These overseas destinations DON'T welcome visitors...

- **Kahndaq** in the Middle East is reputed to be the birthplace of magic, but its rulers have no love of western politics or Super Heroes.
- The western European kingdom of **Markovia** is home to a deadly superhuman weapons program and infested with vampires.
- **Bialya** in the Middle East has been dominated by tyrants for centuries.
- The Eastern European principality of **Vlatava** has endured Soviet occupation, decimation by the Spectre and civil war between democratic forces and royalists loyal to Count Vertigo.

BEST KNOWN FOR

Exploding – just as Kal-El, a.k.a. Superman, escapes in a rocket ship

THE POWERS OF KRYPTONITE

The radioactive element created in Krypton's destruction has several different forms.

GREEN
Exposure drains Superman's powers; high doses can kill him.

RED
Causes random outbursts in Superman's behaviour for up to 48 hours.

BLUE
Has same effect on Superman clone Bizarro as Green Kryptonite does on the Man of Steel.

GOLD
Contact with this can permanently prevent Superman from using yellow sunlight for his powers, making him ordinary – and vulnerable.

TOUGH BREAK

Superman arrives on Earth soon after **Krypton's destruction,** but the light from the planet's **explosion** does not reach our world for another **27 years.** As an adult, a sombre Man of Steel is able to watch the **death** of his **own homeworld** via a telescope.

TOP 5

Sights of Krypton

It's too late now to book that holiday to Krypton, but here's what you might have seen...

1. **KANDOR:** Krypton's beautiful capital, until bottled and taken away by Brainiac.
2. **FIRE FALLS:** Lava spills dramatically over cliffs dotted with patches of the Blood Bloom plant, and inhabited by fish-snakes and giant birds of prey!
3. **ARGO CITY:** Saved under a dome by Jor-El's brother and Superman's uncle, Zor-El. Later found by Brainiac, shrunk, and added to his collection of bottled cities.
4. **KRYPTONOPOLIS:** After Brainiac takes Kandor, Kryptonopolis becomes Krypton's capital. It is the birthplace of Superman.
5. **FORT ROZZ:** A maximum-security prison accidentally sent into the Phantom Zone, it becomes a base for evil General Zod and his cronies.

BACK FROM THE DEAD!

New Krypton is created using the lost city of **Kandor,** built up into an entire planet using Brainiac technology and **Sunstone crystals.** It occupies the same orbit as Earth, but is hidden from view on the **opposite side** of the **Sun!**

TOP 3

Wonders of Kryptonian Wildlife

1. **METAL-EATING MOLES:** Large golden moles that chew through metal!

2. **DRANGS:** Flying horned serpents that can knock down buildings. They hatch from eggs with shells made of Red Kryptonite!

3. **THOUGHT-BEASTS:** Fearsome predators that carry out telepathic attacks.

FAST FACTS

LOCATION: Formerly orbiting the red sun Rao

CAPITAL CITY: Kandor; later Kryptonopolis

NOTABLE INHABITANTS: Kal-El (Superman); Kara Zor-El (Supergirl); Jor-El; Lara Lor-Van; General Zod; Thara Ak-Var (Flamebird); Doomsday

CURRENT STATUS: Destroyed, but perhaps slowly reforming

WOW!

100,000

The number of Kryptonians who survive the planet's demise. They are trapped when Brainiac miniaturises the city of Kandor and encloses it in a bottle.

DOOMED WORLD!

Superman's home planet Krypton possesses hugely **advanced technology** and some of the universe's **finest minds.** It also faces **unavoidable destruction...**

IN REAL LIFE

In 2012, DC Comics asked the astrophysicist Neil deGrasse Tyson to pinpoint a real location for planet Krypton. Tyson picked out the constellation Corvus. Tyson also appeared as himself in a Superman comic!

KRYPTON IS DYING. FROM WITHIN. AND THERE IS NOTHING I, OR ANYONE, CAN DO ABOUT IT.

Lara, Jor-El and baby Kal-El

JLA FILES

DEATH OF A PLANET

Krypton is destroyed by a series of explosions within its core; explosions that produce the radioactive material Kryptonite. Superman's father, Jor-El, believes that the explosions have been triggered by a nuclear device detonated many years before, during a civil war known as the Clone Wars.

BIG HEAT!

A hellish, burning world ruled by **Darkseid,** Apokolips is crafted to be an **engine of destruction,** fuelled by **fear and hate.**

AARGH!

No one on Apokolips is lower than the ***Hunger Dogs.*** These ***starving hordes*** live in the section of the planet called ***Armagetto,*** and are used as slaves, hunted for sport and even ***burned for fuel!***

JLA FILES

BEYOND OUR REALITY

The world of Apokolips exists outside the Multiverse, ripped away from the fabric of reality when the Old Gods died. As such, it is isolated from the cosmos – unless you know how to navigate beyond the edge of all known universes!

DID YOU KNOW?

Boom Tubes are small devices that generate a tunnel from any given point in one universe to another. They are most often used to travel between two planets that exist outside the Multiverse: Apokolips and New Genesis.

FEMALE FURIES!

These female warriors are trained by Granny Goodness. They are the elite fighting force of Apokolips and their ranks have included:

STOMPA: A super-powerful brawler who crushes foes with her antimatter boots!

BIG BARDA: A former leader, she abandons the team to escape Apokolips.

LASHINA: Her electrical whips are part of her uniform; takes over as leader when Barda quits.

BERNADETH: Sister of Desaad; cunning, and plotting for power; uses a deadly "fahren knife".

MAD HARRIET: An animalistic berserker warrior happy to rend you limb from limb!

ALTERNATE EARTHS

A team of **Steppenwolf's agents,** residing on a version of Earth-2, use the term **"Hunger Dogs"** as their codename. One of them, **Brutaal,** seemingly kills Steppenwolf.

DID YOU KNOW?

On the edge of the Omniverse, there is a barrier, the Source Wall, that prevents any being from understanding the true nature of all creation. Many beings from Apokolips have tried to break through this barrier, but none have succeeded.

TOP 4

Unpleasant Sites

If you're unfortunate enough to find yourself on Apokolips, here are some great places to avoid...

1. **THE NECROPOLIS:** The underground labyrinth home of the mindless Dreggs – bring a map!
2. **THE ORPHANAGE:** Run by the ever-malevolent Granny Goodness – don't stay long!
3. **FIRE PITS:** Dotted about the planet, these constantly spew fire, molten lava and hellish heat – keep your distance!
4. **ARMAGETTO:** The slum home of the Hunger Dogs – throw them a bone!

TOP 5

Servants of Darkseid

All that exists on Apokolips serves Darkseid!

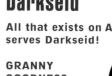

1. **GRANNY GOODNESS:** Trains the new recruits for Darkseid's armies.

2. **DESAAD:** Darkseid's chief torturer.

3. **MANTIS:** Former leader of a humanoid insect colony.

4. **KANTO:** Darkseid's favourite assassin.
5. **STEPPENWOLF:** Darkseid's uncle and loyal general.

YESSS!

An ancient hunger from the realm of imagination attacks ***Apokolips.*** This ***galactic entity*** feeds on star systems, but the lack of a ***nourishing life-force*** on the planet forces it ***to retreat!***

MADE IN APOKOLIPS

This dark world is a wellspring of wicked weaponry...

DEVILANCE'S LANCE:
A multipurpose, cosmic killing tool.

DR BEDLAM'S ANIMATES:
Provide physical form for his evil energy.

THE JUSTIFIERS' MIND-CONTROL HELMETS:
Cancel conscience and enhance cruelty.

BERNADETH'S FAHREN KNIFE:
A super-hot assassin's blade.

DARKSEID'S MASS THOUGHT-CONTROL UNIT:
Sifts human minds in search of the ultimate secret.

APOKOLIPS IS MY ***SOVEREIGN DOMINION*** AND SHALL REMAIN ***FOREVER*** SO!

Darkseid

HOME OF THE NEW GODS

A lush, green planet blooming with life, **New Genesis** is ruled by the **New Gods.** This race of **immortal beings** is energised by **the Source** – the **wellspring of all reality!**

PLANETARY WARS
New Genesis was formed afte[r] the destruction of the Old Gods at the same time as its hellish twin planet Apokolips i[n] the Fourth World, a universe outside the Multiverse. The two planets have been at war ever since. New Genesis is bombarded with energy from the Source, giving its inhabitants great powers.

POWER UP!

The Forever People combine their will and summon the powerful being Infinity Man, who tells them that they have been chosen to battle Darkseid's oppression and Highfather's autocratic rule.

PLACES OF INTEREST

SUPERTOWN: The floating capital city of New Genesis, built by Highfather to be a celestial home of divine perfection.

THE UNTAMED WILDERNESS: Home to beings called "Primitives", who reject the celestial city and live on the surface of New Genesis.

INSECT EMPIRE: Living deep beneath the surface of New Genesis, the Bugs humanoid insect race is led by a queen, known as the All-Widow.

ASYLUM OF THE GODS: A home for any New Gods who go insane.

SINGULARITY STOCKADE: A Multiversal prison specially designed to negate the powers of its prisoners.

HANDLE WITH CARE!

The New Gods have **living computers** called **Mother Boxes** that can access the energy of **the Source** and use it to **alter reality!**

Noble Bug
Insects can be ***heroes*** too... ***Forager,*** of the Bug race, sacrifices himself to ***save Earth*** from the embodiment of the ***Anti-Life Equation!***

Q&A

Q: Who rules New Genesis?

A: Highfather. As Izaya the Inheritor, he was once a warrior of New Genesis. After losing everything he loved to the forces of Apokolips, Izaya travelled into the Source and returned as Highfather. He became the ruler of New Genesis, and tried to forge a pact of peace with Darkseid by exchanging their sons.

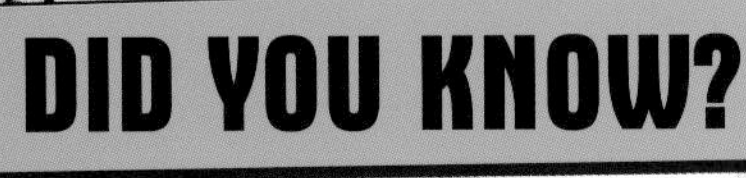

DID YOU KNOW?

When Highfather's sense of duty becomes greater than his love for his son, Scot, his conscience leaves him, becoming Infinity Man. Lacking a conscience, Highfather's rule has since become more autocratic.

Q&A

Q: Who are the Forever People?

A: Originally mortal beings from Earth, the Forever People were selected by Highfather and recreated on New Genesis! Returning to Earth, these amazing beings battle evil wherever they find it!

IN REAL LIFE

The planet of New Genesis – along with the New Gods, Darkseid, and the planet Apokolips – was a crucial part of trail-blazing writer and artist Jack Kirby's "Fourth World" saga, published by DC Comics from 1970 to 1973.

WOW!

127,420

The diameter of New Genesis in km (79,175 miles) – more than 10 times the size of Earth.

TOP 4

Highfather's favourites

All citizens of New Genesis are under Highfather's care, but some he has given special attention to...

1. **MISTER MIRACLE:** Highfather's son, taken by Darkseid at birth.
2. **LIGHTRAY:** Known as the Shining Star of New Genesis.
3. **TAKION:** A human being infused with cosmic awareness.
4. **FORAGER:** Heroic member of the Bugs insect race of New Genesis.

DID YOU KNOW?

Darkseid introduces microbe-sized **Bugs** to New Genesis, vainly hoping they will **consume** the planet's **food supplies.** They start out tiny but in time assume **human form** and build their own **colonies.**

WHAT THE..?!

The Source is a sentient power, and once merged Apokolips and New Genesis into one planet!

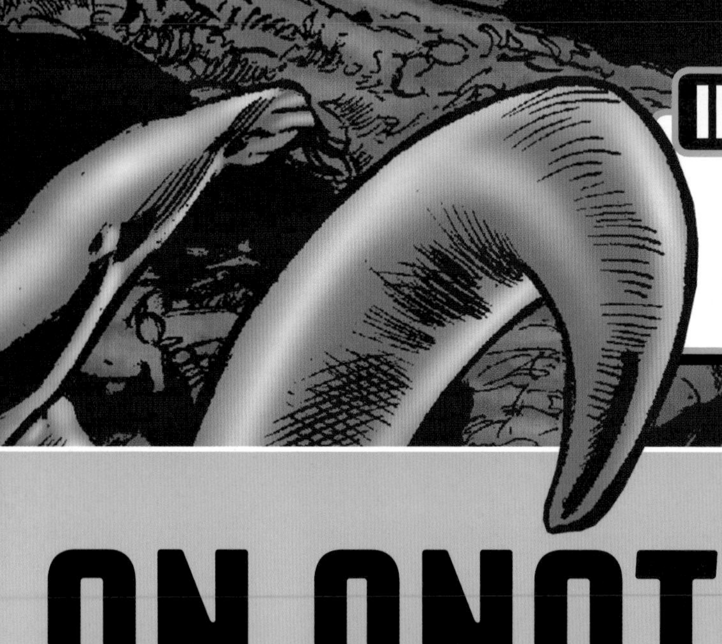

IN NUMBERS

4.5
The distance in light years from the planet Rann to Earth.

YESSS!

The Green Lantern Corps are stranded in a ***dying universe*** and ***under attack*** from ***light-wielding Lightsmiths.*** The Lightsmiths are about to take over ***Mogo,*** but this ***sentient planet*** surprises everyone by absorbing all the Lightsmiths' energy and using it to ***drive them away.***

ON ANOTHER PLANET

It's a **big universe** out there, with many **alien worlds** to discover. But will their inhabitants offer a **hand** – or **tentacle** – of friendship, or **stick a ray gun in your face?**

DID YOU KNOW?

Thousands of years ago, a **complex civilisation** exists on **Mars,** but **overuse** of resources turns the planet **red.** The subsequent destruction of the Martians and their settlements leaves only a handful of survivors – including J'onn J'onzz, the **Martian Manhunter,** and M'gann Morzz, a.k.a. **Miss Martian.**

WHAT THE..?!

When settlers arrive on the planet **Dryad,** they think it has no **human** or **animal** life. Then they see the **"boulders"** that dot the landscape **walking and talking!**

JLA FILES

THE PLANET OA
Oa is the home of the Guardians of the Universe, and the base for their Green Lantern Corps. The actions of the being Relic destroy Oa, but the Lanterns' Citadel doubles as an escape rocket. This not only takes the wounded Guardians to safety, it also preserves something of Oa's technology for the future.

DASTARDLY DEED

Daxam is the home of a race descended from Kryptonians. They gain the same powers as **Superman** if exposed to a **yellow sun.** Unfortunately their **powers** make them **a target,** and the entire population of the planet is almost **wiped out** by shape-shifting alien **Durlans.**

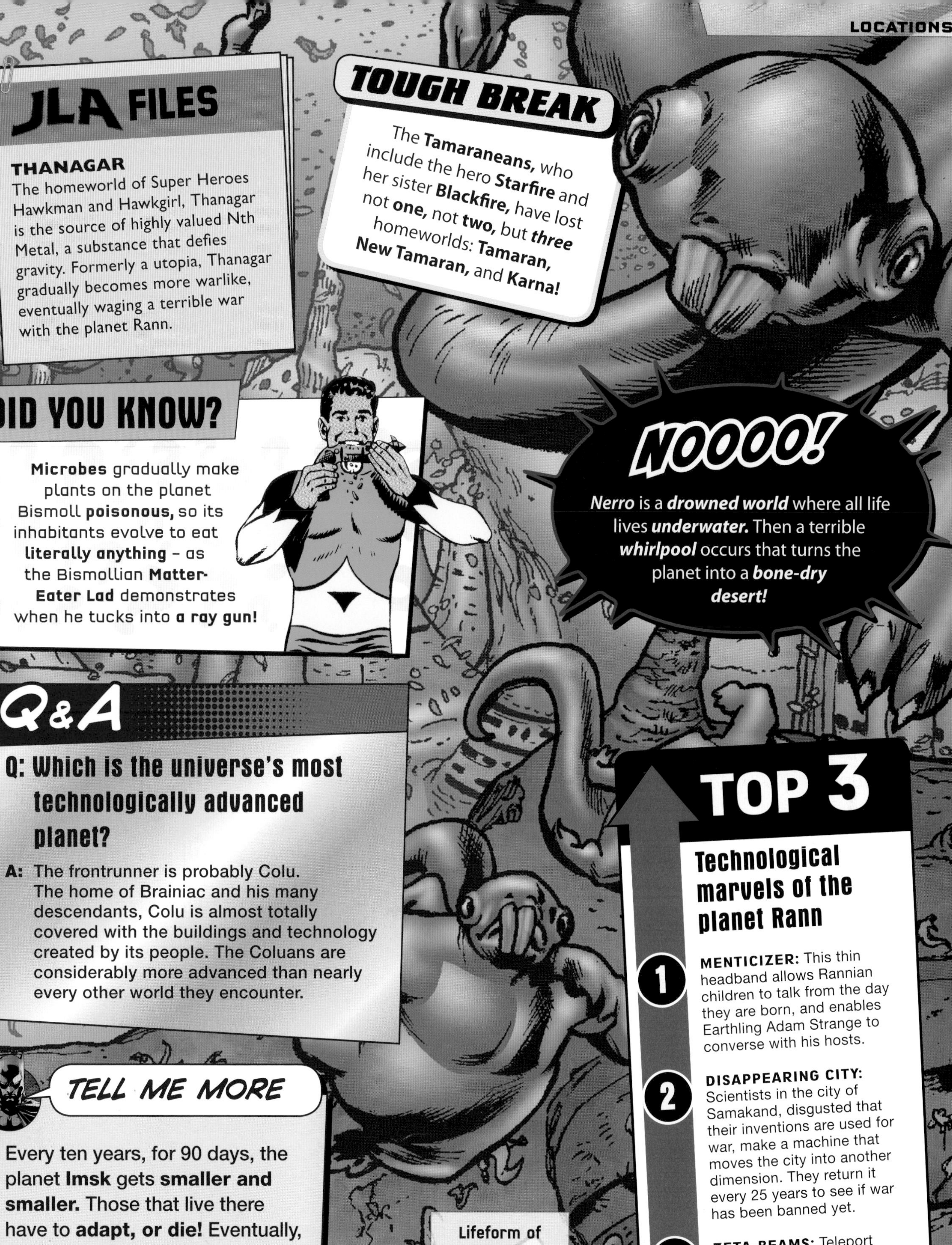

JLA FILES

THANAGAR
The homeworld of Super Heroes Hawkman and Hawkgirl, Thanagar is the source of highly valued Nth Metal, a substance that defies gravity. Formerly a utopia, Thanagar gradually becomes more warlike, eventually waging a terrible war with the planet Rann.

TOUGH BREAK

The **Tamaraneans,** who include the hero **Starfire** and her sister **Blackfire,** have lost not **one,** not **two,** but ***three*** homeworlds: **Tamaran, New Tamaran,** and **Karna!**

DID YOU KNOW?

Microbes gradually make plants on the planet Bismoll **poisonous,** so its inhabitants evolve to eat **literally anything** – as the Bismollian **Matter-Eater Lad** demonstrates when he tucks into **a ray gun!**

Nerro is a ***drowned world*** where all life lives ***underwater.*** Then a terrible ***whirlpool*** occurs that turns the planet into a ***bone-dry desert!***

Q&A

Q: Which is the universe's most technologically advanced planet?

A: The frontrunner is probably Colu. The home of Brainiac and his many descendants, Colu is almost totally covered with the buildings and technology created by its people. The Coluans are considerably more advanced than nearly every other world they encounter.

TELL ME MORE

Every ten years, for 90 days, the planet **Imsk** gets **smaller and smaller.** Those that live there have to **adapt, or die!** Eventually, the Imskians evolve to be able to **shrink at will!**

Lifeform of planet Nerro

TOP 3

Technological marvels of the planet Rann

1. **MENTICIZER:** This thin headband allows Rannian children to talk from the day they are born, and enables Earthling Adam Strange to converse with his hosts.
2. **DISAPPEARING CITY:** Scientists in the city of Samakand, disgusted that their inventions are used for war, make a machine that moves the city into another dimension. They return it every 25 years to see if war has been banned yet.
3. **ZETA-BEAMS:** Teleport people – and even entire planets – across space.

TOP 7 WEIRD ZONES

PHANTOM ZONE: Intangible, timeless area used to imprison Kryptonian criminals.

SHADOWLANDS: Land of dark demons and source of shadowmatter.

META-ZONE: A dimensional region inhabited by futuristic humanoids observing Earth.

ILLORAN: A parallel world where evolution has run wild, producing human butterflies and winged gorillas!

GHOST ZONE: The annex of the Phantom Zone and location of Prometheus' Crooked House.

MIRROR WORLDS: Infinite reflected dimensions, warping the natural laws of existence.

FAST FACTS

LOCATION: Everywhere and nowhere; the conventional rules of physics seldom apply to these uncanny domains.

HOW TO GET THERE: By super-science, magic, sheer accident or having the wrong kind of enemy.

BEST ADVICE: Get back home any way you can!

DID YOU KNOW?

When the first gods died, the clash created worlds of light (New Genesis) and darkness (Apokolips). These planets exist in their own dimension, inaccessible to normal space/time except by Boom Tubes or Metron's Mobius Chair.

JLA FILES

VANISHING POINT

A citadel outside the space-time continuum, Vanishing Point exists in the very last frozen moment of the universe before it is destroyed. Time travellers such as Rip Hunter and the Linear Men have used this fortress to access any point in history.

HA! HA! THE FLASH WILL NEVER FIND ME IN THIS MIRROR WORLD!

Mirror Master

WHAT THE..?!

The Dreaming contains a Grand Library housing every book that has never been written!

AARGH!

The ***Realm of Satanus*** is a Hell-like plane populated with ***lesser demons*** constantly battling to win ***more power*** for themselves.

UNKNOWN REALMS

Our universe, and **our Earth,** are linked to an **infinity of dimensions** and **parallel worlds:** arcane realms that only a very few **lucky** – or **damned** – souls **ever see!**

TOP 3

Other Dimensions

1 **ANTIMATTER UNIVERSE:** The physical opposite of our cosmos, where evil rules and the Weaponers of Qward dominate; the birth dimension of the terrible Anti-Monitor.

2 **NETHERSPACE:** A timeless, fourth-dimensional purgatory; water-filled and ruled by evil Aquaman-double Thanatos.

3 **FIFTH DIMENSION:** Populated by energy-sprites, like Superman annoyance Mr Mxyzptlk and Batman irritant Bat-Mite, whose science is magic.

SITTING IN LIMBO

Spirit World is a shadowy realm linking many realities. It is a corridor and waiting room for departed souls unable to reach Heaven or Hell. Many evil spirits and monsters gather here.

TOP 5

MAGICAL REALMS

They all have links to Earth...

1 **SKARTARIS:** A timeless pocket dimension seemingly located beneath the Earth.

2 **GEMWORLD:** A former chaos-dimension colonised by mystics and magical beasts, who flee Earth to escape the rule of science.

3 **MYRRA:** Ruled by wizards and defended by mystic champion Nightmaster.

4 **YS:** An unchanging mirror of our dimension used by the Warlock of Ys to capture unwary human victims.

5 **THE DREAM STREAM:** A metaphysical border region policed by the Sandman, who ensures that nightmare monsters don't escape into our waking world!

Q&A

Q: Where can you go if Heaven or Hell exclude you?

A: The Dreaming. Constructed from and fuelled by the unconscious thoughts of the living. Magical countries inside the Dreaming include the Nightmare Realm, the 12 factions of Gemworld and the provinces of Faerie.

NOOOO!

The ***Elder Gods*** are locked in a ***dungeon dimension*** sealed by the ***Alabaster Gate,*** created long ago by ***Earth's mages.*** They wait for ***Earthly magic*** to fail, and enable them to ***feed*** upon ***humankind!***

TELL ME MORE

Psychic Dorothy Spinner of the Doom Patrol has a spooky connection to the Dreaming. When she is upset or scared, nightmares escape from her imaginary Dream Country to attack the real world.

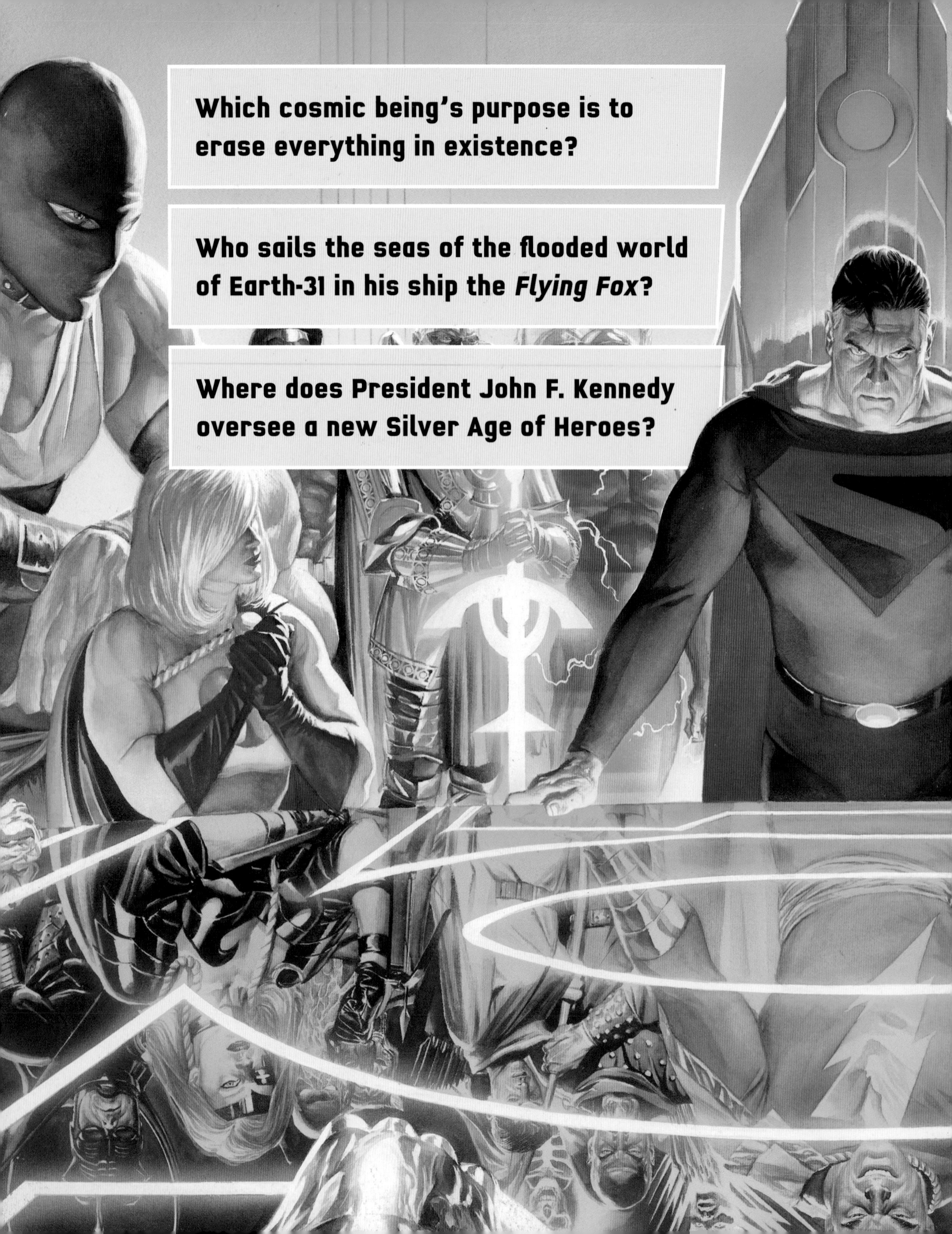
Which cosmic being's purpose is to erase everything in existence?
Who sails the seas of the flooded world of Earth-31 in his ship the *Flying Fox*?
Where does President John F. Kennedy oversee a new Silver Age of Heroes?

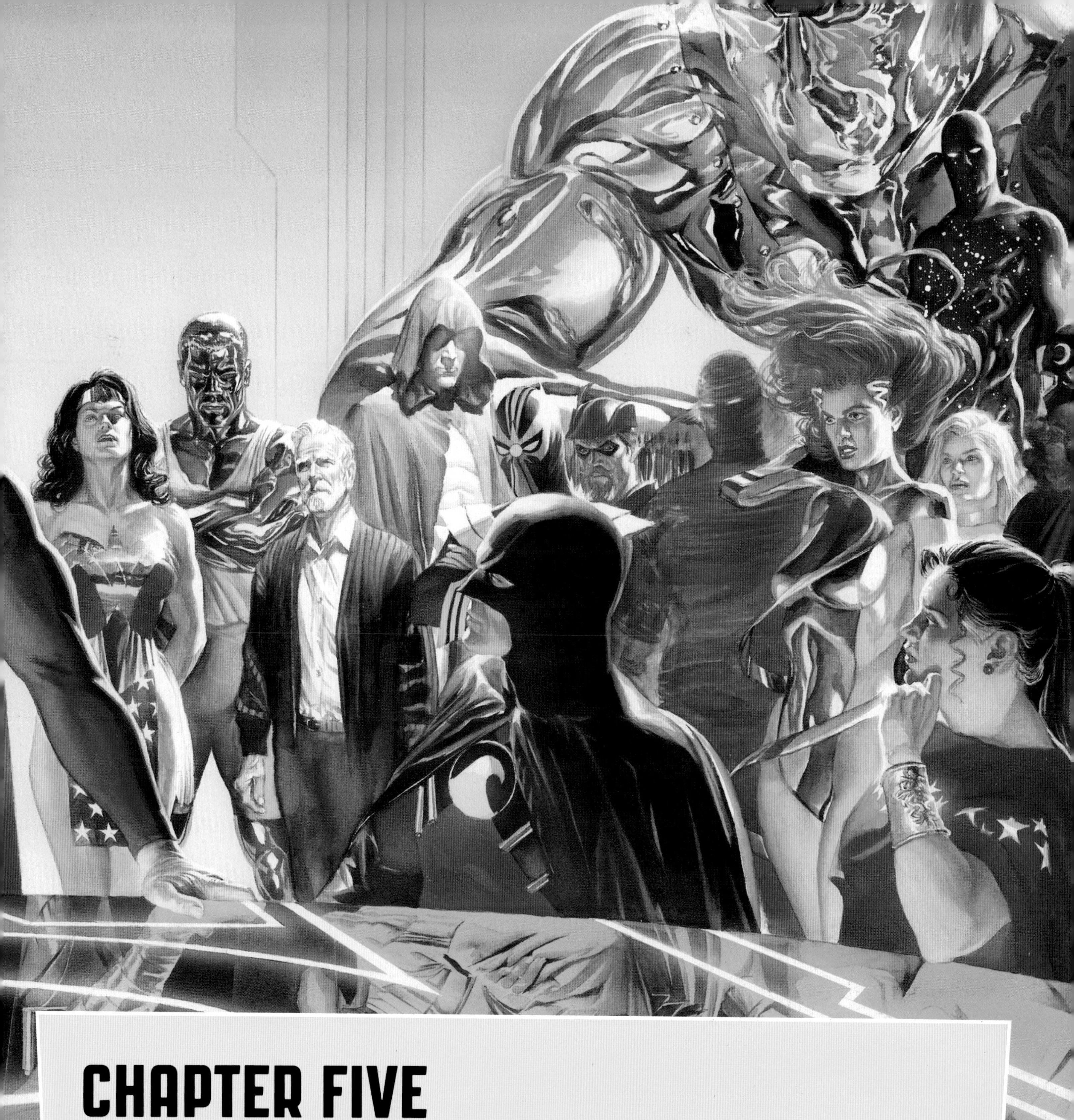

CHAPTER FIVE
THE MULTIVERSE

INFINITE EARTHS

AARGH!

Hal Jordan is temporarily driven ***insane*** by the power of ***Parallax, avatar of Fear!*** The former ***Green Lantern*** embarks on a mission to ***fix everything*** he thinks is ***wrong with reality*** – wiping away and rewriting ***entire histories.***

WELCOME TO YOUR DOOM!

TELL ME MORE

Infinite realities cascade across eternity, each one almost exactly like the other, but slightly different. Each reality has its own Earth, that may be slightly – or hugely – different from its neighbour.

The Anti-Monitor

BAD DAY

Supergirl saves **Superman** by battling the reality-extinguishing **Anti-Monitor.** But her bravery comes at a cost – **her own life!**

BACK FROM THE DEAD!

The recreation of the **Multiverse** triggers the rebirth of the **Anti-Monitor,** previously destroyed by the **Superman of Earth-2!**

CRISIS OF TWO EARTHS!

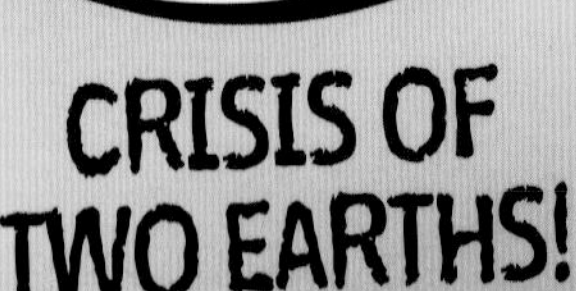

When the super-villains of Earth-1 and Earth-2 team up to conquer both universes, the only force that can stop them is the combined might of two worlds – the Justice League of America and the Justice Society of America!

A SUITABLE JOB FOR A SUPERMAN

The Superman of Earth-2, last seen in battle with the Anti-Monitor, returns to warn the heroes that reality is wrong, that everything is broken and evil! In the course of this new crisis, many parallel Earths return to existence, and the Multiverse begins to heal!

CRISIS ON EARTH-3

When the Crime Syndicate, an evil version of the Justice League, becomes bored with its own Earth-3 reality, it turns its attention to the heroes of Earth-1 and Earth-2. The three teams prove evenly matched, so the villains are eventually contained, rather than defeated.

NOOOO!

The Flash, taunted by his bitter enemy ***Reverse-Flash,*** runs back in time to save the life of his ***mother.*** By doing so, he alters ***all of history*** – but ***not*** for the ***better!***

JLA FILES

THE ANTI-MONITOR
An impossible being created when the Multiverse was born, the Anti-Monitor craves only to spread the unreality of his existence by erasing everything that exists!

BACK FROM THE DEAD!

Kid Flash becomes lost in time, forgotten by everyone. Only when **The Flash** is able to remember him is his sidekick **reborn!**

TOP 10

Supermen

Most Earths have their own Superman, though some are more "super" than others...

1. **ULTRAMAN:** The ruthless leader of the Crime Syndicate on Earth-3.
2. **OVERMAN:** A Nazi Superman brought up by Adolf Hitler on Earth-10.
3. **SUPERDEMON:** Fights evil on the magical world of Earth-13.
4. **HYPERIOUS:** Hiding behind a mask, little is known of the Superman of Earth-8!
5. **SUPERCHIEF:** This Iroquois warrior leads the Justice Riders on the Wild West frontier world of Earth-18.
6. **SUPER-MARTIAN:** Earth-32's Super-Martian fights evil as a member of the Justice Titans!
7. **SAVIOR:** The Superman of Earth-34 and leader of the Light Brigade.
8. **SUNSHINE SUPERMAN:** Leader of hippy heroes Love Syndicate of Dreamworld on Earth-47.
9. **SUPREMO:** The greatest hero of the "pseudoverse" of Earth-35.
10. **GOLD SUPERMAN:** A Super Hero robot built by genius Dr Will Tornado on Earth-44.

CRISIS? ...WHAT CRISIS?!

The Multiverse is a **vast place,** with an **infinite number of realities,** all of which are continually being **erased** and **rewritten!**

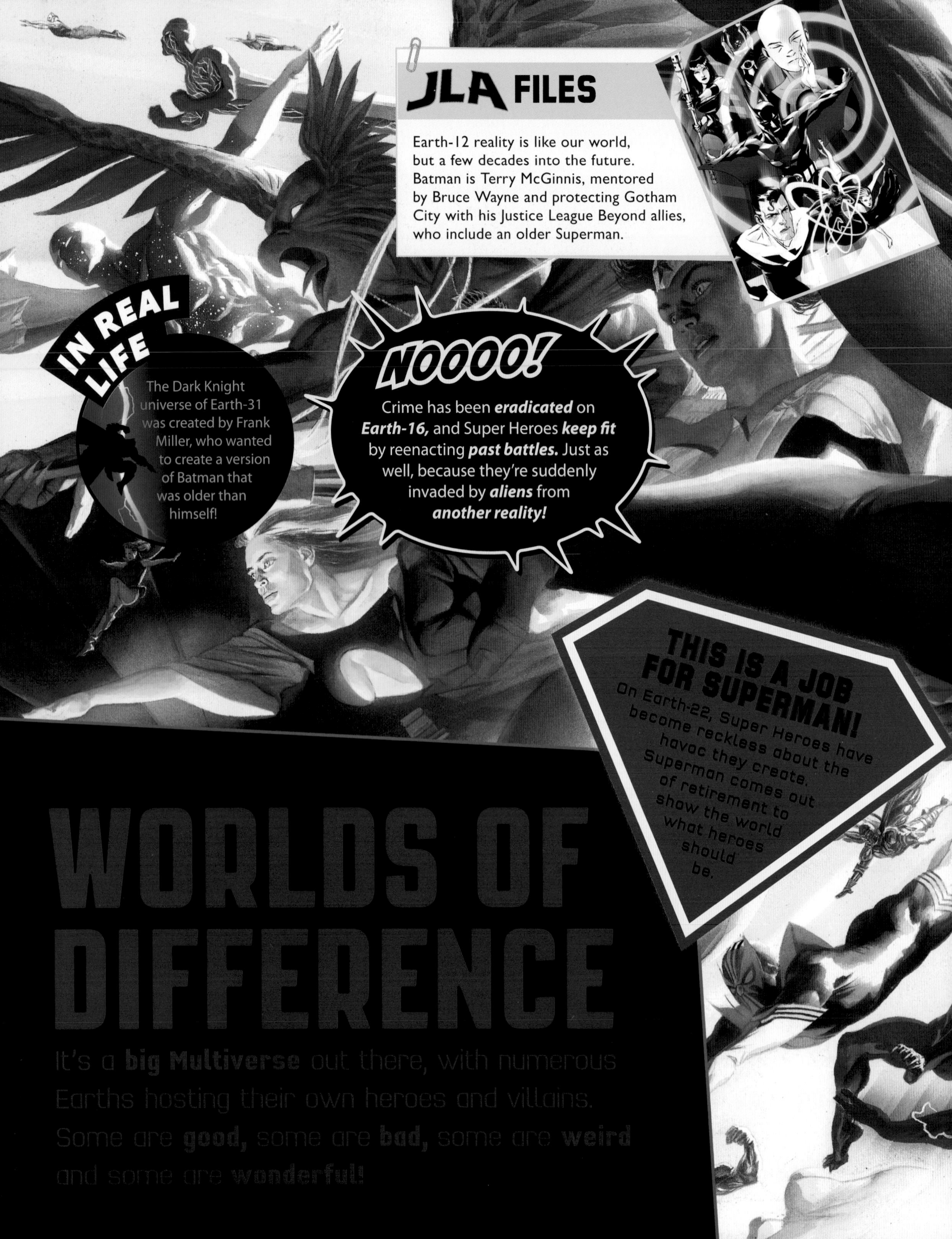

JLA FILES

Earth-12 reality is like our world, but a few decades into the future. Batman is Terry McGinnis, mentored by Bruce Wayne and protecting Gotham City with his Justice League Beyond allies, who include an older Superman.

IN REAL LIFE

The Dark Knight universe of Earth-31 was created by Frank Miller, who wanted to create a version of Batman that was older than himself!

NOOOO!

Crime has been ***eradicated*** on ***Earth-16,*** and Super Heroes ***keep fit*** by reenacting ***past battles.*** Just as well, because they're suddenly invaded by ***aliens*** from ***another reality!***

THIS IS A JOB FOR SUPERMAN!

On Earth-22, Super Heroes have become reckless about the havoc they create. Superman comes out of retirement to show the world what heroes should be.

WORLDS OF DIFFERENCE

It's a **big Multiverse** out there, with numerous Earths hosting their own heroes and villains. Some are **good,** some are **bad,** some are **weird** and some are **wonderful!**

WE HAVE BEEN AWAY FOR A WHILE. THAT WAS OUR MISTAKE.

DASTARDLY DEED

On **Earth-3,** Thomas and Martha Wayne, and their young son Bruce, are shot by **Alfred Pennyworth** as part of a plot by their eldest son, **Thomas Jr.** He then becomes **Owlman,** ruling Gotham City with an iron fist!

WHAT THE..?!

Earth-5, or **Thunderworld,** is the home of the **Marvel Family.** They have to leap into action when **Doctor Sivana** creates an artificial day of the week by **importing time** from other universes. He plans to use it to kill **Captain Marvel** and take over the Multiverse with a **Legion of Sivanas!**

DID YOU KNOW?

Earth-13 is a mystical world where days are 13 hours long and years last 13 months. It is protected from threats – such as a vampire invasion – by Etrigan, alias Superdemon, and the League of Shadows.

YESSS!

The powers of the **Quantum Superman** of **Earth-4** are so **overwhelming** that he has to control them with **medication.** He lets it wear off to help **Superman** cure a dying **Lois Lane.**

★ TEAM PLAYER ★

The **Justice Guild** of **Earth-11** comes from a world where the **Amazon race** enables women to take the **lead** in society. Its members include **Batwoman, Superwoman, Aquawoman** and **Wonderous Man.**

WHEN GOOD GUYS GO BAD

The **Batman** of **Earth-52** can't keep up with his rogues gallery, so he forcibly absorbs **The Flash's Speed Force** and becomes the **Red Death,** delivering **lethal justice!**

JLA FILES

MULTIVERSAL TRUTHS
On Earth-51, Kamandi is the Last Boy on Earth in a world ruled by animals. He and his friends Ben Boxer, alias biOMAC, and Tuftan, a humanoid tiger, reach the Island of the God Watchers and discover clues that point to the existence of the Multiverse!

Ben Boxer (biOMAC)

GOOD DAY

Blood League vampires launch an invasion of **Earth-13,** until the sorceress Annataz replaces their **bloodlust** with a craving for **coffee!**

KAMANDI!! WE MADE IT! "THE ISLAND OF THE GOD WATCHERS!"

Tuftan

WHAT THE..?!

Earth-47, otherwise known as **Dreamworld,** is the home of the **Love Syndicate,** where the 1960s live forever and **all is groovy!**

BAD DAY

Earth-42's tiny **Justice League heroes** have never faced weapons before, until the **Legion of Sivanas** kills Aquaman, Cyborg and Martian Manhunter!

NOOOO!

Earth-10 is a world under ***Nazi rule,*** with the Kryptonian ***Overman*** as its ***chief enforcer!***

Kamandi

TOUGH BREAK

Earth-19 is a world in which **Jack the Ripper** hunts for victims in 19th-century **Gotham City.** Bruce Wayne, fighting crime on the streets as **Batman,** is **convicted** of being the **notorious killer!**

YESSS!

On Earth-21, **President John F. Kennedy** is alive and oversees a new **Silver Age of Heroes.**

DID YOU KNOW?

Frozen by the **Time Trapper** in the 19th century, the people of **Earth-18** still achieve **air travel** and a **telegraph internet.** This frontier world is protected by the **Justice Riders,** who include **Superchief, Bat-Lash, Madame .44, Strongbow** and **Johnny Thunder.**

NOOOO!

On Earth-43, ***Batman*** is investigating a series of murders, when he gets ***bitten by a vampire*** and turned into one himself. He then has to battle the vampires' infamous leader – ***Dracula!***

WILD WORLDS!

Throughout the Multiverse there are worlds **beyond imagining,** where **the impossible** happens all the time and **myth and legend** become **everyday reality!**

JLA FILES

On Earth-30, the rocket containing baby Kal-El lands in the Ukraine, and Superman becomes a hero of the Soviet Union! His power enables Moscow to spread its influence across most of the globe. In the U.S., Lex Luthor devotes his life to finding a way to stop the Communist Superman, much to the annoyance of his neglected wife, Lois.

DID YOU KNOW?

Earth-31 is a world flooded by environmental **disaster. Batman** is **Captain Leatherwing,** a privateer patrolling the high seas in his ship the *Flying Fox*, whose crew includes young **Robin Redblade.**

IN REAL LIFE

Earth-33 is our own world – where Super Heroes only exist in comic books, chronicling the happenings of other universes. The only power on this Earth is the human imagination, which makes ideas reality and creates new imaginary worlds.

Q&A

Q: How did the Statue of Liberty get to America?

A: On Earth-1876, it was delivered by Clark Kent. Kent amazed visitors – and the world – at the 19th-century Centennial Exposition in Pennsylvania by flying in as the Super Man, holding the statue's famous torch.

INDEX

ARTISTS' ACKNOWLEDGEMENTS

Dan Abnett, Daniel Acuna, Neal Adams, Dan Adkins, Jack Adler, Christian Alamy, Oclair Albert, Mario Alberti, Enrique Alcatena, Michael Allred, Marlo Alquiza, Brad Anderson, Brent Anderson, Murphy Anderson, Marc Andreyko, Android Images, Ross Andru, Jim Aparo, John Arcudi, Ulises Arreola, Mark Askwith, Mahmud Asrar, Michael Atiyeh, Brian Augustyn, Tony Aviña, Brian Azzarello, Mark Badger, Jim Balent, Darryl Banks, Matt Banning, Mike W. Barr, Eddie Barrows, Jim Barry, Sami Basri, Cary Bates, Moose Baumann, John Beatty, Scott Beatty, C.C. Beck, Tony Bedard, Dave Bednar, Jordie Bellaire, Ed Benes, Bengal, Joe Benitez, Ryan Benjamin, Joe Bennett, Eddie Berganza, Jordi Bernet, D. Bruce Berry, Liz Berube, Otto Binder, Steve Bissette, W. Haden Blackman, Alex Bleyaert, Blond, Will Blyberg, Craig Boldman, Brian Bolland, James Bonny, Brett Booth, Geraldo Borges, Brett Breeding, Norm Breyfogle, E. Nelson Bridwell, Mark Bright, Pat Broderick, John Broome, Bob Brown, Daniel Brown, Joe Brozowski, Ed Brubaker, Rick Bryant, Brian Buccellato, Rebecca Buchman, Rick Burchett, Chris Burnham, Jack Burnley, Kurt Busiek, John Byrne, Stephen Byrne, Peter Calloway, Robert Campanella, Giuseppe Camuncoli, Greg Capullo, Nick Cardy, Russell Carley, Matteo Casali, Richard Case, Joe Casey, Joey Cavalieri, Joe Certa, Keith Champagne, Ernie Chan, Bernard Chang, Jim Charalampidis, Travis Charest, Amy Chu, Tom S. Chu, Chris Chuckry, June Chung, Ian Churchill, Vicente Cifuentes, Yildiray Cinar, Matthew Clark, Dave Cockrum, Andre Coelho, Gary Cohn, Gene Colan, Jerry Coleman, Vince Colletta, Amanda Conner, Will Conrad, Gerry Conway, Darwyn Cooke, Heath Corson, Jeromy Cox, Saleem Crawford, Shawn Crystal, Chuck Cuidera, Paris Cullins, David Curiel, Fernando Dagnino, Rodolfo Damaggio, Gene D'Angelo, Tony S. Daniel, Alan Davis, Dan Davis, Shane Davis, Shawn Davis, Andrew Dalhouse, Marc Deering, John Dell, Jesse Delperdang, J. M. DeMatteis, Tom Derenick, Ruben Diaz, Dan DiDio, Andy Diggle, Digital Chameleon, Dick Dillin, Paul Dini, Steve Ditko, Chuck Dixon, Rachel Dodson, Terry Dodson, Peter Doherty, Derec Donovan, Les Dorscheid, Arnold Drake, Gustavo Duarte, Christian Duce, Jo Duffy, Gerry Duggan, Dale Eaglesham, Scot Eaton, Gabe Eltaeb, Steve Englehart, Mike Esposito, Mark Evanier, Jason Fabok, Nathan Fairbairn, Romulo Fajardo, Jr., Ray Fawkes, Wayne Faucher, Carla Feeny, Raul Fernandez, Eber Ferreira, Julio Ferreira, Nick Filardi, David Finch, Bill Finger, Fabrizio Fiorentino, Sholly Fisch, Michael Fleisher, Robert Loren Fleming, Sandu Florea, Jon Forte, Gardner Fox, Romona Fradon, Gary Frank, Derek Fridolfs, Mike Friedrich, Richard Friend, Jenny Frison, John Fuller, Carl Gafford, Eric Gapstur, Lee Garbett, José Luis García-López, Pat Garrahy, Alé Garza, Sterling Gates, Stefano Gaudiano, Drew Geraci, Sunny Gho, Carmine Di Giandomenico, Dave Gibbons, Joe Giella, Keith Giffen, Dick Giordano, Jonathan Glapion, Patrick Gleason, Gina Going, Al Gordon, Jordan B. Gorfinkel, Alan Grant, Jamie Grant, Devin Grayson, Tom Grummett, Wade Von Grawbadger, Justin Gray, Mick Gray, Dan Green, Michael Green, Timothy Green II, Robert Greenberger, Sid Greene, Mike Grell, Renato Guedes, Jackson Guice, Yvel Guichet, Andres Guinaldo, Greg Gula, Larry Hama, Edmond Hamilton, Cully Hamner, Scott Hanna, Ed Hannigan, Jeremy Haun, Doug Hazlewood, Russ Heath, Don Heck, Scott Hepburn, Jack Herbert, Heroic Age, Phil Hester, John Higgins, Hi-Fi Design, David Hine, Bryan Hitch, Rick Hoberg, Nansi Hoolahan, Sandra Hope, Richard Horie, Tanya Horie, Alex Horley, David Hornung, Dylan Horrocks, Mike Huddleston, Adam Hughes, Rian Hughes, Gregg Hurwitz, Jamal Igle, Stuart Immonen, Carmine Infantino, Mark Irwin, Tony Isabella, Geof Isherwood, Mikel Janín, Klaus Janson, Jorge Jimenez, Phil Jimenez, Jock, Geoff Johns, Dan Curtis Johnson, Drew Johnson, Jeff Johnson, Mike Johnson, Gerard Jones, J. G. Jones, Kelley Jones, Malcolm Jones III, Arnie Jorgenson, Ruy José, Dan Jurgens, Justiniano, John Kalisz, Mike Kaluta, Bob Kane, Gil Kane, Robert Kanigher, Jeff Katz , Stan Kaye, Joe Kelly, Karl Kerschl, Barbara Kesel, Karl Kesel, Jessica Kholinne, Matt Kindt, Lovern Kindzierski, Jeff King, Tom King, Jack Kirby, Barry Kitson, George Klein, Todd Klein, Scott Koblish, Scott Kolins, Don Kramer, Andy Kubert, Joe Kubert, Aaron Kuder, Paul Kupperberg, Greg Land, Andy Lanning, Michael Lark, Ken Lashley, Stanley Lau, Carol Lay, Jae Lee, Jim Lee, Stan Lee, Jeff Lemire, Paul Levitz, Richmond Lewis, Rob Liefield, Steve Lightle, John Livesay, Victor Llamas, Scott Lobdell, Jeph Loeb, Alvaro Lopez, Aaron Lopresti, Lee Loughridge, Adriano Lucas, Eric Luke, Emanuela Lupacchino, Tom Lyle, Mike Machlan, José Wilson Magalhaés, Kevin Maguire, Rick Magyar, Doug Mahnke, Marcelo Maiolo, Guy Major, Francis Manapul, Tom Mandrake, Clay Mann, Seth Mann, Guillem March, William Moulton Marston, Laura Martin, Roy Allan Martinez, Christy Marx, Ron Marz, José Marzan, Jr., Randy Mayor, Dave Mazzucchelli, Dave McCaig, Trevor McCarthy, Tom McCraw, Scott McDaniel, Luke McDonnell, Tom McGraw, Ed McGuiness, Dave McKean, Sean McKeever, Mark McKenna, Mike McKone, Bob McLeod, Lan Medina, Linda Medley, Javier Mena, Jaime Mendoza, Jesús Merino William Messner-Loebs, Joshua Middleton, Rodolfo Migliari, Mike Mignola, Danny Miki, Matt Milla, Bryan Q. Miller, Frank Miller, Jack Miller, Dan Mishkin, Steve Mitchell, Lee Moder, Doug Moench, Sheldon Moldoff, Travis Moore, Rags Morales, Jack Morelli, Tomeu Morey, Moritat, Grant Morrison, Win Mortimer, Paul Mounts, Patricia Mulvihill, Jonboy Myers, Todd Nauck, Paul Neary, Mark Nelson, Diogenes Neves, Don Newton, Dustin Nguyen, Tom Nguyen, Fabian Nicieza, Troy Nixey, Ann Nocenti, Graham Nolan, Mike Norton, Kevin Nowlan, Ivan Nunes, John Nyberg, Bill Oakley, Sana Oback, Sonia Oback, Ben Oliver, Glynis Oliver, Patrick Olliffe, Santiago Olmedo, Dennis O'Neil, Glen Orbik, Jerry Ordway, John Ostrander, Juan Ortiz, Carlos Pacheco, Greg Pak, Jimmy Palmiotti, Arnold Pander, Jacob Pander, Mark Paniccia, Pete Pantazis, George Papp, Yanick Paquette, Charles Paris, Sean Parsons, Fernando Pasarin, Martin Pasko, Allen Passalaqua, Paul Pelletier, Mark Pennington, Andrew Pepoy, Benjamin Percy, George Pérez, Harry G. Peter, Will Pfeifer, Khoi Pham, Sean Phillips, Claude St. Aubin, Joe St. Pierre, FCO Plascencia, Al Plastino, Alberto Ponticelli, Whilce Portacio, Francis Portela, Howard Porter, Mark Poulton, Joe Prado, Bruno Premiani, Kelley Puckett, Steve Pugh, Jack Purcell, Wil Quintana, Frank Quitely, Jay David Ramos Tom Raney, Norm Rapmund, Fred Ray, David Vern Reed, Ivan Reis, Rod Reis, Jonny Rench, Paul Rivoche, Darick Robertson, Andrew Robinson, Gerry Robinson, James Robinson, Jerry Robinson, Denis Rodier, Marshall Rogers, John Romita, Jr., Alex Ross, George Roussos, Stephane Roux, Adrienne Roy, Bob Rozakis, Joe Rubinstein, Greg Rucka, Nei Ruffino, P. Craig Russell, Matt Ryan, Jesús Saíz, Gaspar Saladino, Tim Sale, Joseph Samachson, Daniel Sampere, Alejandro Sanchez, Peter Sanderson, Rafa Sandoval, Kurt Schaffenberger, Ira Schnapp, Mark Schultz, Rob Schwager, Ethan Van Sciver, Petra Scotese, Nicola Scott, Trevor Scott, Steven T. Seagle, Bart Sears, Stjepan Šejić, Mike Sekowsky, Miguel Sepulveda, Jerry Serpe, Buzz Setzer, Declan Shalvey, Liam Sharp, Scott Shaw, Jim Shooter, Joe Shuster, Jon Sibal, Jerry Siegel, Bill Sienkiewicz, Gail Simone, Louise Simonson, Walt Simonson, Alex Sinclair, James Sinclair, Paulo Siqueira, Jeremiah Skipper, Steve Skroce, Sibin Slavković, Andy Smith, Bob Smith, Brett Smith, Cam Smith, Matthew Smith, Sean Smith, Tom Smith, Peter Snejbjerg, Ray Snyder, Scott Snyder, Ryan Sook, Chris Sotomayor, Aaron Soud, John Stanisci, John Statema, Joe Staton, Peter Steigerwald, Brian Stelfreeze, Roger Stern, Cameron Stewart, Dave Stewart, Karl Story, Carrie Strachan, Lary Stucker, Curt Swan, Duane Swierczynski, Bryan Talbot, Billy Tan, Romeo Tanghal, Jordi Tarragona, Rick Taylor, Greg Theakston, Art Thibert, Roy Thomas, Jimmy Thompson, Frank Tieri, Bruce Timm, Anthony Tollin, Peter Tomasi, Alex Toth, Billy Tucci, Michael Turner, James Tynion IV, Peter Vale, Lynn Varley, Brian K. Vaughan, Rick Veitch, José Villarrubia, Dexter Vines, Daniel Vozzo, Matt Wagner, Ron Wagner, Mark Waid, Brad Walker, David F. Walker, Lee Weeks, Joe Weems, Len Wein, Greg Weisman, Dean White, Glenn Whitmore, Mike Wieringo, Wildstorm FX, Freddie E. Williams III, Rob Williams, Scott Williams, Joshua Williamson, Bill Willingham, Mary Wilshire, Matthew Wilson, Judd Winick, Stan Woch, Marv Wolfman, Walden Wong, Tatjana Wood, Wally Wood, Pete Woods, William Wray, Gregory Wright, Jason Wright, Bernie Wrightson, Annie Wu, Tom Yeates, Tom Ziuko.

The publishers have made every effort to identify and acknowledge the artists and writers whose work appears in this book.

DK | Penguin Random House

Senior Editor: Alastair Dougall
Senior Designer: Anne Sharples
Project Art Editor: Jon Hall
Designers: David Ball, Rosamund Bird
Jacket Design: Jon Hall
Picture Research: Alexander Evangeli
Senior Pre-Production Producer: Siu Chan
Senior Producer: Zara Markland
Managing Editor: Sadie Smith
Managing Art Editor: Vicky Short
Art Director: Lisa Lanzarini
Publisher: Julie Ferris
Publishing Director: Simon Beecroft

Dorling Kindersley would like to thank:
Amy Weingartner, Josh Anderson, Mickey Stern and Melanie Swartz at Warner Bros. Global Publishing.
Doug Prinzivalli, Mike Pallotta, Courtney Jordan and Leah Tuttle at DC Entertainment.
Ann Barrett for the index.

First published in Great Britain in 2018 by
Dorling Kindersley Limited
80 Strand, London WC2R ORL
A Penguin Random House Company

DORL39613
Wonder Woman created by William Moulton Marston.

18 19 20 21 22 10 9 8 7 6 5 4 3 2 1
001–307686–Sept/18

A CIP catalogue record for this book is available from the British Library.

ISBN: 978-0-24131-424-1

Printed and bound in China

A WORLD OF IDEAS:
SEE ALL THERE IS TO KNOW

www.dk.com